Thirst

Thirst

God and the Alcoholic Experience

James B. Nelson

Westminster John Knox Press
LOUISVILLE • LONDON

Scripture quotations are from the New Revised Standard Version of the Bible, copyright © 1989 by the Division of Christian Education of the National Council of the Churches of Christ in the U.S.A., and from *An Inclusive-Language Lectionary, Year C* © 1985 by the Division of Education and Ministry of the National Council of the Churches of Christ in the U.S.A., and are used by permission.

Excerpt from "The Lost Thought," by Emily Dickinson is reprinted by permission of the publishers and the Trustees of Amherst College from *The Poems of Emily Dickinson*, Thomas H. Johnson, ed., Cambridge, Mass.: The Belknap Press of Harvard University Press, copyright © 1951, 1955, 1979 by the President and Fellows of Harvard College.

Book design by Sharon Adams
Cover design by Eric Walljasper, Minneapolis, MN

First edition
Published by Westminster John Knox Press
Louisville, Kentucky

This book is printed on acid-free paper that meets the American National Standards Institute Z39.48 standard. ∞

PRINTED IN THE UNITED STATES OF AMERICA

04 05 06 07 08 09 10 11 12 13—10 9 8 7 6 5 4 3 2 1

Library of Congress Cataloging-in-Publication Data

Nelson, James B.
    Thirst : God and the alcoholic experience / James B. Nelson.
      p. cm.
    Includes bibliographical references and index.
    ISBN 0-664-22688-4 (alk. paper)
      1. Alcoholism—Religious aspects—Christianity. 2. Twelve-step programs—Religious aspects—Christianity. 3. Alcoholics—Rehabilitation—Biblical teaching. 4. Church work with alcoholics. I. Title.

HV5186.N45 2004
361.8'33292—dc21

2003053765

For my alcoholic and nonalcoholic companions on this journey. You have been God's givers of life.

Contents

Preface

Gratitude, it is frequently observed, is the core dynamic of the Christian life. Ours is a "eucharistic" life with an ethic shaped by thanksgiving. To that I want to add my conviction—shared by countless alcoholic companions of varying spiritual persuasions—that gratitude is also the core dynamic of recovery. In chapter 1 I present my rationale for writing this book, a task some authors assign to the preface. My words in this spot are simply ones of very real gratitude.

Some years ago Stephanie Egnotovich, executive editor of Westminster John Knox Press, and Davis Perkins, president and publisher of the Presbyterian Publishing Corporation, encouraged me to pursue this project. I assured them that it would come "in the fullness of time." They may not have suspected that "the fullness" would be quite this long, but they have given warm and patient support, and in editorial counsel Stephanie Egnotovich has guided me skillfully. Thank you.

I find it difficult to express adequately my gratitude to the following friends, each of whom read the entire manuscript and gave me marvelous encouragement along with wise suggestions: Charles Englehart, Douglas Federhart, Jerry Gill, Lark Hapke, Stuart Holland, Wilys Claire Nelson, Mári Sörri, and Sterling Vinson. They have left constructive marks on many pages. Thank you.

My professional-spiritual home for many years was United Theological Seminary of the Twin Cities. Faculty, staff, and student colleagues there stood by me with amazing grace through struggle and in rejoicing. In years since recovery (and retirement), they have invited and challenged me to teach a summer school course (with the able partnership of Karen

Smith Sellers) and to speak at Spring Convocation and workshops on the present subject. Thank you.

My other spiritual communities have been several and are of enduring importance. First Congregational Church of Minnesota (U.C.C.) in Minneapolis held Wilys Claire and me with life-sustaining love during critical years. More recently, Southside Presbyterian Church in Tucson and two other clusters of searching friends, "The Thought Club" and "The Journey Group," have been valued partners. My men's groups in both Minneapolis and Tucson have known me well and have cared in unforgettable ways. And there are other special friends, not part of these groups, whose grace has etched deep marks on my life and these pages. Thank you.

My recovery groups have been indispensable. I do not intend in any sense to speak *for* them nor directly *of* them. But *without* them neither would this project have life nor, perhaps, would I. What else can I say? Thank you.

I come to my family. Our children, Stephen and Mary, were adults and living far away when my drinking became alcoholic. They worried from a distance, as did our daughter-in-law Denise, and distance brought its own particular hardships during the active disease. In the years of recovery, the loving support of these three has been tangible and has meant the world. Thank you. And, I want to add, I am grateful to be a sober grandpa for my two delights, Kristin and Bryan, who have known me only in that way.

Wilys Claire—partner, wife, friend, soul mate of fifty years—has been through it all—"up close and personal," as they say. I have deliberately refrained from attempting to write her story in this book. I could not. A hospital staff chaplain with experience on the chemical dependency unit, she was professionally knowledgeable about alcoholism long before I was, and, unfortunately, saw it coming. The very occasional references to her in these pages do justice neither to the depth of her pain during my active disease nor to her enormous gifts to me in recovery. If some day she chooses to write her own story as a spouse of an alcoholic, it will convey her incisive insights that unfailingly enrich me. And, if some day she should write of the wounding and healing she experienced, I hope I can be as supportive as she has been to me in this present process. She has been, and is, magnificent—my most significant companion on this journey. Thank you.

At some point during the month I was a patient at the treatment center, I received a phone call from a friend, Alan Johnson, then on the national staff of the United Church of Christ. As I shared with him some of the spiritual meanings this treatment experience was bringing, he commented, "I suspect that the Thirtieth Psalm is speaking to you as never before." I confessed that I did not remember what the Thirtieth Psalm was but after the call went to look it up. It has been a treasure ever since.

While the psalm later came to be part of the ritual for the feast honoring the rededication of the temple, it is clear that the writer's initial intent was profoundly personal. This poem was an act of gratitude for recovery from a serious illness. Read through the eyes of an alcoholic, it conveys remarkable insight into the dynamics of denial and the despair of alienation. Most of all, however, it puts words to the profound gratitude one feels to God and to all those who have embodied that healing Presence for life received once more. I invite you to read words from it with the alcoholic's experience in mind.

> Sing praises to God, O you saints of God,
>   and give thanks to God's holy name.
> For God's anger is but for a moment;
>   and God's favor is for a lifetime.
> Weeping may tarry for the night,
>   but joy comes with the morning.
> As for me, I said in my prosperity,
>   "I shall never be moved."
> By your favor, O God,
>   you had established me as a strong mountain;
> you hid your face,
>   I was dismayed.
> To you, O God, I cried . . .
> "What profit is there in my death,
>   if I go down to the Pit?
> Will the dust praise you?
>   Will it tell of your faithfulness?
> Hear, O God, and be gracious to me!
>   O God, be my helper!"
> You have turned for me my mourning into dancing;
>   you have loosed my sackcloth
>   and girded me with gladness,
> that my soul may praise you and not be silent.
> O Sovereign, my God, I will give thanks to you for ever.
>   (Ps. 30:4–12, Inclusive Language Lectionary)

"The Big Book" of Alcoholics Anonymous puts it simply: "The age of miracles is still with us."[1]

Chapter One

Silence and Speech

A Short Story

That memorable imbiber W. C. Fields began one of his autobiographical accounts something like this: "I was born of poor but dishonest parents. They were in the iron and steel business—my mother ironed and my father stole." My own story is not nearly so interesting or unconventional, but it does set the stage for the reflections in these pages.

I grew up in a middle-class, Midwestern, small-town, respectably Presbyterian—and teetotaling—family. I didn't have even a taste of alcohol until my first weeks in college, but then and there I made up for lost time. A couple of years later and disgusted with my own weekend binge drinking, it struck me that alcohol did *not* enhance my life, and I chose not to drink for another twenty years. I don't recall having struggled with that decision, nor do I recall difficulty with the quitting process. Neither seemed to be a big issue. I just realized that whenever I drank I tended to drink too much, embarrassed myself, and felt rotten the next day. The thought that I might be a candidate for addiction never crossed my mind. I remained abstinent, surprisingly as I think about it, even during my tour of duty as an enlisted man in the army.

However, about age forty, when my family and I were living in England for a year on sabbatical leave, I began drinking wine socially as was the very civilized custom among the Oxford folk. I liked the ambiance of it all in the college's Senior Common Room. I liked the taste of claret, sherry, and port. Most of all, I liked how it felt and what it did to me.

1

Even though I usually wanted more alcohol than I actually drank, my drinking remained fairly moderate for perhaps a dozen years. But in my fifties my solitary drinking increased as did my use of hard liquor. While professionally I continued to function quite well, the disease was taking its toll more personally. My marriage was under stress, physical and emotional problems were emerging, and close friends were concerned about my drinking. After repeated attempts to moderate my use, after attempting white-knuckled abstinence, after various therapists, after an unsuccessful intervention, after morning drinking and blackouts had become frequent and denial routine, and after a five-and-a-half-day binge locked in a Minneapolis hotel room less than two miles from my home, I finally had to admit that alcohol, this fine gift of God, was now playing for the other team. Concerning me, it had a mean streak, even a killer instinct. So, on the night of April 19, 1993, after room service had ended and the liquor stores had closed, I ran out of vodka and had my last drink.

The following day I arranged for treatment at the Hazelden Center and asked my dean for assistance in arranging cancellation of my seminary and off-campus commitments for the next month. I entered in-patient treatment on April 21, was discharged thirty-one days later, participated in six months of Hazelden's "after care" group therapy, and became a regular participant in recovery meetings.

My disease has been in remission ever since. I am not a recovered alcoholic, nor am I an ex-alcoholic. I doubt that there are such people. Rather, I am a recovering alcoholic trying to live one day at a time, enormously grateful that my disease is not active today.

In abbreviated form that is my story. It's not an unusual one. With a few changes in details it has been told in a million similar versions. But, while I have never kept my alcoholism secret since the day I left for the treatment center, it has taken me quite a while to write about it.

The Struggle to Speak

Years ago—some time before I became seriously alcoholic—I was trying to write a book about sexuality and theology. The conditions were ideal. I had been teaching the subject, was fascinated by the issues, had done my background research, and had the uninterrupted time of a sabbatical leave. I even had enough paper for my typewriter.

But I simply could not get started. The book's subject was academic, to be sure, but it was also personal. I felt vulnerable. I feared that many readers would find my book too academic, and academics would find it too personal and self-revelatory. For a time I felt paralyzed. After several aborted attempts, I gave up and turned to other projects for three months. Then, beginning once more, I wrote furiously for the last months of my leave time in order to complete the project. That process has become familiar to me once again.

In that earlier process I discovered something that André Maurois described well. He observed that the need to express oneself in writing typically springs from unresolved inner conflicts. It is not a matter of having found an answer to the problem, Maurois said, but rather having discovered the problem and desiring a solution. The solution that typically comes, however, is not a resolution of the problem but rather a deeper consciousness of the issues. It is a consciousness born of having wrestled with the attempt to express the problem.[1]

At some point early in my recovery I knew that some day I would need to write about my alcohol addiction, if for no other reason than self-understanding. Often we don't understand ourselves well until we try to explain ourselves carefully and honestly to others, and this is certainly true concerning my alcoholism. On this matter two quite different writers speak to me. Anne Lamott says it with characteristic directness and whimsy:

> [G]ood writing is about telling the truth. We are a species that needs and wants to understand who we are. Sheep lice do not seem to share this longing, which is one reason they write so very little. But we do. [2]

In her memoir *At Seventy* May Sarton gives voice to similar convictions:

> [W]riting is for me a way of understanding what is happening to me, of thinking hard things out. I've never written a book that was not born out of a question I needed to answer for myself. [3]

I needed to write before the vividness of my active alcoholism had dimmed, but also only after some years of recovery had given me perspective. So I set a marker in my mind: after five years I would put words to paper. My fifth sobriety anniversary came. I was retired and had ample time to write. I also had competing commitments. Further, whenever I tried to put words about alcoholism to paper, I discovered more ways of organizing my desk or thought of additional household chores and the compelling needs of the world to which I must attend. My inventiveness was astonishing. But the main reason for the delay was not difficult to find: a book about the interplay of theology, addiction, and recovery was just plain frightening. Everything about it was just too personal.

Guidelines for Speech

Along the way I discovered several wise and useful texts in St. Mark—in this case St. Mark Twain, hardly a spiritual saint but surely a canonized writer. The first is his observation that there are two kinds of people in the world: people who divide people into two kinds of people and people who don't. In spite of all of the important differences between those of us coping with addiction and those who have not encountered this problem, there is finally only one kind of people—human people, God's people. Drunk or sober, never personally affected by chemical addiction or living with that issue, we are much more alike than different. Getting clear about this helped me begin writing.

Twain's second useful observation is this: as a reminder that he should speak for himself and not on behalf of all others, he observed that the only persons authorized to say *we* believe such-and-such are, of course, the pope, the king or queen, and the person with tapeworms. Everyone else should say *I*. True enough, and humility lightens the load. I do not have the obligation, the wisdom, or the authority to speak on behalf of addicted and recovering people in general. In spite of our commonalities, each of us is unique. Nor am I authorized to speak on behalf of any re-covery movement or organization. There are good reasons, which I shall comment on shortly, why the major recovery movement has "anony-mous" in its title. Nor do I speak theologically for any of the Christian churches, though my faith home is there. I shall try to speak for myself, but always with the hope that there are bridges to others' experiences and reflections.

Adam, Twain also observed, was the only person who, when he said a good thing, really knew no one had ever said it before. (Twain apparently meant this to apply only before Eve's creation.) If and when any "good things" appear in the following pages, the influences and voices of many others doubtless will be present. Chemical dependency is a social disease. I did not contract my alcoholism in solitary splendor. My genes, relation-ships, and environment had something to do with it. Likewise, for many of us recovery is a very social process. Though bookstores typically dis-play recovery literature in the "Self Help" section, that notion did not ap-ply to me. My solitary attempts to break the back of my own alcoholism were dismal failures, and to this day my recovery is dependent on the gifts of many, many others. So also, what I write here makes no pretense to uniqueness. I am, as the letter to the Hebrews said, "surrounded by so great a cloud of witnesses" (Heb. 12:1). Thank God.

My Hopes in Speaking

Thus, getting to this book has been quite a process. But why write about this alcoholism business at all? One reason—I have already mentioned it —is quite selfish: *self-understanding*. During my active disease I learned something about "the enormous negative power of the unspoken."[4] The proverbial elephant in the living room that everyone tries to ignore haunts families of alcoholics, and no one is more interested in keeping the elephant out of sight than the alcoholic. But if we fear something so much that we cannot even name it, how can we ever understand it? If, after persistent inquiry, our resulting understanding is not a package of neat answers, it *can be* (as Maurois said) at least a much better awareness of what the real issues are.

Beneath my desire for self-understanding, I suspect, is *the desire for existence itself*. In *Neurosis and Treatment*, Andras Angyal states, "To be is to mean something to someone else. . . . A poem written in a language that no one can read does not exist as a poem. Neither do we exist in a human way unless someone decodes us."[5] Sometimes alcoholics talk about their experience of the disease as "a living death" or as "feeling as if I were dying." While the physical problems and suicidal risks of unchecked alcoholism can and often do lead to biological death, here I am talking (as is Angyal) about *the sense of existence*.

One of the most desperate things about my own alcoholic drinking was the fear that I was losing existence itself. To be sure, I was less alive in terms of energy. To be sure, my enthusiasm for life was diminished. But it was more than that. At times I found myself doubting and even losing my sense of *being real*. This feeling, of course, was directly connected to the secrecy I needed for protecting and practicing my addiction. Increasingly I was afraid of being known by the intimate others in my life, and the result was a growing fear, even dread, of nonexistence.

On the other hand, a fundamentally important part of recovery is regaining the sense that *I really am*. And this in turn is directly related to letting other people know *who* I am—sometimes in fear and trembling, but with the confidence that existence is far better than nonexistence. I find it a compelling motive for self-disclosure.

Even so, why should I inflict my own needs on others through the printed page? A personal journal shared with a few close friends could suffice. But I write for print with the hope that these pages might be useful also to others who wrestle with the same demons and angels.

Many of us know ourselves as persons of faith—yes, sometimes doubt-filled faith, sometimes bad faith, sometimes idolatrous faith, sometimes faltering faith, but faith nevertheless. We cannot live, it seems, without placing our trust and confidence in something that makes it worthwhile getting up in the morning. But this trust or confidence in something is not self-explanatory. It raises as many questions as it seems to answer. Indeed, it is "faith seeking understanding," and this classic definition of theology by Anselm is relevant many centuries after he said it.

Let me be clear about what I am *not* doing. This book is not "recovery literature." Bookstore shelves hold many volumes of daily meditations and emotional/spiritual guidance for those recovering from addictions. Personally, I have found some of these helpful, and I use several with regularity. But their primary intention is not theological exploration. For those of us who wonder about and struggle with the faith questions underlying this particular experience, we also need more *theology*, and there is still surprisingly little in print.

If this book is not recovery literature, neither is it a "how to" book for chemical dependency counselors and clergy. These pages offer no guidance for the helping professional concerning effective interventions, recovery support, or family dynamics. Such literature is important, but it already exists in abundance and in quality.

Finally, this book is not an attempt to recommend a certain theological approach or framework to treatment centers or recovery groups. Such is not necessary for recovery. Recovering people have diverse religious and nonreligious backgrounds, and some people carry lasting religious damage. Hence, a more generalized "spiritual" approach is utterly appropriate for those contexts.

On the positive side, these pages are for people who want to use the lenses of theology (especially Christian theology) to look at their own addiction and recovery or that of others they care about. It is for people who want to "think theologically" about life and its important events, including addiction and recovery. It is for people who know that their personal stories, somehow touched by addiction and recovery, are best understood as part of a larger faith story. It is for people who are forever "religiously curious" and who find life richer and deeper in the exploration of that dimension. It is for those who find themselves with a spiritual thirst that will not go away—one that keeps leading them to deeper levels of experience—and for those who sense that both addiction and recovery are expressions of that very human spiritual thirst.[6]

One of theology's tasks is to probe behind the obvious. Things are seldom what they seem. At this point, faith and science have much in common; both challenge the conventional secular mind that takes things quite literally and asks few questions about what lies beneath the surface. As Martin L. Smith puts it, "The profane mind reacts to immediate appearances and asks no further questions; the religious mind keeps on asking questions in search of the deepest meanings behind all appearances."[7] Indeed, the scriptures of the world's major religions seem to agree. The ancient Upanishads, for instance, tell us that the gods hate the obvious and love the obscure. Likewise, for Christian theology the most important things are not obvious, the prime example being the claim that the supreme revelation of divine love for the world can be seen in a grisly execution. That is not a problem to be solved but rather a mystery to be probed. So, digging behind the obvious facts of alcoholism for its deeper meanings should be a natural task for theology.

If we need more theology on this subject, we also need more of it done from the inside. What we now have (not much in quantity) has been written by empathetic and experienced but *nonaddicted* professionals. I am truly grateful for their work, as my references in the pages that follow will indicate. At the same time, as I read them I find things missing—nuances, feelings, pieces of the experience—stuff of common conversations among recovering addicts. A seasoned and sensitive male obstetrician can tell us important and valuable things about childbirth— except those things that come only from experiencing it through one's own body. So we also need the birth mother's own story and reflections. Likewise, it is time for more of us who are in recovery from alcohol and other drug addictions *and* who care about theological reflection to speak out.

A friend prominent in the chemical dependency field frequently argues that what we need is more *public alcoholics*. He means recovering people willing to go public, for chemical addiction is the one major disease in America that does not have a visible and vocal constituency. Unlike HIV/AIDS, cancer, lung disease, multiple sclerosis, or diabetes, chemical addiction still has no effective, identifiable group of constituents—folk actually dealing with the disease who are willing and able to speak out for research funding, prevention education, and treatment support. We need a significant, visible group of persons willing to say, "I know from my own experience that treatment works, that it is cost effective, and that it needs to be funded."

More public conversation by recovering people also can mitigate some of the persisting fear, shame, and embarrassment about alcoholism. Consider the parallel with cancer. Many of us remember the time when the word "cancer" was seldom spoken. The disease seemed to be a death sentence, and simply pronouncing the word seemed to make one a participant in the sentencing of an innocent victim. Today we are much more open. Now we know that cancers can often be arrested with early detection and treatment. More public discourse about cancer has not lessened the severity of the disease, but it has diminished some of the fear, it has expanded funding and research, and it has made treatment more hopeful.

In a similar way, vastly increased public conversation about mental illnesses have lessened the embarrassment and shame associated with such diseases. Bill Wilson, cofounder of Alcoholics Anonymous, struggled with depression for years during his recovery. In a 1958 article he wrote, "I used to be ashamed of my condition [depression] so didn't talk about it. But nowadays I freely confess I am a depressive, and this has attracted other depressives to me. Working with them has helped a great deal."[8] We understand considerably more about clinical depression than we did years ago. Now we know it as a brain disease, not a self-inflicted condition for which the person should be blamed. Indeed, moralistic judgments will only impede recovery. When Wilson could talk freely about his own depression, he discovered it not only immensely helpful to others but also beneficial regarding his own shame.

Restrictions on Speech

(This section will be of particular interest to those involved in Alcoholics Anonymous, though others may wish to "listen in" on the struggle with anonymity.)

Since the day I entered the Hazelden Center in April 1993, I have chosen to be open with others about my alcoholism. But refraining from writing was appropriate for a considerable time. I needed years to listen, to reflect, and to find some stability in recovery. Now it is time to speak out.

Still, I listen carefully to those recovering people who warn against *any* public speech about one's own addictive experience. Many have good reasons. For some people, still today, job security or professional standing can be seriously threatened by general knowledge of their addiction. Others, for whom economic self-protection may be unnecessary, simply do not wish to be branded. There is reason. Though the heaviest judgments of sin and shame have ebbed, still common are assumptions that a person becomes alcoholic because of weak character, inadequate will power, immaturity, or emotional instability—or all of the above.

Furthermore, some members of Alcoholics Anonymous (A.A.) or Narcotics Anonymous (N.A.) believe that the A.A. anonymity tradition demands our public silence. A word of explanation is in order. In addition to the well-known Twelve Steps toward recovery in A.A., there are Twelve Traditions that guide the communal life of the movement. Tradition 12 says this: "Anonymity is the spiritual foundation of all our traditions, ever reminding us to place principles before personalities."[9] The reference to "spiritual foundation" has to do with humility: "Anonymity is real humility at work. It is an all-pervading spiritual quality which today keynotes A.A. life everywhere. Moved by the spirit of anonymity, we try to give up our natural desires for personal distinction as A.A. members both among fellow alcoholics and before the general public."[10]

These words were based on difficult experience. A.A. was founded in 1935, and within a short time the youthful movement learned the importance of anonymity the hard way. In fact, one of A.A.'s significant forerunners on the American scene faced that lesson much earlier. It was the Washington Total Abstinence Society, a group that arose in the mid-nineteenth century when members of a Baltimore drinking club decided to give up liquor.[11] Originally composed only of alcoholics trying to help each other, it soon broadened its membership to include nonalcoholics and broadened its mission to include contentious public issues. These things contributed to its early demise. But there was one other important factor: the well-publicized relapses into drunkenness of some prominent members. The Washington Total Abstinence Society simply lost credibility.

Years later, the newly developing A.A. movement experienced a similar threat. Freshly into recovery and enthusiastic about it, some members (several celebrities among them) told their stories to the press. Unfortunately, in some of these cases the publicity was followed by relapses into drinking and drunkenness—damaging blows to a youthful A.A. that was struggling to prove itself in a society where moralistic judgments and skepticism about the alcoholic's chances for recovery prevailed.

Now, decades later, with A.A.'s approach well-established as a proven recovery path for countless people, there is little threat to the movement if members speak publicly about their own experience. But I take several principles seriously, and I want to honor them as fully as I possibly can:

1. *The importance of humility.* My alcoholism is a chronic disease. It is, as *Alcoholics Anonymous* ("The Big Book" of A.A.) characterizes it, "cunning, baffling, powerful." While I am enormously grateful that my sobriety has been intact through these years and while I am strongly committed to the program of recovery, I also know that sobriety carries no automatic lifetime warranty. Since alcoholism is a disease marked by the proneness to relapse, we live one day at a time. Humility is always in order.

2. *No one should try to speak for A.A., and surely I do not.* This remarkable international movement—loosely organized and almost completely led by volunteers—has no official spokespersons. That has been important for A.A.'s flourishing. Furthermore, alcoholics notoriously resist imposed leadership; were such to be attempted, it would be like trying to herd cats. Thus, Tradition 2 states that there is but one ultimate authority—a loving God speaking through the group conscience. "Our leaders are but trusted servants; they do not govern."[12] Even the Twelve Steps (though taken very seriously by the vast majority of A.A. members) are not mandated but rather "are *suggested* as a program of recovery."[13] Because my own recovery experience is so intimately tied to A.A., I will be speaking *of* the movement's effects on me, and speaking *about* the theological implications of A.A.'s approach to recovery. This, however, is far different from speaking *for* or *on behalf of* the organization—which no member has a right to attempt.

3. *Confidentiality is a high trust and must be strictly observed.* I believe there is an important distinction between anonymity and confidentiality. I am free to make choices about my own anonymity or openness as an alcoholic. I am free to reveal to others whatever I choose about my own active addiction and about the steps of my own recovery. Confidentiality, however, is a matter of trust concerning the anonymity of *others*—both in their identities and in their words. Confidentiality means that who is present and what is said at a meeting stays within those walls. Members owe this to each other, and to themselves as well, for recovery needs safe space. It requires safety for those who do not wish their alcoholism publicly known, and space where all can share freely about the depths of their insanity as active alcoholics and the high hopes to which they now cling.

4. *One's public words about his or her own alcoholism and recovery should be motivated and guided by the aim of service to those affected by the addiction.* Good procedures of biblical understanding interpret one part of Scripture through other parts of Scripture—they are never isolated pieces.

That is a good operating principle for A.A. documents as well. Tradition 11 counsels anonymity in the media as a guard against self-promotion, and in Tradition 12 anonymity reminds us to place principles above personalities. These traditions might seem to preclude any public speech, including writing. *Step* 12, however, contains the missionary mandate: Carry the recovery message to other alcoholics. How do we do this "anonymously"? Surely, it can often be done in the relative anonymity of one-to-one encounters or within group meetings. It is my conviction that sometimes, however, anonymity (though never confidentiality) must bend in favor of the mission: service to those affected by alcoholism. Unless this happens, a rigid understanding of anonymity will unwittingly keep the curtain of silence and even shame drawn tightly around us, and our sorely needed public discussions of both theology and public policy will suffer—to the detriment of all who are affected by this addiction.

Liberation Theology

Throughout this book I will draw on and weave together several sources. One is Scripture and Christian tradition. While the phenomenon of alcoholism itself is doubtless as ancient as the ancient texts, the *concept* of this addiction is modern. Accordingly, we cannot expect the early texts to address the subject as we know it. On the other hand, we *can* expect their theological insights about God in the human experience to shed light on the dark corners of addiction and recovery.

Another source is contemporary wisdom. Those psychologists, physicians, sociologists, and anthropologists who have worked on addiction and recovery issues can, in John Calvin's words, be revealers of "God's common grace." So also can novelists, playwrights, and poets. We should cast our nets as widely as possible when we are fishing for insights.

The third source, already named, is the lived experience of addiction and recovery. All three sources are important, but the lived experience of addicts and recovering persons has been the most neglected theologically.

Keen attention to experience is, of course, a cardinal principle of *liberation theology*, one of the theological "types of speech" that will be evident in these pages. This approach, arising in Central America during the latter third of the twentieth century, holds that the poor and the oppressed are our most important teachers about God's activity. Is it too much of a stretch to say that the addicted and recovering also are our teachers?

Of course, some of those actively addicted are literally poor, living on the streets and sleeping under bridges. Others are materially comfortable even though their addictions gradually take an economic toll. What of those in recovery? Addictions indeed have caused serious economic hardship for some, but not for all. However, the same might be said of African Americans or of white women or of gay, lesbian, bisexual, and transgendered persons in this society—groups from which other liberation theologies have arisen. Sometimes economic poverty is a major facet of oppression; sometimes it is not.

People of color, women, and sexual minorities, however, have been oppressed for reasons of their very being, reasons they have not chosen. Is chemical addiction in that category? No, some would say, for the oppression felt by the addicted is from their self-inflicted wounds. I will challenge that contention later. For now, I simply invite you to move with me into a theologizing style indebted to the liberationists in several ways.[14]

One is the recognition that *theology is a second moment* for people of faith. The first moment is life itself. Our lived experience has precedence over theological reflection. Theology comes afterward, attempting to understand and serve life. Some of us have succumbed to chemical addiction, a fact that has enormously changed our lives and those around us— that is "the first moment." And some of us addicted folk have gotten into recovery, and again our lives and those around us have been significantly changed—still the first moment. "The second moment" comes when we ask what all this means when seen through eyes of faith. What has God to do with this—the One who is our Creator, Redeemer, and Sustainer? And how will our theological reflections help to serve life now?

In addition, liberation theologies remind us that (whether we are conscious of it or not) *all theologies are bound to specific histories and life experiences.* There are no universal theologies. All theologies are particular attempts by believers to make sense of life's challenges and to respond to them in faith. Thus, there is no need to apologize for such a specific theological focus as addiction and recovery, as if more authentic theology were done in detachment from this messy concreteness. A theological probing of why some of us have been addictive drinkers can be as fruitful for serving life as the most exalted reflection on a "more pure" theological issue like the resurrection of Christ. In fact, faithful probing of a drunk's release from alcohol obsession might be a particularly useful way of grasping the ongoing reality and specificity of Christ's resurrection.

In the third place, liberation theology reminds us that *theology is essentially a social enterprise.* It is not fundamentally an individual and specialized intellectual task, but rather—at its most genuine—an outgrowth of life in community. Yes, I am a theological professional who has written these words in the solitude of his study. But I am also acutely aware of the community of recovering people who continue to teach me and who point me to the presence and activity of the Holy. These are my Spirit-filled teachers, and I try to listen to them carefully.

Why listen? Those who have experienced oppression have keen ears and wide eyes, hearing and seeing things that others might miss. They more likely see and hear God lifting up the lowly, filling the hungry with good things, and sending the rich away empty (Luke 1:51–52). Furthermore, truly listening to anyone invariably communicates a sense of worth and dignity that the other deserves. Dietrich Bonhoeffer's warning from the underground seminary is a reminder: "Many people are looking for an ear that will listen. They do not find it among Christians, because these Christians are talking where they should be listening. But [the one] who can no longer listen to . . . brother [or sister] will soon be no longer listening to God either. . . . This is the beginning of the death of the spiritual life, and in the end there is nothing left."[15]

Along with the wisdom of recovering people, I will draw (as I said earlier) on that of social scientists and medical professionals in the addiction field. Theology as "second moment" involves understanding our "first moment" experience as fully as we can. Though Western European theologies typically have taken philosophy as their partner, more frequently social science has been the ally of Latin American and other liberation theologies as they have attempted to understand the experience of the oppressed. Similarly, the social and medical sciences will be our partners in trying to see the experiences of addiction and recovery through eyes of faith.

"The function of freedom," Toni Morrison declares, "is to free someone else, and if you are no longer wracked or in bondage to a person or a way of life, tell your story. Risk freeing someone else."[16] In that statement lies the power of liberation theology, and also an invitation to narrative theology—to telling the story.

Narrative Theology

While narrative or story has been a popular theological theme for some years, there is still little agreement about what it means and how narrative should function theologically. Nevertheless, "fools rush in," and the lack of scholarly agreement need not deter us. What *I* mean by narrative theology in these pages is several things.

For one thing, I mean *the healing significance of storytelling and story hearing for the recovering alcoholic.* Healing is a time-honored theological issue, and its connection with story is ancient. Today, typical A.A. meetings are full of personal narratives. "Our stories," says the Big Book, "disclose in a general way what we used to be like, what happened, and what we are like now." Thus there are the "drunkalogues" that recall—sometimes with rollicking humor ("we absolutely insist on enjoying life"), sometimes with touching pathos—the drinking days and what the depths of the active disease were like for us.[17] And there are recovery stories that not only celebrate in gratitude what happened to release us from alcoholism's grip, but that also wrestle candidly with the ongoing struggles of sobriety.

A.A. members readily attest that telling and hearing these stories is healing. The narratives give encouragement and practical advice. They reinforce a sense of belonging and mutual support. Their honesty both relies on and underscores the safety of the group as a society of mutual vulnerability. But there is something more. "The little stories" of each recovering person in the group seem to be spoken and held in the context of "the big story"—the A.A. story that recovery is possible and that there are certain ways it can happen.

Likewise, narrative theology would have us place our little stories of recovery in the larger context of "the big story"—the story that the community of faith tells about God. Drunkenness and recovery may be a strange story, but the gospel is at least as strange. It is a story of divine vulnerability, a story about God's caring more about us than we care about ourselves, a story of divine life-giving even in the midst of death.

Narrative theology for alcoholics can be illuminated by the ways stories have been used with other illnesses. In recent years the literature about illnesses such as cancer, HIV/AIDS, and clinical depression has been marked by a good bit of narrative writing by people with those diseases. No longer are we content only with attempts at objective description—as if the experience of the person with the disease were quite beside the point. Now we recognize how critical for healing it is to hear the personal, subjective narrative reflection.

Arthur Kleinman, a pioneering interpreter of this phenomenon, makes the distinction between *disease* (the organic reality) and *illness*, which "refers to how the sick person and members of the family or wider social network perceive, live with, and respond to symptoms and disability."[18] Definitions of an illness (what a particular disease *means*) are shaped by a host of cultural beliefs and values, including an interpretation of the stigma that may be attached to a particular disease.

Sick people, usually influenced by the attitudes they perceive around them, develop "illness narratives." These are personal interpretations of what the disease means to them, and these interpretations in turn greatly affect the ongoing experience of the disease. But these illness narratives can be harmful, compounding the organic disease itself. When this is the case, they keep the sick person trapped in guilt, shame, fatalism, or self-destructive attitudes. But a critical part of the healing process is "remoralization"—a fresh construction of the narrative that helps the person deal more creatively with the disease and the changes it is bringing to his or her life.

That process has been central to my recovery. At Hazelden I struggled mightily with the guilt and shame I had brought to the treatment center, finally causing my exasperated counselor to tell me that my recovery would be stymied until I understood my problem as a disease. He was urging me to reconstruct my illness story in a nonmoralistic, nonjudgmental way that could hold promise for the future.

Healing is a major reason why throughout history religious communities have relied on storytelling. The same holds for recovery groups. And whether in religious or recovery contexts, the narratives typically have a common format: what we used to be like, what happened to us, and what we are like now. It is the testimonial.

We are rediscovering what St. Augustine demonstrated in his *Confessions* many centuries ago: autobiography itself can be a theological statement. At the very least, when we are reflective in our stories about ourselves, we reveal what is ultimately important to us. John Barbour writes, "At its [autobiography's] heart lies *bios*. *Bios* in autobiography does not mean simply the temporal span of organic existence, but the 'sense of life' of an individual: *all that gives meaning and purpose to a person's existence in time*.'[19] Thus, in telling her story, the person is not simply reciting a series of events, however significant they might be. She is also disclosing what it is that really gives her *life* and what makes life worth living for her. She is, in short, telling the story of her faith—the story of what she most deeply trusts.

At a recovery meeting I introduce myself saying, "My name is Jim, and I'm an alcoholic." Therein lies a story of my self-understanding. But I understand my own little story only if I place it within the framework of a larger story where the two accounts interact. That larger piece for me is surely the story of my recovery movement. Also, and still larger, is the story of the church, the narrative in many different versions that we Christians tell about God.

For me, these three narratives—my personal one, A.A.'s story, and the church's story—interact, each illuminating the other. It is a dynamic familiar to John Calvin, who began his *Institutes of the Christian Religion* by observing that all true wisdom has two parts: knowledge of God and knowledge of the self. True and sound wisdom, Calvin believed, had to do with the relations between those biblical narratives about the identity of God and the narratives that people tell each other to express their self-understandings.[20]

H. Richard Niebuhr writes, "Revelation means for us that part of our inner history which illuminates the rest of it and which is itself intelligible." His analogy for revelation is the experience of reading a difficult book, trying to follow a difficult argument, and then coming upon "a luminous sentence." That one sentence furnishes a base from which we can look backward over what we have read, also move pages ahead, and get some grasp of the whole book. "Revelation is like that."[21]

The fundamental "luminous sentence" in my own inner history is God's story told in Hebrew and Christian Scriptures and in the history of the church. This sentence throws light on the rest of my narrative— including both my alcoholism and my recovery. Connecting those stories is a major purpose in these pages.

Consider, for example, a familiar story from the book of Genesis in the Hebrew Scriptures. It begins, "Jacob was left alone; and a man wrestled with him until daybreak" (Gen. 32:24). It is a story about struggle, about wrestling with powers in the darkness, about wounding. It is a story about staying with the struggle until blessing comes. It is a story about receiving a new name, and about limping into the sunrise. It is a gripping story for many who have been living through prolonged spiritual struggles.

As an alcoholic I find it a particularly powerful narrative. We alcoholics know well about flawed characters, and we can identify with Jacob. We know about struggling in the darkness with a power, our disease, that has threatened to overcome us. In recovery we have stayed with the struggle, demanding blessing. The blessing we receive is inseparable from the new name given us: "My name is Jim, and I'm an alcoholic." And in recovery we still limp, for our wounds have been deep, but we know that we are limping into the sunrise. It is a moving story.

However, we live with multiple stories and that complicates things. Yes, I am an alcoholic. I am also a Protestant Christian, white, male, North American, of Scandinavian descent, military veteran, middle-class, married, parent, grandparent, retired seminary professor. Each of these particularities contains a narrative, and each is a lens through which I see my story of addiction and recovery. And each of them shapes my story of God.

That makes generalizations risky. So I must try to speak as specifically and confessionally as I can—for (Mark Twain reminds me) I am neither pope, nor royalty, nor do I have tapeworms. But whenever elements of my stories connect with those of the reader, I am grateful—whether it is through the narratives about addiction and recovery, or the narratives about God, or hopefully both.

I believe that all addictions have certain important commonalities. Whether they are "substance addictions" (alcohol, various other drugs, tobacco, food, etc.), or "process and behavior addictions" (sex, gambling, work, shopping, religion, relationships, etc.), all share certain dynamics. But there are also important differences among them. So I will focus on chemical addictions and, especially, on alcoholism. Alcohol was, in the current jargon, my "drug of choice." It is the story I know from experience. But when meaningful connections occur between my experience and that of readers affected by other addictions, I give thanks.

Finally, a narrative approach can give theology passion. These days we crave some passion in our literature, whether it be theology or fiction. Literary critic Roxana Robinson observes that as the globe is warming, the literary world seems to be cooling down. "A century ago, books engaged the heart as well as the mind, and when we read, emotion seized us, took us over, broke us down. Who could sit dry-eyed through the death of Pere Goriot? Who was unmoved by Anna Karenina's despair?"[22] But now, she laments, such deep engagement with life is rare.

Instead of the emotion that reminds us of our own vulnerabilities and sufferings, there is coolness and detachment. Perhaps we have been numbed by seemingly endless horror. Faulkner once observed that writing is about the human heart in conflict with itself. Though few contemporary writers seem to speak of the human heart, we still have those organs, and what they symbolize is fundamental to our humanity. So we thirst for good stories of the heart. We also need revealing narrative theologies that speak to the heart and create connective tissues among us.

A Paradoxical Theology

Folks in recovery are well-advised to keep things simple. A close friend gave me an important bit of advice the day before I began treatment. He himself had been through treatment for alcoholism a few years earlier. A practical, down-to-earth man who knew my academic penchant for examining all sides of an issue, he said, "Jim, don't ask questions. Just do what they tell you to do." His advice was extraordinarily important for me, even when it was not easy. During that month of treatment and in the years since, I have profited many times by remembering those words. Sometimes a luminous simplicity is nurtured by desperation.

But these years of sobriety have also taught me that—in some other ways—issues in addiction and recovery are often complex and paradoxical. In fact, part of the profundity in any truly probing human story is its paradoxical nature. I had to learn this. I grew up with the notion that life was filled with simple oppositions: people were either good or bad; things, either true or untrue; decisions, either right or wrong. College, army, marriage, parenting, and theological study changed all that. I learned that paradox is central to understanding both life and Christian faith. After all, my basic theological studies took place in the 1950s when Søren Kierkegaard and Karl Barth were standard theological fare. While a reconstructed liberalism remained part of me, I did become convinced that the gospel could not be understood without seeing it paradoxically. What I had yet to learn was the centrality of paradox to my own deepest personal experiences, and alcoholism has been my most demanding and persuasive teacher.

The word *paradox* comes from the Greek, literally meaning "beyond" (*para*) "opinion" (*doxa*). It points to a reality that goes beyond our typical, simple linear thought. The word also ordinarily signifies a conjunction of terms that appear to be contradictory or absurd when used together, but in reality are not. Each term actually needs the other.

I have organized these chapters around a number of paradoxes that I have experienced in alcoholic addiction and recovery. I also find them part and parcel of the Christian faith, characteristic of its countercultural, subversive wisdom. In both realms they now seem unavoidable to me. When I ignore them or dualistically break the terms apart into either/or propositions, I do so at great risk. And it is a very real risk for an alcoholic: when my sobriety is threatened so is my life, for active alcoholism is a predictably life-shortening disease.

That nineteenth-century Danish radical Kierkegaard taught us that when thought is driven to its limits, when we attempt to discover what thought finally cannot rationally comprehend, we are left with the absurd. But the absurd—which can be expressed only in paradox—is the road to faith.

As an alcoholic I have learned more about the absurd than I ever thought I would need to know. It is, after all, absurd to be a drunk. And in a different way recovery is absurd—it is a mystery. As a matter of fact, the term "recovering alcoholic" for many years would have been viewed as an oxymoron. The two words were thought to be simply contradictory, for alcoholics just did not recover. Today we use both words in one breath, and "recovering alcoholic" no longer sounds strange. But the reality itself is still deeply paradoxical for, in spite of better scientific understanding, both addiction and recovery remain pervaded by mystery.

As is Christian faith itself. To be sure, as a late archbishop of Canterbury used to say, the doors of the church ought never be so low that we must leave our heads outside when we enter. Indeed, any theology worth the name calls for demanding, careful, and rigorous thought. But that does not mean that the faith itself is a reasonable matter. The same archbishop once preached on the end of the world. Following worship a woman said to him at the door, "Your Grace, I so much enjoyed that sermon," to which he responded, "But Madam, you weren't supposed to enjoy it."[23]

There is mystery and paradox at the heart of faith itself. As the apostle Paul says, what the world calls wisdom is simply foolishness to God, and what the world calls foolishness and weakness is God's power for salvation.[24] That sounds strangely like A.A.'s discovery—power comes to alcoholics only when they move deeply into their own powerlessness—a true paradox.

Chapter Two

God Thirst and Alcoholic Thirst

Spirituality and Religion

Because of the pervasive influence of Alcoholics Anonymous and its kindred organizations, it is now both commonplace and highly significant to speak of recovery from addiction as a *spiritual* process. "Addiction/Recovery" shelves in the bookstores are amply stocked with daily meditation books and volumes on recovery spirituality. What is typically missing from our common awareness, however, is the recognition that *addiction* no less than recovery is a spiritual matter. Without that understanding we are left speaking about addiction only in medical and psychological terms, and the result is the confusing package of a spiritual solution for a nonspiritual problem.

Granted, to speak of chemical addiction as a spiritual phenomenon sounds strange. Its origin is likely genetic in some measure. It develops from changes in brain chemistry. It is psychological and emotional. It involves relationships and social environments. Addiction is all of these, but in what sense is it spiritual? And, for that matter, what is spirituality?

While *spirituality* is an immensely popular concept in our time, its meanings seem procrustean, covering anything and everything. Sometimes we are more certain about what it is not. Recovery group conversations often contrast it with religion: "Religion is for people who are afraid of going to hell. Spirituality is for people who have been there." Though I can understand some of the feelings and experiences lying behind such statements, an either/or approach does not help us.

Historically, in fact, the spiritual approach of A.A. was grounded in "organized religion." Bill Wilson and Dr. Bob Smith (the cofounders of A.A.), trying to understand their own recoveries and searching for a viable approach to reach others, found their initial anchorage in the Oxford Group. Founded in 1908 in both Europe and America as "The First Century Christian Fellowship," it was a theologically conservative, nondenominational, evangelically oriented attempt to recapture the spirit of what its members believed to be early Christianity. The movement peaked in the early 1930s and late in that decade changed its name to Moral Rearmament.

For a time this body provided both the religious grounding and the conceptual home for Wilson, Smith, and their early recovering companions. Indeed, the movement clearly articulated several fundamentals that would later become central to A.A.: the necessity of a Higher Power, of conversion, and of group support. However, the initial band of recovering alcoholics gradually became disenchanted with the Oxford Group's approach. Its penchant for absolutism in belief structure and its aggressive evangelism were just too much for "a bunch of drunks." Though he had repeated contacts with national Oxford Group leaders and other religious notables, and though he had a powerful "conversion" experience while withdrawing from alcohol in the hospital, Bill W. never completely lost his skepticism about religion. It was a persisting mistrust that would mirror the experience of many other recovering people.

Several major critiques of religion (especially of Christianity, the background of most A.A. members) were frequently voiced in the early A.A. movement and continue to the present. For one thing, religion is denominational and divisive. Split into competing groups with each claiming superiority, religion offers no common ground for recovering people. A drunk looking for help does not want to be asked about religious labels or affiliations. Such a person needs a group with only one requirement for membership: the desire to stop drinking.

Furthermore, some have found religion rigid and doctrinal. Most religious groups, it is said, are filled with unquestionable doctrines that separate the sheep from the goats. But alcoholics do not do well with absolutes. Bill W. complained that the problem with religious groups was "their claim how confoundedly right all of them are," so he moved toward an approach that made suggestions rather than proclaiming absolutes.[1]

Related to this criticism is a third: religion is perfectionistic. It is for people who claim or aspire to holiness. Some of us who are recovering people, however, know that perfectionism was our problem and cannot be our answer. It was one of the major dynamics behind our drinking, and if we are to get sober and stay sober it will not be through a program for saints but through a humble fellowship of sinners.

Finally, religion as experienced by many alcoholics is moralistic and judgmental. Quick to interpret alcoholism as a moral problem, as a failure of character and will power, such religion is quick to judge the alcoholic accordingly. But people seeking recovery typically carry a heavy load of guilt and shame already, and instinctively shy away from those who would add more to that burden. They recoil from a religiosity that seems more interested in eternal salvation than in support and healing now.

All of this adds up to a heavy indictment: religion is divisive, doctrinally rigid, perfectionistic, and moralistically judgmental.[2] I would not wish such religion on any person hoping for recovery—indeed on *anyone*. Even those of us whose experience has been much more positive (as mine has been) do well to remember what good theology has always known: religion is a highly ambiguous and risky venture. The source of amazingly creative goodness and self-sacrifice, it is also one of the most dangerous of all human enterprises, for it tempts its adherents to confuse themselves with God.

Because of this mixed picture, more generic and neutral definitions of both spirituality and religion are helpful. I suggest these: our *spirituality* is our response to our human sense of incompleteness—whatever form that response might take. *Religion*, on the other hand, is the communal expression of that response—when persons bound together by similar spiritualities develop group patterns of nurturing, expressing, extending, and preserving those experiences.

Those are exceedingly broad definitions, though I think useful ones. They mean that all of us are inescapably spiritual, even though that spirituality takes extraordinarily different shapes. And most of us are religious as well (even if not in traditional ways), for it seems natural that we seek some kind of communal support and some kind of ritualization for our spiritualities. In later chapters we will look further at the religious and communal dimensions of both addiction and recovery. In this chapter, however, I want to focus on the spiritual: our incompleteness, our desire— yes, our thirst.

One standard dictionary gives three meanings for *thirst*: the discomfort that arises from the need for water; a craving for alcohol; or any craving or strong desire.

Ultimately the word comes from an Indo-European base meaning "to be dry." I find it an important metaphor for both alcoholism and for the fundamental yearning behind every spirituality, including that which can bring recovery. We alcoholics surely know the experience of craving "our drug of choice." And though we might express it in a thousand different ways, we also know what the psalmist was speaking of: "As a deer longs for flowing streams, so my soul longs for you, O God. My soul thirsts for God, for the living God. When shall I come and behold the face of God?" (Ps. 42:1–2).

The Core of Spirituality

A haunting sense of incompleteness, a yearning for completion, an uncertainty craving for certainty, a brokenness hungering for wholeness—these things seem to lie at the bottom of our human spirituality. Human beings are, as Karen Armstrong says, "compelled to search for hidden meaning and to achieve an ecstasy that makes them feel fully alive."[3]

Hence, *desire* is at the core of our spirituality, a burning desire for that which promises to bring us closer to completion and certainty and wholeness, a desire to connect with what feels most life-giving. Some ancient Greeks spoke of it this way: "We are fired into life with a madness that comes from the gods and which would have us believe that we can have a great love, perpetuate our own seed, and contemplate the divine."[4] As Ronald Rolheiser puts it, "There is within us a fundamental dis-ease, an unquenchable fire that renders us incapable, in this life, of ever coming to full peace. This desire lies at the center of our lives, in the marrow of our bones, and in the deep recesses of the soul."[5]

The search for, naming of, and reflecting on this desire lie at the heart of all great literature and art, all philosophy and psychology, and, surely, all theology. It is a restlessness, a disquiet, a hunger, "a wildness that cannot be tamed, a congenital all-embracing ache that lies at the center of human experience."[6] It is that of which St. Augustine spoke in his oft-quoted prayer: "Thou hast created us for thyself, O God, so that our hearts are restless until they find their rest in thee."[7]

Restlessness of heart comes in varied shapes and sizes. Sudden feelings of physical and emotional intensity bubble up in the presence of someone we love. We feel an ache saying good-bye to a friend we won't see again for a long time. We sense that all scientific discovery, artistic creation, and philosophical insight arise out of the passion for the unknown. And, once in a while, we feel almost a palpable ache for this nameless presence. God is both source and destiny of this ache, this yearning, this desire.[8]

Many of us experience this as a thirst. It is a yearning we can't quite name and yet are quite aware of. It is Augustine's restlessness and longing for home. It is the despised Samaritan woman thirsting for "the living water" as she encounters Jesus at the well: "Sir, give me this water, so that I may never be thirsty or have to keep coming here to draw water." (John 4:15). It may even be part of the thirst Jesus felt on the cross. Somehow, this desire seems close to the core of our humanity. Whether we are conscious of it or not, whether we give words to it or not, there is a huge God-shaped hole in each of us, wanting to be filled.

It is the *imago dei*, the image of God in which we are created. In other words, our creatureliness is *deiform* in shape. We have originated from God and our spiritual DNA is stamped with the traces of the divine.[9] Deep calls to deep, like calls to like, and we feel the pull of our primordial connection with the holy Source and sacred Ground of our being. That thirst is at the core of our humanity. But as St. Augustine observed, this sense of lack, this yearning to be filled can lead either to God or to a frustrated and destructive sense of inadequacy.[10] Addiction is a clear example of the latter. Our spiritual capacity is indeed neutral.

Superficial religious interpretations would have us believe that desire as such is evil. A fairly common Western misunderstanding of Buddhism identifies *tanha* as the cause of life's dislocation and equates *tanha* simply with "desire." Just eliminate desire, then, and the root of life's problems is removed. The same idea is reflected in George Bernard Shaw's *Heartbreak House* when Ellie exclaims, "I feel now as if there was nothing I could not do, because I want nothing." This moves Captain Shotover to his only noticeable passion in the play: "That's the only real strength. That's genius. That's better than rum."[11]

If desire itself is the problem, the Buddhist Eightfold Path that eliminates all desire from life would appear to be the remedy. However, as Huston Smith aptly observes, to shut down all desire would be to die, and death is not a very good solution to life's fundamental problem. Furthermore, "there are some desires the Buddha explicitly advocated—the desire for liberation, for example, or for the happiness of others. *Tanha* is a specific kind of desire, the desire for *private* fulfillment."[12] Thus, for the Buddhist it is not the energy of desire per se that is the problem, but only those desires that close the self in on the self, increasing one's separateness from all else.

However, desire has been intrinsically suspect not only in certain interpretations of Eastern religions, but also in some versions of Christianity. At least in formal doctrine, Protestants have had more difficulty with this than Roman Catholics. Doubtless it goes back to the Protestant Reformation wherein the yearning for God was mistrusted because it was seen to encourage human effort to reach the Holy One. By blessing human endeavor it then undercut the message of God's radical grace. Catholics, on the other hand, were less suspicious of a place for human effort. The great doctors of the faith Augustine and Aquinas actually blessed desire as intrinsic to our humanity and hence God-given. In actual pieties, however, both Catholics and Protestants have been ambivalent, for desire so frequently seems bodily and visceral, even (God forbid!) sexual, hence something alien to true spirituality.

But spirituality always is a matter of the total self—the body and its desires included. The ancient philosophical dualism that split spirit from body, mind from matter, is alien to the best in Hebraic and Christian traditions. Since spirit is neither ethereal nor disembodied, both God and alcohol can be sensuous *and* spiritual experiences.

Spirituality, then, has to do with how we deal with that basic human desire experienced in the totality of our beings—how we handle our yearnings, our hunger for connection, our restless yearning to find a place called home in the universe. It is about *eros*, that dimension of our love born of desire. Spirituality is not necessarily mystical, esoteric, churchly, or otherworldly. Nor is it the domain of the exceptionally religious or of New Age people. It is universal. We emerge from our mothers' wombs not serene but kicking and screaming, and our spirituality throughout a lifetime consists in how we pattern and direct that desire. "And how we do channel it, the disciplines and habits we choose to live by, will either lead to a greater integration or disintegration within our bodies, minds, and souls, and to a greater integration or disintegration in the way we are related to God, others, and the cosmic world."[13] Whether creative and integrative or destructive and disintegrative, it is still our spirituality.

Spirituality inevitably involves *faith*. As a Christian, I can speak of faith as confidence and trust in God, whom I have experienced primarily through the community of Jesus Christ. Faith is not fundamentally assent to doctrinal "truth," though it involves belief. It is more a matter of trust and dependence. It is more a gift than an achievement. That is a fairly typical Christian description.

But we can also legitimately speak of faith in a more general and "formal" way. Thus Paul Tillich says, "Faith is the state of being ultimately concerned. The content matters infinitely for the life of the believer, but it does not matter for the formal definition of faith."[14] Whatever engages our ultimate concern—whether it be the God revealed in one of the religious traditions, or our own success and security, or our family, or our nation, or the bottle—whatever we really trust in and depend on to slake our fundamental desires, that is the object of our faith. Martin Luther said it simply: whatever your heart clings to and relies on, that truly is your god.

Whether we are traditionally religious or militantly atheist or something in between, we appear to be inescapably spiritual, fated with the thirst for completion. By the same token, we are fated to live by faith. We cannot move through the day without patterning our lives around whatever powers or realities we really trust in, rely on, and believe to be ultimately significant. Nicholas of Cusa observed that God is the minimum as well as the maximum: the little things of ordinary days are no less sacred than the great issues of our existence. So we exhibit our faith in little ways no less than big ones, and our spirituality gives shape to the dailiness of our lives just as to our more dramatic moments and decisions. And all of this informs our addictions and our recoveries.

Thirst: Divine and Demonic

The "drunkalogue" stories we tell each other in recovery groups typically speak of the *what* and the *how* of our past alcoholic drinking. However, we seldom address the *why* of it. Our reluctance is not hard to understand. The *why* feels so complex and mysterious. Indeed, it also seems so circular: Did I become alcoholic because I drank too much, or did I drink too much because I was alcoholic?

At one level, of course, the *why* is a matter of scientific inquiry. Those who study alcoholism in the laboratory will tell us about its physiology. They will speak of the concentration of alcohol in the blood, the rate of absorption, and the development of tolerance (the need to drink more to obtain the same effect). They will tell us also about the experiential dynamics of craving. We alcoholics learned that the ingestion of alcohol produced pleasure in us (how much pleasure seems partly determined by heredity). But the pleasure is short-lived and is followed by feelings of discomfort (the degree of which may also be linked to heredity). Then what happens? Psychiatrist Donald W. Goodwin captures it with startling simplicity: "[T]he alcoholic drinks for two reasons: to achieve the pleasure and to relieve the discomfort. The same substance that produces the happy feeling also produces the unhappy feeling and is required both to restore the one and abolish the other."[15] The name for the unhappy feeling is *craving*, and nothing is as effective in abolishing it as the drug that produced it in the first place.

Some people describe craving as an experience of "discomfort," but that description is far too mild. My experience and that which others tell of was more than discomfort. It was pain. (A bar on Payne Avenue in St. Paul is named, fittingly, "The Payne Reliever.") And in addition to acute physical distress it was the strong emotional sense of drivenness, of being taken over.

What is the pleasure we seek in the first place? The descriptions given by alcoholics are as numerous and varied as the stars in the sky: to relax, to have fun, to forget, to connect, to reward myself, to drown my sorrows, to get up my courage, to feel like one of the group, to loosen up, to feel convivial and social, to get a rush, and, for many males, to feel like a man. The list could go on and on.

And what is the thirst behind the thirst? In one way or another, each explanation seems to be but a variation on the theme: "I was thirsty because I was feeling incomplete, and alcohol helped me feel more whole, more connected, more alive." Is alcohol, then, a way of searching for God, the ultimate source of wholeness and life? A positive answer may seem too facile, too generalized, indeed too characteristic of one like myself given to the theological enterprise. But similar responses come from many others.

Listen to a philosopher. Bruce Wilshire is speaking of our primal human hunger for the ecstasy of finding our lives significant. When our primal needs have not been satisfied early in life, we are unsure of what they are and what would satisfy them: "Because these unmet primal needs still exist, a signal of alarm at *something* impending . . . will continue to sound, muffled and unplaceable, creating a vague, pervasive restlessness." Then we act erratically and impulsively trying to appease our hunger, and this is addiction.[16]

Listen to a novelist. Thomas Wolfe writes in *Look Homeward Angel*, "In all the earth there was no other like him, no other fitted to be so sublimely and magnificently drunken. . . . Why, when it was possible to buy a God in a bottle, and drink him off, and become a God oneself, were men not forever drunken?"[17] Bill Wilson, perhaps paraphrasing Wolfe, later wrote, "Before A.A. we were trying to drink God out of a bottle."[18] Like members of the cult of Dionysus, we were trying to become divine by consuming the god; it was communion.

Listen to a psychiatrist. Gerald G. May observes, "After twenty years of listening to the yearnings of people's hearts, I am convinced that all humans have an inborn desire for God. Whether we are consciously religious or not, this desire is our deepest longing and our most precious treasure."[19] It might be that we have repressed this desire. Or it might be that we feel it in different ways—as a yearning for fulfillment or completion. But whatever shape it takes, May argues, it is a longing to love and to be loved, and a desire for the Source of love, God. When this same yearning is distorted, it is the origin of our most destructive urges and actions. Then it is the soil from which addiction grows.

Finally, here is Carl Jung writing to Bill Wilson two weeks before the psychiatrist's own death in 1961. Jung was speaking of Roland H., a difficult alcoholic patient with whom he had worked decades earlier. Roland was able to be abstinent for a year under Jung's care in Switzerland, but returning to the U.S. he reverted to alcoholic drinking. Back in Switzerland once again, Roland was informed by Jung that there was no "cure" for his alcoholism and his only hope was a thoroughgoing spiritual transformation.

Jung wrote to Wilson saying he had become convinced that only some deep spiritual conversion could save Roland from utter alcoholic destruction. He explained that he had not been able to communicate to his patient how central spirituality is to recovery, for he feared that Roland would misinterpret his talk about this subject: "How could one formulate such an insight in a language that is not misunderstood in our days?" But, as Jung explained to Wilson, the fundamental dynamic of the disease was spiritual: "[Roland's] craving for alcohol was the equivalent on a low level of the spiritual thirst of our being for wholeness, expressed in medieval language, the union with God. . . . You see, alcohol in Latin is *spiritus* and you use the same word for the highest religious experience a well as for the most depraving poison. The helpful formula therefore is: *spiritus contra spiritum.*"[20] Because in its fundamental dynamic, alcoholism is longing for the Spirit, it finally takes the Spirit to counter the spirits.

There is a thirst behind the thirst. Some of us—and not only theologians—will name it the desire for God.

The thirst in the foreground, the thirst of which we are most conscious, seems almost infinitely varied in its shape. So does the experience of craving. Sometimes the desire is mystifying even when it is imperiously insistent. The emptiness inside seems like a bottomless pit. The character in Saul Bellow's *Henderson the Rain King* describes it this way:

> Now I have already mentioned that there was a disturbance in my heart, a voice that spoke there and said, *I want, I want, I want!* It happened every afternoon and when I tried to suppress it it got even

stronger. It only said one thing, *I want, I want, I want.* And I would ask, "What do you want? But this is all it would ever tell me. . . . Through fights and drunkenness and labor it went right on, in the country, in the city. No purchase however expensive would lessen it. Then I would say, "Come on, tell me. What's the complaint, is it Lily herself? Do you want some nasty whore? It has to be some lust?" But this was no better a guess than the others. The demand came louder, *I want, I want, I want, I want, I want, I want!* And I would cry, begging at last, "Oh, tell me then. Tell me what you want!"[21]

If we are practicing alcoholics, we may not know the deeper source of that insistent desire within, but at least we know we crave *alcohol.*[22] Craving goes beyond mere liking. I *liked* alcohol, of course—its flavor, its looks, the cool condensation on the glass. All of these things I found highly pleasant, but craving is more than that. It seems also different from heightened desire. I *desired* alcohol on certain occasions, even strongly desired it—at lunch, before dinner, in the evening, before bedtime, with companions or relaxing alone, when I was happy or when I was sad. But more than liking and more than desiring, my alcoholic experience was that of *craving* alcohol. As I reflect back on my experience, I perhaps never did have a "normal" relationship with the substance. From the beginning of my drinking, even when I was able to stop, I always wanted more. It was an urge more powerful, less rational than any other I have known.

The alcoholic's craving can be associated with a romantic image, or a trembling in the belly, or the distinctive taste of a martini, or the anticipated tingling buzz in the brain, or the picture of cold wetness of the can in hand—or with no particular image at all. The variations are many. According to one psychiatrist, "It can be an inchoate urge, almost without mental content or imagery, verbal thought, visual images, or a total experience including smell, taste, vision, and even physiological effects. To a large extent, the nature of the urge or compulsion depends on the predominant way each individual thinks."[23]

The distinction between *desire* and *lust* now becomes critical. Often we think of desire as any itch (bodily or emotional) that demands scratching. Then lust is simply highly intense desire. But the Latin root of the word suggests that desire is that dynamic of being drawn to something that truly fulfills our deepest needs, in contrast to an attraction that simply satisfies or gratifies transient wants. "The aim of desire is not so much to satisfy our craving for fleetingly pleasant sensations as to awaken in us an abiding and sensitive yearning for all that we require to flourish spiritually."[24] I can experience lust for a new house, for sex, for better appearance, for certain achievements. But desire goes beyond a house to a home, beyond sex to love, beyond appearance to health, beyond achievement to respect. In my alcoholic craving I thought I was experiencing intense desire, but that was not so. What I did experience was a potent and unrelenting lust—yet anything I did in attempting to quell it finally was incapable of satisfying my desire.

"The Ruins of Our Search for Transcendence"

After suffering decades of desert wandering and endless plagues, the people of Israel were (like the practicing alcoholic) restless, irritable, and discontent. While Moses was climbing Mount Sinai to receive God's revelations for this community of faith, their discontent overflowed. The book of Exodus records what happened:

> When the people saw that Moses delayed to come down from the mountain, the people gathered around Aaron, and said to him, "Come, make gods for us, who shall go before us; as for this Moses, the man who brought us up out of the land of Egypt, we do not know what has become of him. Aaron said to them, "Take off the gold rings . . . and bring them to me. . . . He took the gold from them, formed it in a mold, and cast an image of a calf; and they said, "These are your gods, O Israel, who brought you up out of the land of Egypt!" (Exod. 32:1–4)

A core conviction of monotheistic faith is that God alone deserves our ultimate loyalty. Only God should have our ultimate concern; only God deserves to be the object of our utmost desire. But my desire for alcohol became lust, and my thirst for the Spirit became confused with my thirst for spirits. I found my solution in a golden calf.

Monotheistic faith has often portrayed God as a "jealous" deity, brooking no competition and tolerating no rivals. The first commandment of the Decalogue says it: "You shall have no other gods before me." Though at times both Hebrew and Christian faiths have expressed this crudely, suggesting an unattractive divine petulance, the point is fundamental. When we place absolute trust in anything other than the universal source of life, it will backfire. That is precisely what happens in alcoholism.

Yet the issue is complex, and one of the reasons for complexity is the fact that most, if not all, of our experiences of the divine presence are *mediated*. I doubt that even most disciplined mystics have unmediated experiences of the Holy. Often encounters with the Holy are mediated by language, stories, traditions, images, metaphors, icons, liturgies, and interpretations gleaned from faithful companions. Sometimes the divine comes to us in nature's beauty, energy, and vastness. Frequently the most compelling sense of God comes through human flesh—in the mundane touches of beloved and familiar lives, in movements of history, in the heights and depths of our bodily experienced days. And that points to the core meaning of *incarnationalism* in its general sense: we experience the infinite through the finite. And that can include alcohol. The psalmist sings,

> "You cause the grass to grow for the cattle,
>   and the plants for people to use,
> to bring forth food from the earth,
>   *and wine to gladden the human heart.*"
>   (Ps. 104:14–15, italics mine)

The difficulty, of course, is in knowing the difference between the finite experience that conveys the life-giving sacred energy and that which is contrary to it. As my alcoholism progressed, my thirst for God increasingly became transmuted into a thirst for the seemingly *godlike* experiences that alcohol induced. Alcohol gave me a sense of well-being and connectedness—and wasn't that an experience of God? Alcohol released me from the nagging sense that I was never good or competent enough—and wasn't that God's grace? Alcohol dissolved my worries about the future, allowing me to live in the present—and wasn't that a divine gift? At my core there was a thirst, a thirst for whatever would fill the emptiness.

It was deceptive because the finite stuff in which I gradually placed my ultimate trust was not evil in itself. Alcohol is not evil. There is general agreement on this in Alcoholics Anonymous. Even when the Big Book's wording on occasion seems to condemn the substance ("we deal with alcohol—cunning, baffling, powerful!"), the A.A. approach (unlike the early temperance movements that castigated "demon rum") typically recognizes that alcohol is not bad in itself. For the alcoholic it has *become* demonic, but for many others it remains a good.

Here is a critically important theological affirmation. Creation is *good*—positively, unambiguously good. God looked at everything created and declared it very good. Yes, the creaturely can become demonic, but that is a distortion of its created goodness and not an intrinsic evil. The symbolism for this in Christian tradition is the devil as a fallen angel. The devil is not pure evil, but rather fallen goodness. This issue will bear further discussion in chapter 4, but at this point it is important to recognize that when alcohol becomes demonic it is a *distorted goodness*, something good gone awry.

Why insist on this? When I was a child, our family's standard table grace began, "God is great and God is good. . . ." It is quintessentially solid, basic theology, for in a sense all theology is but commentary on God's greatness and goodness. The divine greatness means, among other things, that there is no cosmic dualism—no independent force of evil that exists over against the Holy One. God's goodness means, among other things, that everything given existence from the hand of the Creator is positively good. As Augustine liked to say, "Whatever is, is good."

All of this is important in very practical ways for the alcoholic. If we describe anything as *intrinsically* evil, our language, attitudes, and actions become dualistic. We are in war. It is good against evil, the righteous against the unrighteous. Such perceptions play havoc in human relations, and they are lethal in international affairs.

Such perceptions are also bad news for recovery. If I can externalize the problem and locate it "out there" then *I* do not have to change. If the fundamental problem lies in alcohol itself, then I only need to avoid the evil substance. But that is a recipe for trouble, for we live in an alcohol-soaked society, and we who are recovering need to learn to live with the substance all around us. It is *we* who must change if there is to be lasting recovery.

I had known and affirmed all of these things before I became an active alcoholic. I never actively doubted them nor disavowed them, but the disease does strange things to one's fundamental beliefs. They remain in the mind but lose reality and force in life itself. And the insidious change comes through a deceptive but powerful idolatry.

How can we describe that idolatrous urge—the temptation to believe as infinite that which is only finite, to absolutize that which is only relative, and in doing so to make the good into something demonic? Daniel Day Williams describes what happens. The demonic attracts us because it is fascinating. It grabs our interest, excites us, makes us feel passionate energy. Beyond this, we perceive the demonic as revelatory. It seems to disclose the depth and power of things. But there is always distortion in this revelation. The demonic gains its power to exploit and destroy by making us see falsely. And then the demonic becomes aggrandizing, demanding increasingly more of our attention and loyalty. Its craving becomes insatiable.[25]

All of this was true for me with alcohol. Initially, I was fascinated with its ability to both soothe and excite me. Drinking seemed to open up new meanings. When I was relaxed with alcohol, I thought I could understand people and situations more clearly. But it became more and more deceptive. It was a lie. I couldn't understand more at all—my insight was drastically diminished. Even then alcohol had the power to delude me. While it gave me less and less, at the same time it demanded more and more from me—more attention, more devotion, more love. My thirst was not assuaged. The more I drank the thirstier I became.

Yet my thirst for alcohol never eradicated my thirst for God. Whether that is true for other alcoholics, I can only speculate. One could argue that some alcoholics have been so thoroughly overtaken by the disease that every vestige of desire for greater wholeness, every yearning for something transcendent, has been completely erased. The *only* thing they want is another drink. But I question that, and for two reasons.

First, I doubt it because of the stories I hear. They are reports from alcoholics who have lost virtually everything—family, home, work, possessions, self-respect—everything. When trying to articulate *why* they wanted so much to keep drinking even in those extremities, they typically convey the conviction that—even then—alcohol was not an end in itself. It was a means to something else. And that something else had to do, even if in a terribly inverted way, with a larger and more connected self.

So it is, even when the solution is so circular and so self-defeating. In Saint-Exupery's classic fairy tale, the little prince visits a strange land inhabited by "a tippler." The boy asks the tippler what he is doing, and the man replies that he is drinking. When the little prince then asks why he is drinking, the man replies that he drinks so that he may forget. "Forget what?" asks the prince. "Forget that I am ashamed," replies the tippler. Wanting to help him, the prince then asks the man what he is ashamed of. "Ashamed of drinking," comes the reply.[26] I know that vicious circle from experience, and I strongly suspect that every alcoholic does, regardless of how thoroughly the disease seems to have taken over. That larger, truer thirst never seems to vanish completely.

My second reason is theological: I believe that the image of God in us is never destroyed. The *imago dei* is not a substance, a thing that we possess. Rather, it is a relational reality. It is our connectedness to God. Even when we, by our own actions or will, try to sever all relationship with God, the Holy One does not sever the relationship with us. The *imago dei* may be defaced, but it is never eradicated. Even when we are taken over by an addiction so strong that God consciousness feels utterly alien to us, the point of contact is never lost. And that is why, for all of the understandably celebrative and exuberant language of a "new creation," our salvation is best understood as the *transformation* of what is, rather than its replacement by something totally new. Paul's enduring words say it best: "For I am convinced that neither death, nor life, nor angels, nor rulers, nor things present, nor things to come, nor powers, nor height, nor depth, nor anything else in all creation [including addictions], will be able to separate us from the love of God in Christ Jesus our Lord" (Rom. 8:38–39).

If addictions are, in John Bradshaw's apt phrase, "the ruins of our search for transcendence," those ruins remain as haunting reminders in us, and the reminders sometimes prompt the cry for help.[27] The psalm sung at the beginning of each monastic hour in religious orders for over a millennium and a half is a cry for help. It is even a scream: "Oh come and rescue me, God, Yahweh come quickly and help me!" (Ps. 70:1, Jerusalem Bible). "The insight is constant: Our darkness . . . is *a thirst* . . . for 'God,' for 'the spiritual,' for whatever might alleviate this painful side of the human condition, for whatever might somehow fill the empty hole in our human be-ing."[28]

The Spirit can teach us an immense amount in every thirst we experience, every desire in our lives.[29] If I am—as I was—full of anxious desires to keep working and working to please others no matter what it cost, the Spirit may some day prompt me to ask, "What is the desire behind that desire?" If I discover that I desire approval and esteem through being seen as conscientious, considerate, and capable, what is the desire lying deeper than that desire? I may discover the craving to be cherished for exactly who I am, regardless of what I do. And if I drink to deal with these things, what is the thirst behind that thirst?

It is through pressing such questions that the Spirit takes us deeply into our own woundedness out of which our drivenness and addictions arise. The Spirit leads us out into the wilderness, sometimes for years of wandering. "In that day the beautiful young women and the young men [and others of us as well] shall faint for thirst" (Amos 8:13). But this is also the place where the basic healing of our souls can occur. Carl Jung is frequently quoted as saying that the gods have now returned to us in our diseases.[30] Our diseases often do seem to arise from some profound, mysterious place, and in journeying deeply into them we sense that "the gods" themselves suffer with our sickness. Finally, however, it is not *the gods* who suffer. It is *God*. It is the Holy One who is wounded with our wounds. Indeed, that is the story of the cross.

Once, in our drinking days, we were blind, but now we begin to see. In recovery we gradually grasp the meanings behind our desires and begin to decipher the language of our thirst. Then we understand, in a way we could not have predicted, that our thirst has led us closer to home. It truly is as Augustine prayed: "[O]ur hearts are restless until they find their rest in thee."[31]

Chapter Three

Disease and Sin

What is Alcoholism?

Alcoholism wears many different faces. One portrait depicts an impoverished family in Limerick, Ireland. Frank McCourt describes his own home in *Angela's Ashes:*

> When Dad gets a job Mam is cheerful and she sings . . . "Could it be true, someone like you, could love me, love me?" . . . When Dad brings home the first week's wages Mam is delighted she can pay the lovely Italian man in the grocery shop and she can hold her head up again. . . . When Dad's job goes into the third week he does not bring home the wages. On Friday night we wait for him and Mam gives us bread and tea. The darkness comes down and the lights come on along Classon Avenue. . . . On the morning of the fourth Friday of Dad's job Mam asks him if he'll be home tonight with his wages or will he drink everything again? . . . Mam keeps at him. I'm asking you, Are you coming home so that we can have a bit of supper or will it be midnight with no money in your pocket and you singing . . . sad songs? He puts on his cap, shoves his hands into his trouser pockets, sighs and looks up at the ceiling. I told you before I'll be home, he says.[1]

Each alcoholic's story is unique, but there are common themes. My addiction did not involve poverty or depriving my family of food or losing jobs. But there were absences, and promises sincerely made but broken, and sad songs.

According to a standard definition, alcoholism is compulsive drinking in spite of repeated negative consequences. The alcoholic's "insanity" is repeating the same actions over and over again while expecting different results. Contrasted with nonalcoholic "problem drinkers," alcoholics usually have these characteristics:

1. Compulsive, repetitive alcohol use, often in ritualized ways.
2. Tissue tolerance: over time, increasing amounts of alcohol are required for the desired effects.
3. Withdrawal symptoms (ranging from restlessness and irritability to severe hangovers) when alcohol is no longer used.
4. Increasing dependence, both psychological and physiological, on alcohol.
5. Craving for alcohol and obsessive thinking about drinking.
6. Loss of control: the inability to stop once drinking has begun, and loss of control over alcohol's effects.[2]

Regarding the number of alcoholics in the United States, the best estimates hold that about 70 percent of adults drink and about 12 percent (20 percent of men and 8 percent of women) drink heavily. Among these "problem drinkers" is a subgroup of alcoholics, estimated at around 5 percent of the general population in men and slightly less than 1 percent in women.[3] Thus, at least ten million Americans are likely in some stage of alcoholism. With the exception of caffeine and nicotine, more people are addicted to alcohol than to all other chemicals combined.[4]

For years I was aware of having other addictions. Caffeine dependence, of course. After all, I was a Minnesota Scandinavian. Nicotine? After twenty-some years on cigarettes I eased my conscience by switching to the pipe but knew I was still inhaling. Both stimulation and blessed calm came from the coffee cup and the pipe. But alcohol? I had not the slightest inkling that I would become addicted and certainly did not intend that. No one ever does. The cost of membership in that club is just too high. When I began to use alcohol moderately and regularly, I did so simply because (for a variety of reasons) it made me feel good. After some years, however, I depended on alcohol not just to feel good but to feel *normal*. Finally there came the "oops phenomenon"—the surprising, wrenching realization that I was hooked.[5]

When a person gradually "progresses" from being a voluntary to a compulsive drinker, it is because of brain changes. The neurotransmitters are especially affected, and dopamine, the primary transmitter of pleasure feelings, provides a good illustration. Alcohol causes its intense release, resulting in powerful feelings of pleasure. However, the brain seeks homeostasis, a constant level of cell activity. When extended alcohol use provides artificially high levels of dopamine, the brain decreases its own production. Then, when alcohol is removed, and with it that extra dopamine, the person not only feels the lack of pleasure but also fatigue, irritability, depression, and possibly physical pain: withdrawal. To the addicted person it is clear that relief will come only through the use of more alcohol, and that judgment seems vindicated, for drinking *does* produce relief. It is the picture of the hijacked brain and the dynamic of craving. Lord Byron's words fit my alcoholic experience remarkably well:

> My very chains and I grew friends,
> So much long communion tends
> To make us what we are.[6]

As alcoholism progresses, psychological symptoms become more severe.[7] I became preoccupied with alcohol—always aware of when and where I could have the next drink. At the same time, self-deception had shifted into high gear. Inwardly I tried to convince myself that my alcohol preoccupation was simply my freely willed desires, not an out-of-control obsession. However, I was plagued by too many reminders of the depth of the problem: Wilys Claire's pleas and anger, my trembling hands and red eyes, my night sweats and night terrors, and then blackouts and frightening gaps in memory.

There was a constant cloud of guilt to endure and a dreadful secret to protect—and to deny. The vicious circle had arrived. I was aware that things were wrong and that my ability to act on my best values and wisdom was diminishing. But I bargained internally to persuade myself that this was not a real loss—it was just circumstantial and wouldn't happen again. Yet, the slide continued, the bargaining began to lose its efficacy, and I began to dislike myself for it all. But this dislike was a clear signal that I needed more alcohol to banish those feelings.

The progression is deceptively gradual. Barbara S. Cole, an addiction therapist and recovering person, describes this aspect: "Like lights dimming in indistinguishable increments, our precious attributes fade. . . . When it happens this slowly, others can barely tell that our souls have been robbed of their light."[8] Because it is all so gradual, even those close to us can seldom help us. The damage becomes hurtful before they realize it, and they withdraw from us in confusion, pity, or disgust.

Medical problems also mount. The stomach is commonly afflicted with gastritis, inflammation of the lining, and the alcoholic seeks relief with—surprise—more alcohol. The liver frequently swells up, and its cells no longer make their necessary products efficiently; cirrhosis can develop in time. Sexual inhibitions are often reduced, but at least regarding men Shakespeare was right: drink "provokes the desire, but it takes away the performance."[9] With muscular weakness, increasing memory impairment, and sometimes permanent brain damage, alcoholism can negatively affect almost every organ in the body.

What Causes Alcoholism?

Physiological and genetic factors. While the causes of alcoholism in any particular case will likely be multiple, it is now widely accepted that genetic factors likely increase the risk.[10] As the quip (worthy of a bumper sticker) would have it, "There are no lifeguards at the gene pool." Studies of family histories show statistically significant increased risks when there is alcoholism somewhere in the family. Though environmental influences are hard to assess, additional research—for example, on adopted children raised by nonalcoholic adoptive parents—gives further credence to genetic factors. Those adoptees with an *alcoholic biological parent* (though the child was removed from the birth home shortly after birth) have significantly higher incidences of alcoholism than those without addicted biological parents. Other research has dealt with twins. When one identical twin is alcoholic, the other twin (with, of course, identical genes) is much more likely to be alcoholic also. Such is not the case with fraternal twins.

I find the cumulative evidence persuasive. Regarding alcoholism, while genes do not *predetermine* anything, it strongly appears that they do *predispose*. Though my own parents were abstinent, there was alcoholism elsewhere on both sides of the family. That by itself did not make me addicted. But there were other factors. For one, I chose to use repeatedly a potentially addictive substance that caused the sorts of brain changes I have described. And, as those changes occurred, my freedom to stop using alcohol progressively diminished.

In addition to the physiological factors, another cluster of components is significant to the development of chemical addiction. Though difficult to separate neatly, it divides roughly into three groups: the psychological and emotional, the sociological and cultural, the religious and spiritual. In the previous chapter I introduced the religious and spiritual factors, which will be the main focus of the rest of this book. However, let me comment on the others, for they are inextricably related to our major focus.

Psychological and emotional elements. Alcohol has a stunning popularity in most parts of the world because it is a proven anesthetic for emotional pain. I found that so. I could count on alcohol to desensitize my hyperactive, self-judging conscience and numb my doubts about self-worth. One does not have to be emotionally disabled to become an alcoholic. Most people found me quite healthy, and I usually felt that way myself. However, from the vantage point of recovery, I can recognize a portrait, one fairly common among the addicted. The picture shows a vague uncertainty about my worth, a constant need to prove myself, yet the difficulty of receiving affirmation. It shows me living with the sense that some day the hidden, unknown parts of myself would become visible for all to see and I would be exposed as the fraud I really was. The portrait shows me acting as though I were really fine, but not trusting my feelings. It is a picture of pleasing others at my expense, and finding it difficult to share these deepest feelings with anyone, for there were no words to express them.

Years of psychotherapy had helped me better understand those persisting emotional issues rooted in the past, but it had not erased them. In his research on childhood homes of adult alcoholics, Howard Clinebell found four destructive parental patterns: "heavy-handed authoritarianism, success-worship, moralism, and overt rejection."[11] The family of my childhood years scored high on the first three, and along the way I acquired a generous dollop of perfectionism. For some years alcohol miraculously soothed these troubled waters, though as my disease progressed the calm became increasingly short-lived. But while it worked it was magical. The apostle Paul advised Timothy that a little wine was good for his stomach. I always treasured that apostolic blessing, and with good alcoholic reasoning thought if a little was good, more would be better.

Yet there is an obvious dilemma. Clinebell describes it succinctly: "Alcoholics drink so much because they hurt so much, but their excessive drinking increases the painful feelings that made alcohol so attractive in the first place. Thus a vicious, self-feeding cycle of increased drinking to overcome the painful effects of previous excessive drinking is established."[12]

But do emotional factors *cause* alcoholism? The picture is unclear. Donald Goodwin reminds us, "Frustrated, unhappy, insecure, lonely people drink to feel less frustrated, unhappy, insecure, and lonely. . . . The fallacy in the reasoning is a simple one: most people are frustrated, unhappy, insecure, or lonely some of the time but do not become alcoholic."[13] We are on safer ground if we think in terms of *contributing* factors instead of *causal* ones. We are on safer ground if we also keep the door open for a healthy dose of mystery.

Sociological and cultural elements. Patterns of alcohol use and misuse differ markedly in different social and cultural climates, and that suggests their importance in understanding alcoholism. Though drinking is very acceptable among both Irish and Jewish people, the Irish are far more likely to become alcoholic. If you are Asian and live in Asia, your chances of becoming alcoholic are very slim. But if you live in France you are statistically at considerable risk, much higher in fact than if you live in Italy, even though the wine flows freely in both countries. In the United States, city dwellers and suburbanites are more susceptible than small-town and country folk. Some occupations appear riskier: writers and reporters have a much higher rate than mail carriers and farmers. And in every known society, men are at higher risk than women—a fact to be examined more carefully in chapter 5.

Certain sociocultural factors supported my drinking. I was male, of Scandinavian descent, and a city dweller—all risk factors. Most of my friends and associates drank, and we live in a society where alcohol is easily available, relatively inexpensive, and glamorized by the media. The list of supportive factors could be expanded. However, the puzzle remains. The great majority affected by the *same* social factors have not become alcoholic. Students of the subject will continue to compile statistics, finding significant correlations. And there is still mystery. Precisely to what extent and why these things are significant is still very imprecise—and likely will remain so as long as there is human freedom.

To summarize, the causal factors for alcoholism are multiple and not yet understood with any exactitude. There are physiological factors: alcohol itself has biochemical properties that make it potentially addictive, and because of genetic predisposition apparently some people's bodies are simply more vulnerable. There are also psychological factors and sociocultural elements. And there are profound spiritual dynamics. So, is alcoholism a disease or a sin? Both or neither? And does it finally matter what we call it?

Disease, Sin, and Everything in Between

Various positions on the disease/sin issue have been identified.[14]

In my own version I see five options, starting at the sin side of things and moving toward the disease side:

1. *"It's purely sin."* Addiction is caused by personal failings that become habituated in a stubborn sinful pattern. It is voluntary, personally chosen sin, not disease. This is the position of certain fundamentalists.
2. *"It begins as sin and becomes disease."* Chemical addiction begins as personal sin, then gradually develops into an obsessive-compulsive disease process. The Salvation Army believes *all* drinking is sinful. The Roman Catholic Church believes that only *excessive* drinking is sinful. However different these two groups are, they agree that alcoholism begins with sin and gradually becomes a disease.
3. *"Addiction is sin and disease all mixed together."* While the Big Book of A.A. does not use the word "sin" and prefers "illness" to "disease," this third option seems to be its position. Moral failures contribute to the mental obsession with drinking *and* purely biological factors result in abnormal physical responses to alcohol. The elements converge.
4. *"Addiction is disease resulting from sin, but that sin is outside a person's responsibility."* Addictions do result from powerful forms of *social* sin —abusive family systems, sexism, racism, poverty, the alcohol and drug-soaked culture in which we live—but sinful social systems are beyond the individual's control. The person is largely a victim.
5. *"Addiction is purely disease; sin is not a factor."* It is not wrong to drink alcohol as such, but a certain percentage of those who do are biologically programmed to develop the disease of alcoholism. Sin is not in the picture. It is a matter of disease pure and simple.

Disease or sin? Those on one end of the continuum believe alcoholism is purely sin—a failure of the will, weak moral character, and deeply habituated bad actions. On the other end are those who say it is clearly a disease with all of the medical criteria, including identifiable causes (biological programming and brain changes), prognosis, and symptoms. Then there are positions holding various mixes of disease and sin. Sin or disease? What is at stake and why does it matter what we call it? To take liberties with Shakespeare, would addiction by any other name smell the same?

The Birth of the Disease Model

Over the years A.A. has shown little interest in the theory of alcoholism as a disease. The Big Book pragmatically focuses on the person (the alcoholic) rather than the thing (alcoholism). True, the volume begins with a chapter entitled "The Doctor's Opinion" in which Dr. William Silkworth (known in A.A. as "the little doctor who loved drunks") describes alcoholism as an allergy with predictable physiological characteristics. And in later chapters the Big Book characteristically describes alcoholism as "an illness which only a spiritual experience will conquer." But it rests content at this point. Admittedly, medically sophisticated modern investigations into the disease theory had not really begun when the Big Book was written. But even today many recovering people likely would place little importance on exactly *what* it is they have as long as there is a way to deal with it.

So why bother? I have found the disease concept to be of enormous practical significance in my own recovery, particularly in confronting the paralyzing effects of shame and guilt. Thus, I want to understand it as fully as I can—where it came from, what it claims, how it functions personally and socially, and what it all means theologically. As philosophers have long taught us, some very important things are "necessary but not sufficient." Even if the disease concept alone is not sufficient, I find it necessary.

Surprising though it may be, the perception of alcoholism as a disease is well over two centuries old. In this country, Dr. Benjamin Rush deserves the pioneering credit. Physician-General of the Continental Army and signer of the Declaration of Independence, he was also the first American expert on alcoholism. Coming out of an alcoholic family and witnessing the alarming incidence of drunkenness in the army, Rush broke from the traditional view that excessive drinking stemmed from moral depravity or mental illness. Well aware that he was swimming against the cultural stream, he publicly advocated viewing alcoholism as a self-contained disease, the only hope for which was permanent sobriety achieved through "religious, metaphysical, and medical" influences. Working independently about the same time, an English physician, Thomas Trotter, likewise described alcoholism and characterized it as a disease. Rush and Trotter together are probably the originators of the "disease concept" of alcoholism.[15]

A hundred years later, in 1870, the American Association for the Cure of Inebriates was founded. The first four tenets in its statement of principles were these:

1. Intemperance is a disease.
2. It is curable in the same sense that other diseases are.
3. Its primary cause is a constitutional susceptibility to the alcoholic impression.
4. This constitutional tendency may be inherited or acquired.[16]

Further, the association's statement of principles criticized the punitive, penal approach to inebriety and called for the creation of special medical institutions where alcoholics could be viewed as patients and treated scientifically. During the late nineteenth and early twentieth centuries a host of such institutions were in fact created and proceeded with various "cures" for this still little-understood disease.

However, the real flowering of the disease concept awaited the decades of the 1930s and 1940s. Dr. Silkworth's view of alcoholism as an *allergy*, while not a fully developed view of the addiction as a primary and progressive disease, was "the first modern medical concept successfully used by large numbers of alcoholics as a metaphor to understand what happened to them and to explain why they could no longer drink."[17] Because it was so helpful, this allergy-illness view found its way into A.A.'s basic literature where it coexists with the movement's other understanding of alcoholism's origins—emotional and spiritual maladjustment.

The 1940s proved to be a critical decade for the disease concept. Two figures stand out. One is Marty Mann, a recovering alcoholic and accomplished professional writer who mounted a national campaign to replace the notion of moral degeneracy with an understanding of alcoholism as a treatable disease. In thirty-five years of tireless travels, organizing activities, political savvy, and spellbinding oratory she became "unquestionably one of the most successful public health reformers in American history."[18] Mann's scientific collaborator was Yale scientist Dr. E. M. Jellinek, who made the first breakthrough study of A.A. members, documenting the patterns of their alcoholism. Jellinek's research established the predictable progression of the disease with such symptoms as blackouts, tolerance, and withdrawal distress.

In spite of the research by Jellenik and others, the disease concept that emerged between the late eighteenth and the mid-twentieth centuries was more of a governing image, a perspective, than a thoroughly scientifically validated reality. It was a metaphor that provided a new public way of talking about alcohol problems and creating institutions appropriate to deal with them. For individuals struggling with alcohol, the disease concept became a way to understand their vulnerability and their need for total abstinence, and, for many, a way to release paralyzing guilt and shame. To the culture at large the concept provided an alternative paradigm to drunkenness solely as sin and moral degeneracy.

Now in the twenty-first century, the disease concept of chemical dependency is still a work in process. Though it is persuasive to most health care professionals, it still lacks some of the rigorous scientific verifiability true of many other diseases. What is remarkable is its power to survive countless attacks over the years and its extraordinary usefulness to people's recoveries.

Advantages of the Disease Concept

Dr. Paul O., a recovering alcoholic physician well-known in A.A. circles, writes, "I choose to believe alcoholism begins as far back as . . . conception. . . . Alcoholics drink for all the same reasons [that others do] plus one additional reason more important than all the other reasons combined: the disease, alcoholism, makes them drink."[19]

When "Dr. Paul" begins "I *choose* to believe . . ." his words are both honest and realistic. Still lacking the status of scientific inevitability, the disease concept is a choice. But, along with many others, I find it a compelling choice for these reasons:

1. *Alcoholism fits the criteria for a disease and has been defined as such by leading medical and health organizations.* Among a host of other medical and professional groups, the World Health Organization, the American Medical Association, the American Psychiatric Association, and the American Society of Addiction Medicine all have proclaimed that alcohol addiction is a disease. What do these medical professionals mean by that?

First, consider *disease* itself. This description is fairly representative: "the condition has a clear biological basis; is marked by identifiable signs and symptoms; shows a predictable course and outcome; and the condition or its manifestations are not caused by volitional acts."[20]

Alcoholism appears to qualify. There are authenticated and biologically based risk factors. There are identifiable signs and symptoms: withdrawal, development of tolerance to the substance, unsuccessful attempts to control one's use of alcohol, increasing preoccupation with it in both time and energy, and continued use in spite of adverse consequences. Furthermore, alcoholism has a predictable course and outcome: loss of control, increasing social and employment difficulties, growing health problems, and, if the addiction is not arrested, a downward spiral resulting in major incapacitation and eventual death.

But what about the statement "the condition or its manifestations are not caused by volitional acts"? This is a key issue for both sides of the debate. If this criterion were interpreted to exclude any ailment to which volitional acts *contributed*, then smoking-induced lung cancer could not be considered a disease. In addition to having the genetic factor, a person must choose to drink alcohol over a period of time to become an alcoholic. Certainly volition is involved at this point. The real question, however, is about the major manifestations of the disease *once it is a reality*. Continued drinking in spite of regular bad consequences is a major manifestation of alcoholism. But over against the belief that this is a matter of moral weakness, the disease concept maintains something else. A cardinal feature of the addiction is that, regardless of genuine and repeated attempts and in spite of every effort to mobilize their willpower, addicted persons are simply unable to control the use of the substance once that use has begun. I know. My will power, strong in other areas of my life, failed miserably with alcohol.

   2. *Alcoholism as a disease is marked by brain changes that explain otherwise inexplicable behavior.* Alcoholism is not just the result of bad habits. Nor is it just a stupid way of dealing with life's problems. Consumption of alcohol by those susceptible to this disease actually creates changes in the brain's chemistry and functioning (which I have described earlier). When my brain was "hijacked" I was no longer free to act in certain ways. Though I had long prized rational discussion and logical argument, regarding alcohol I was no longer free to respond to these approaches. Nor to urgent pleas about my drinking. Nor to psychotherapy. Over a decade I was a patient of several different capable therapists, and I was more alcoholic at the end of that time than at the beginning.

   The changes in the brain best account for why alcoholics frequently relapse, returning to drinking for no apparent reasons or for ludicrous ones. Such changes best explain why alcoholics will drink for virtually any reason—when things are going well, when things are going poorly, when they are happy, when they are sad. There seem to be no other explanations for these behaviors.

   Furthermore, these organic brain changes also help us understand why alcoholics cannot safely return to drinking even after years of sobriety. When alcoholics do attempt to drink moderately after even long periods of abstinence, their moderation is almost always short-lived. They quickly return to the worst condition of their previous active alcoholism.

   3. *The disease concept helps us to distinguish between cause and effect.* Did I become alcoholic because I drank too much, or did I drink too much because I was alcoholic? Most people probably would say it was the former. I would agree, but only in one sense: as one who was vulnerable to the disease, *any* alcohol was too much for me.

Because of the tolerance effect, most alcoholics drink more and more as their disease progresses. As time passes, organic brain changes require more alcohol to produce the same desired effects. But the amount consumed per se does not determine whether one is alcoholic. Indeed, not all heavy drinkers are alcoholic, and some alcoholics drink less than some nonalcoholic drinkers.

In any event, I believe the larger truth of the matter is that I drank too much *because* I was alcoholic. Most recovering alcoholics seem convinced similarly about themselves, and the same belief is widely shared by addiction and recovery professionals. Why? The evidence is experiential, overwhelmingly so. We who are seriously vulnerable to the disease simply find ourselves drinking more and more *without intending to do so*. The disease progressively destroys our control over the substance. It is a phenomenon that nonalcoholics may find difficult to understand. It truly is a strange experience, but to alcoholics it is all too real, and the disease concept helps me to understand it. The basic explanation is disarmingly simple: "You are an alcoholic, and that is what alcoholics do."

Furthermore, the disease concept holds that alcoholism is a "primary disease." It is not the secondary effect of, for example, a dysfunctional childhood family. Admittedly, with addiction cause and effect are hard to sort out in such things as early life experiences. Research (such as Clinebell's, mentioned earlier) does testify to *correlations* between certain patterns in early family life and later alcoholism, and I believe such patterns may well be *contributing* factors. I believe they were for me. But contributing factors are different from direct causes.

While still drinking I persuaded more than one therapist that we should not be talking about my problems with alcohol. I was not dissembling. I was really convinced that if we dealt successfully with the "fundamental" problem (my childhood family issues) then secondary problems (like alcohol use) would evaporate. Finally I encountered a therapist who would not listen to my theory and instead insisted that we begin with my *primary* disease—alcoholism—and leave other issues until later. That approach did not please me one bit, but it was exactly what I needed.

Is there an "alcoholic personality"? Here is another cause and effect question. Do some individuals have psychological patterns that destine them to alcoholism if they drink? While alcoholism has sometimes been viewed as itself a symptom of an underlying psychopathology, there is little evidence for this. Drawing on extensive research and clinical work, David E. Smith and Richard B. Seymour write, "Recent treatment and recovery experience has generally shown that, while many addicts may also have mental health problems as well as being addicted, these problems are coexisting within a dual-diagnosis . . . [rather] than in a cause-effect relation to one another."[21]

The emotional problems alcoholics often exhibit, though sometimes thought to cause the disease, are more typically the result. But this is confusing, not the least to members of A.A. The Big Book, written by medical lay people and published before there was much research into disease theories, seems to want it both ways: alcoholism is an illness (a physiological condition comparable to an allergy) *and* it is caused by certain emotional conditions and character orientations.

Regarding the latter, the Big Book frequently names selfishness as "the root of our troubles."[22] While it is true that active alcoholics appear to be markedly self-centered, it is by no means clear that selfishness is the cause or even makes a significant contribution to the development of the addiction. What, then, is the likely connection between the two? An obsessive-compulsive disease simply forces the person's own needs front and center.

My own case may illustrate. During the time my drinking was most compulsive, I was relentlessly focused on ways to keep my habit alive. Considerations for others' needs had to take a back seat to my own—a dependable supply of alcohol and places and times to drink it. That was self-centeredness with a vengeance, but a self-centeredness dictated by cravings endemic to a progressive disease.

To be sure, alcoholic drinking did many things to my personality. It made me feel withdrawn, confused, and insecure. Then it made me preoccupied with covering up those feelings so that others wouldn't notice. Mine became a selfish, neurotic alcoholic personality, but that personality did not cause the disease. It is truer to say that I became that way *because* of my alcoholism. Dr. Paul O., observing that the so-called "alcoholic personality" emerges, if at all, after the disease has developed, goes on to say, "If this were not so, it would be possible by psychological testing to prevent alcoholism by identifying and treating pre-alcoholics, and NASA would not have sent to the moon a man who later developed alcoholism."[23]

4. *Understanding alcoholism as a disease markedly undercuts moralistic judgments and blaming, thus enhancing the chances for recovery.* By their own accounts, those people who worked hardest on the disease concept shared a common passion. They desperately wanted to alleviate the destructive, invidious effects that flowed from understanding the addiction as moral depravity or willful misconduct. In an earlier time, such interpretations

commonly judged, ridiculed, punished, and ostracized the chemically dependent. When these interpretations persist today, as they sometimes do, their consequences are not quite as blatant as a century ago. Nevertheless, such understandings seriously underestimate the physiological side of addiction. They undercut the gains that the disease concept has brought in accessible and hopeful treatment. And they alienate many addicted people from potentially significant spiritual and religious resources.

Early in my treatment, as I mentioned briefly in chapter 1, my wise counselor began to hammer home the disease message. "Jim," he would say, "you have come here with a huge load of shame and guilt, and it is paralyzing you. Until you internalize the fact that you have a disease, your recovery will not go anywhere. You are not responsible for being an alcoholic, any more than a diabetic is responsible for being diabetic. But now that you *know* you are an alcoholic, you *are* responsible for your recovery, just as diabetics are responsible for their diets and their insulin. Can you understand that?"

I truly needed to hear that. For years I had known about alcoholism as a disease, but I couldn't apply that understanding convincingly to my own case. After all, *I* was now an alcoholic! Possibly that meant something about a disease. But certainly it meant that I was a moral failure and defective down to my core. It was only when I could gradually absorb my counselor's words that my shame and guilt began to release their stranglehold. To understand that I was not willfully bad or weak, but rather dealing with a serious-but-manageable disease came as an immense relief.

During my month in treatment a number of letters and cards came applauding my courage for taking this step. It did not feel to me like courage at all. It felt like desperation. A.A.'s book *Twelve Steps and Twelve Traditions* quite accurately characterized my feelings: "Then, and only then, do we become as open-minded to conviction and as willing to listen as the dying can be. We stand ready to do anything which will lift the merciless obsession from us."[24] A decade later I would not revise that picture, and I hear my recovering companions saying the same. Our halting steps toward recovery were taken more in despair than in courage. We became willing to listen, yes, but it was because we suspected we were dying. Yet in retrospect I also see that if recovery is to occur, there must be hope rather than despair. For many of us that hope came in the startling message that we were not morally degenerate after all. We had a disease that could be arrested.

5. *The disease theory reduces our tendency to see evil as "out there" and external to ourselves.* The ancient Hebrews had a religious practice that inspired our term *scapegoating*. The book of Leviticus records it this way:

"Then Aaron [the priest] shall lay both his hands on the head of the live goat, and confess over it all the iniquities of the people of Israel, and all their transgressions, all their sins, putting them on the head of the goat, and sending it away into the wilderness . . ." (Lev. 16:21). The temptation to externalize evil is probably as old as human self-consciousness. If we can somehow identify the problem as existing "out there" rather than "in here," we can load it onto someone (or something) else and drive it away, out of sight—into the wilderness.

Scapegoating finds fertile ground in all sorts of human discomforts. There are white folks with a tenuous hold on social position and security who find reassurance in racism. Some "straight" males who are unsure of their own sexual feelings bash gay men. Some religious fundamentalists angry about their own uncertainty and dubious virtue project the blame for theological and moral decline onto all who disagree with them.

What about scapegoating and alcoholism? A sad personal memory of mine involves a close relative. During the time he was a patient in an alcoholism treatment center, I was drinking heavily, was denying my own disease, and was still several years away from my own treatment. I did not feel empathy for him—I couldn't. Nor did I reach out with support—I couldn't. I simply tried to ignore him, distancing myself as fully as possible, deeply fearing that what I saw in him was also in me. Since entering recovery, I have asked his forgiveness and he has been utterly gracious. Our relationship is closer, more real than ever before, and we are companions on the recovery journey. All of that is to be celebrated.

But when we cannot face the darkness within, scapegoating has a mighty estranging power. I need to remember that part of the above story. Alcoholics can suffer from it in many ways. For example, certain religious groups that exalt self-control and personal discipline are sometimes tempted to personify "evil," piling it onto the goat and driving the animal away. In this case, the active alcoholic is the one driven away with condescending pity or thinly disguised disgust. But if we are persuaded that alcoholism is more adequately understood as disease than as moral failure, we are dealing with something quite different than we had thought.

Criticisms of the Disease Concept and a Few Rejoinders

As well as naming my reasons for supporting the disease concept, I want to name the primary objections, as I understand them, and respond to those arguments.

Objection No. 1: The disease concept is an unscientific myth with destructive consequences. A vigorous opponent, philosopher Herbert Fingarette, considers the disease theory a well-advertised "myth," neither scientifically valid nor helpful to people. "It promotes false beliefs and inappropriate attitudes as well as harmful, wasteful, and ineffective social policies. . . . The idea that alcoholism is a disease has always been a political and moral notion with no scientific basis."[25]

While I have already argued that the disease theory is scientifically justified, promotes compassion, and opens doors to recovery, I think Fingarette's broadside attack can be useful in one sense. It reminds us that definitions of diseases are never purely scientific nor are they devoid of political and moral content. Even such an apparently objective reality as "the flu" is not as purely objective as it might seem: witness the changing social meanings between the disastrous 1918 influenza epidemic and today.

Essentialism is the term now used for the notion that diseases (and other body phenomena) have objective (essential) characteristics and meanings, and that it is our task to discover those realities and to respond to them appropriately. The contrasting view is *social constructionism*. The constructionist approach recognizes that in significant ways we human beings actually create the meanings and definitions of our bodies in both health and illness.[26]

Before we apply these approaches to alcoholism, consider our bodies themselves. They have their own physical realities—physical appearances, bones and skin, organ systems. The essentialists remind us that there is really something quite objective there. However, there are significant ways of perceiving the body that are not objective at all, and history has seen a variety of such metaphors. St. Paul called the body "a temple." Descartes and Newton called it "a machine." Constructionists remind us that the list of metaphors is long, and each one invites a different response to the body.

I find truth in aspects of both essentialist and constructionist interpretations. When cancer is accurately diagnosed, the malady has not been imagined nor created by any metaphor we might use for it. There is truly something organically there posing a threat to the person. Cancer has its own essential organic reality. The essentialists are right.

Beyond that, however, we still interpret cancer, attaching various labels and meanings to it, and these condition our responses to the disease. Such descriptions change over time and vary among different cultures. The persistence or modification of the labels, images, and metaphors for the disease will depend not only on what we continue to learn about its organic realities but also on the *social usefulness* of the descriptions themselves. The social constructionists are right about these things.

Susan Sontag's examples of the metaphorical naming of diseases are instructive.[27] Tuberculosis, she observes, was the prime example of powerful naming in the nineteenth century. So capricious, so intractable, so mysterious, among diseases in the West it was particularly laden with metaphor. Throughout much of the twentieth century it was cancer that had particular metaphorical power. Both diseases seemed to mean a death sentence and in addition stigmatized and shamed those so afflicted. Thus particular names given to them carried strong meanings. Late in the twentieth century it was HIV/AIDS that supplanted cancer in its metaphorical power, its varied names identifying the disease with gays, with Africans, with punishment, with untouchability, with death, and with the plague. Thankfully, in each of these cases, the punitive metaphors for these diseases have gradually subsided.

So also, social construction has been an important factor regarding alcoholism. To be sure, compulsive, progressively destructive consumption of ethyl alcohol was a reality long before it was called a disease. The disease concept was an interpretation of what was already there. It was a way of naming that reality, a way created gradually over two centuries by numerous people who had their reasons and passions for interpreting it in this manner. It became a particular way of understanding chemical addiction that has ushered in some significantly different responses to it.

Does this mean that when we call alcoholism a disease we are speaking "only" metaphorically, saying it is *like* an authentic disease such as cancer, but not quite that real? No, the reality of any disease does not depend on the thoroughness of our scientific understanding. Nor is its disease status threatened by a candid recognition that more good comes from naming it that way than from calling it other things. Even though the scientific evidence for alcoholism as disease is still less complete than it currently is for some other illnesses, something significant has been happening: the disease concept itself has stimulated additional scientific research, which in turn has established the concept even more securely among medical professionals and the public.

Objection No. 2: The disease concept can lead to a virtual medical monopoly in both understanding and treating alcoholism. What would be wrong with "a virtual medical monopoly"? Consider a simple parallel: lead poisoning. Here is a disease with a defined set of symptoms including headache, abdominal pain, convulsions, and coma. It also has a standard treatment. Alcoholism, too, can be diagnosed by a specific set of symptoms. To say that both lead poisoning and alcoholism are diseases means, among other things, that medical people are supposed to know something about them and may be of great help.[28] I want to affirm that. In developing modern criteria for disease and in applying that to alcohol dependence, the medical-scientific community has vastly increased our understanding of this phenomenon and has contributed much to its effective treatment. I am very personally indebted.

On the other hand, any definition of alcoholism as disease that is *solely* medical in nature quickly becomes reductionistic. Our focus shifts away from the whole person to parts and functions, to genes and neurotransmitters. Deepak Chopra (a physician himself) suggests a parallel, picturing "someone who hears Beethoven's music played on a radio and then begins dismantling the radio in an effort to find Beethoven."[29] Beethoven isn't to be found in the mechanics of the radio, nor is alcoholism to be found simply in neurotransmitters and genetic patterns. Knowledge of the body's nuts and bolts can tell us a great deal. But it cannot tell the whole story of a person dealing with a whole-person disease whose every relationship in life suffers.

Critics also contend that this medical model gives unwarranted power to the medical profession, addiction specialists, and medically oriented treatment centers. Then spiritual resources, if not lost, are seriously underestimated because they are not "scientific." Thus some treatment centers limit their approach to behavior reeducation, diet, and exercise. But any treatment will be deficient if it does not understand that alcoholism, whatever else it is, is a whole-person disease and a spiritual phenomenon.

Some years ago in *Whatever Became of Sin?* psychiatrist Karl Menninger argued that the languages of medicine and law were eclipsing religion in our grasp of basic human issues, and now medicine was winning. A disease model, to Menninger's regret, has become the fundamental understanding of the human predicament. His was an important argument, and coming from a well-known medical professional it carried weight. *West Side Story's* satirical song "Dear Officer Krupke" carries a similar message: if we push the disease model too far we will point our fingers at everyone else, claim victim status, and assume that it is someone else's job to heal us and put us back together.[30]

I, too, resist completely medicalizing alcoholism. But we need not deal with either/or's. While the disease concept is not sufficient by itself, I find it still utterly necessary to a whole-person approach for reasons I have already argued.

Objection No. 3: Alcoholism is caused by self-indulgent behaviors not typically associated with the causes of diseases. Many folk (including some physicians and many religiously oriented people) have trouble seeing alcoholism as a disease because they associate its causes with self-indulgence and pleasure. It just does not deserve to be put in the same category as, say, cancer. While this critique of the disease approach may have a certain visceral appeal, it is full of problems.

The same argument would call into question many other ailments commonly (and rightly) accepted as diseases, including smoking-related lung cancers. The argument would also question whether syphilis and gonorrhea were really diseases because, presumably, they were contracted in pleasurable activities, or even high blood pressure when it is related to diet and lack of exercise. Indeed, to return to an earlier illustration, if some people actually *enjoyed* eating lead, that fact would not change the disease diagnosis of lead poisoning. Likewise, understanding *why* alcoholics drink is important, but their reasons for drinking are not crucial to the matter of naming alcoholism a disease.

This critique also betrays an all-too-common religious suspicion of sensuous pleasure as such. I will explore this more in a later chapter. For now, let us just remember the delight of our Hebrew ancestors in their creation-affirming thanksgivings: "You . . . bring forth food from the earth, and wine to gladden the human heart" (Ps. 104:15); ". . . your kisses [are] like the best wine that goes down smoothly, gliding over lips and teeth" (Song of Solomon 7:9). Let us remember the Gospel writers' perception of Jesus: he was condemned for *not* being an ascetic; he delighted in having his feet perfumed and in creating abundant wine for the wedding party. Those who use an antipleasure position for questioning the disease concept might find certain religious sources to buttress their suspicions, but those sources go against the central testimony of the biblical faith.

A final reason to discount the pleasure critique is often overlooked—or not fully grasped—by nonalcoholics. But it is simple: *persons who are in the throes of alcoholism just do not get much pleasure, if any, from drinking.* Certainly, the desire for pleasure is characteristic of the *beginnings* of an alcoholic's drinking. But that seems true of virtually *everyone* who drinks—people usually do drink for pleasure. However, with the alcoholic that motive shifts with the organic brain changes that are part of the disease. Pleasure gives way to craving. Pleasure is eclipsed by a search for relief from pain. Pleasure is replaced by a desperate desire to maintain some shred of normal feeling. My own experience and the testimonies of countless other alcoholics convince me beyond doubt that in the depths of our addiction drinking was no fun. It was no fun whatsoever.

Objection No. 4: The disease concept understates the person's ability to quit drinking. Fingarette makes this argument: "[A]lmost all people with serious drinking problems have intermittent periods of sobriety during which all metabolic products of alcohol have been excreted. It is implausible that any residual effects, whether physical or psychological, could be so powerful as to override a sober person's rational, moral, and prudential inclination to abstain."[31] It is an argument made by a nonalcoholic who finds the alcoholic experience baffling and irrational. In that sense, he is right: it *is* baffling and irrational.

Doubtless *some* alcoholics, especially early in their disease, have periods of abstinence long enough for their systems to recover from alcohol's metabolic effects. But "almost all people with serious drinking problems"? Hardly. Two of the standard criteria of alcoholism as a disease are increasing tolerance and craving. I experienced both. Progressively, it took more and more alcohol to produce the results I desired. In the year or so prior to my entering treatment I drank frequently in the mornings and at midday as well as later in the day. It had become "maintenance drinking." By this time I was not drinking so much to feel good as to keep from feeling bad. I wasn't looking for highs. I was looking only for normalcy.

Is it "implausible" that even the residual effects of alcohol could be so potent as to overpower one's rational, moral, and prudential thinking? Unfortunately, it is highly plausible. It is alcoholism itself, especially in its later stages, that is implausible.

Without a doubt, it was the most unbelievable experience of my life. Nothing rational or prudential about it, it numbed self-critical ethical reflection. I do not expect nonalcoholics to understand this. I am very glad they have been spared the experience. I only ask them to listen to alcoholics tell their stories, and then acknowledge the utter reality of those stories for the alcoholics. It is not a rational experience. It is a diseased craziness.

Objection No. 5: The disease concept erodes personal responsibility. This critique is closely related to the previous one. Again I turn to Fingarette who claims that it is both misleading and dangerous to consider alcoholism a genetic disorder. Why? "Heavy drinkers without alcoholism in their genetic backgrounds are led to feel immune to serious drinking problems, yet they have the greatest total number of problems. On the other hand, people who do have some hereditary disposition to alcoholism could easily become defeatist. Their risk is higher, and they should be aware of that, but their fate is still very much in their own hands."[32]

The first part of this argument—concerning *non*alcoholic heavy drinkers—is hypothetical. Whether the disease concept gives false reassurance to people who do not find alcoholism in their family backgrounds is problematic. To date the evidence is incomplete. My major concern,

however, is the second argument—that those who know they are at genetic risk for alcoholism might become defeatist and then, presumably,
not exert a real effort to control their drinking.

First, I find this argument simply contradictory. How can it be "misleading . . . to regard alcoholism as a genetic disorder" if one goes on to
acknowledge that, indeed, it *is*—that there are, indeed, those "who do
have some hereditary disposition to alcoholism"?

The phenomenon of denial is the basis for my second critique. Denial
appears to be well-nigh universal in active alcoholics. As is commonly
said, this is the one disease a major feature of which is its ability to convince you that you do not have it. I did not succumb fatalistically to heavier drinking because I had become persuaded that I was a likely alcoholic
through family inheritance. Quite the opposite. I staunchly denied my alcoholism to the end. My increasingly heavy drinking was due to the dynamics of the disease itself, including organic brain changes. It was not
due to a feeling of genetic fatalism.

Nor was it an embrace of the disease concept that delayed my sobriety.
Quite the opposite, it was my moralism. As long as I believed my alcohol
abuse resulted essentially from a failure of willpower and character, I kept
struggling to reform and improve. And I kept resisting treatment. Hadn't
effort and willpower always worked in every other area of my life? In fact,
I firmly believed that any concession that I was alcoholic would be disastrous. It would undercut my self-esteem and shake all confidence in myself. What I needed, I thought, was *more* self-confidence—not less—if I
were to deal successfully with my drinking problem. So I kept struggling
to control my drinking, and I continued to drink.

Believing in alcoholism as a disease did not give me excuses to drink.
Rather, the potent combination of my denial, guilt, and shame effectively
blinded me to the depths of my problem and paralyzed any effort to
change. Howard Clinebell sums it up: "Psychotherapy has shown that
one does not cure irresponsibility or egocentricity by a direct attack upon
them. . . . By increasing their guilt and shame load people tend to become
more self-hating, driven by compulsion, less self-determining, and therefore less capable of being responsible."[33]

Here are the echoes of an ancient theological controversy between St.
Augustine and the British monk Pelagius.[34] The central principle in
Pelagius's moral theology was that God would not command what we are
unable to do. We can do what we ought to do if we try hard enough.
God's grace, he taught, is known in the gift of freedom, in the moral law
as guide, and in Jesus Christ as example. Pelagius clearly wanted to close
the door to easy excuses for irresponsible behavior.

But Augustine found this whole viewpoint infuriating. It made mockery of the depths of disability that people really do experience, and it made a mockery of the radical divine grace we truly need in the face of our paralysis.

Of the two, it is clearly Augustine who speaks to my experience. Emily Dickinson does, also:

> I felt a Cleaving in my Mind—
> As if my Brain had split—
> I tried to match it—Seam by Seam—
> But could not make them fit.[35]

My counselor at Hazelden was right. The breakthrough to recovery occurred only when I came to believe that I *did* have a disease. Only then did the paralysis of shame and guilt begin to lift. It was truly gracious.

Then one other thing happened. I realized that when it comes to alcoholism the perspectives of disease and of sin are not incompatible. True, they are very different. But paradoxically I needed both of them to grasp what I was experiencing. So, let us turn to sin.

Chapter Four

Sin and Disease

Why Sin?

In *Pilgrim at Tinker Creek* Annie Dillard tells of an Inuit hunter's question to the local missionary priest who had come to spread the Christian faith in the Alaskan village. "'If I didn't know about God and sin, would I go to hell?' 'No,' said the priest, 'not if you did not know.' 'Then why,' asked the Eskimo earnestly, 'did you tell me?'"[1]

The Inuit's skepticism is understandable. Over the centuries notions and categories of "sin" have often been wielded by those with more power to control those with less, used by the anxious to defend themselves against those who appeared different, or exercised to equate certain social prejudices with divine judgment. All said and done, why not just abandon sin as a failed concept?

The Big Book of Alcoholics Anonymous almost does that. Knowing the damage "the S-word" had done to so many alcoholics and why so many recovering people recoiled from it, the Big Book's authors at least avoided the term. They knew well that the language of sin had been used judgmentally against countless people struggling with addictions, branding them as weak-willed, flawed, morally pitiful, and unwilling to discipline their lives.

It still happens. So there is good reason why one often hears at recovery meetings, "We're sick people trying to get well, not bad people trying to get good." And "alcoholism is a disease, not a disgrace." Barbara S. Cole protests on behalf of many recovering people when she says that we should not have to live with the burdens of shame and guilt, and it is ridiculous to punish ourselves with a twisted belief system that says we chose this disease. "We did not choose the genes and social circumstances that manifested this disease in us. We did not cause ourselves to become sick. If there were a cure, we would have been the first in line to try it out."[2]

In light of such feelings I can understand why some readers will recoil at my reintroducing sin into this discussion. The simple answer is this: as an alcoholic who stands within the Christian faith and who tries to reflect on his experience theologically, I cannot avoid the notion. But I am quick to add that I find a theological probing of sin in alcoholic experience profoundly *hopeful*. Why? To move beyond the shallow moralistic and judgmental understandings of sin that have condemned so many is to provide relief. To move into understandings of sin that accurately describe the alcoholic's experience can give deep reassurance. And to embrace understandings of our predicament that invite the fullest kind of release is cause for celebration. Kierkegaard observed how comforting it is to know that before God we are all desperate sinners. As an alcoholic I find this true in a special way. Let me try to explain in the pages that follow.

At the risk of repetition, let me say as clearly as I can that the problem for alcoholics and those who care about them is *not* the notion of sin *as such*. It is sin talk of a certain kind: shallow, moralistic, judgmental. It is sin talk that focuses on willful rule breaking. It is those understandings that reduce sin to a failure of the will and hence understand alcoholism as a simple deficiency in willpower.

Linda A. Mercadante begins her useful theological inquiry on alcoholism and sin with these words: "Many people assume there are only two ways to understand the problematic behavior that our society labels as addiction; it is seen either as a failure of willpower and morality or as a disease process. But there are more options."[3] Mercadante is right. The options are not just two. But one important clarification must be made. Theology can offer not only alternative views of addiction but also alternative views of sin itself. And to move beyond the shallow moralism that has condemned so many alcoholics is to move into more healing and life-giving recoveries.

In the previous chapter I argued that the disease concept of alcoholism is enormously important. It has brought hope to countless alcoholics, myself included, and it has demonstrably led to great social gains in the humane treatment of alcohol and other drug addictions. The disease concept is utterly necessary.

But it is not sufficient. A person is never fully described with medical categories alone. A medical description cannot adequately deal with the *spiritual* dimensions of chemical dependency—either in the addiction itself or in the processes of recovery. So, to speak of the spirituality of addiction is to invite theology, and soon we are talking about sin.

Why? I am drawn to the concept *not* just because I spent the larger part of my life in Minnesota, which Garrison Keillor describes as "The Guilt State—where there are more Lutherans than people." Even some of us who have never been Lutherans and who have left Minnesota find the notion of sin critical. For one thing, I need this concept because I cannot join in culture's dismissal of religious language for human dysfunction. It is the refusal to accept what Philip Rieff aptly labeled "the triumph of the therapeutic"—where medicine, psychology, and sociology are seen as the only relevant explanations.[4] To be sure, sin is not the only possible metaphor for addressing the basic human problem, but it is the main one given to me by my heritage.

It is, after all, the general theological category for why things go wrong when they do, and in alcoholism something surely has gone wrong. Actually, every known religion and every decent philosophy has an understanding of something *like* sin. When we try to understand *why* good things have turned bad, why relationships have gone wrong, it is more than idle curiosity. We want to know why so that we might draw on the healing resources that can restore life's goodness.

Different religions conceptualize the issue differently. Those originating in India typically see ignorance as the basic problem and enlightenment as salvation. Chinese religions use metaphors of disharmony; thus salvation involves reconnection with the larger whole. For religions of the Near East, especially Christianity and Judaism, the problem is sin, and salvation is found in divine grace. While I am convinced that the depths of both human and divine are never exhausted by the language of any particular religious tradition, I look for the meanings of my alcoholism and recovery primarily in the language and images of my own tradition.

What Does the Bible Say?

Literally speaking, the Bible cannot tell us a single thing about *alcoholism* and sin.[5] To be sure, the biblical writers were familiar with alcohol *abuse*, but the understanding of alcohol *addiction* is a modern concept. Even so, the attitudes of scriptures toward both the uses and abuses of alcohol will be helpful to us. Beyond that we can draw on those broad principles of biblical theology that shed important light on everything in human experience—including alcoholism.

In the Bible, questions about alcohol use are always part of larger questions. They are not just issues of right and wrong, but rather are matters about how covenanted communities can live with faithfulness. Walter Brueggemann sets the context: the biblical writers were concerned above all about faithful *covenant living* in the midst of competing worldviews. "The Bible does not give a set of rules or provide simple answers for complex moral-social issues. . . . The basic question is, do such practices [as alcohol use] enhance or detract from covenantal living?"[6]

Within this framework of understanding, the Hebrew Bible accepts alcohol as a common fact of life. Though certain ascetic groups practicing complete abstinence are honored in various parts of Scripture, moderate use of alcohol is the general norm. Wine is God's gift to gladden life. In fact, it is a symbol of all other divine gifts. On the other hand, good gifts can be misused. Wine can diminish the covenant-keeping capacity of persons, seducing them to act unfaithfully and destructively. But particular biblical warnings do not in any way suggest that wine is intrinsically bad; rather, in its destructive misuse goodness becomes corrupted. These words from the Apocrypha are representative:

> "[Wine] has been created to make people happy.
> Wine drunk at the proper time and in moderation
>   is rejoicing of heart and gladness of soul.
> Wine drunk to excess leads to bitterness of spirit,
>   to quarrels and stumbling"
>   (Sir. 31:27b–29)

The New Testament's perspective is similar. Here too alcohol use is set within the larger context of covenant faithfulness. Both Jesus and Paul clearly approved of wine in moderation, and both clearly condemned excess. Abundant wine for the wedding feast was a divine gift, and wine symbolized God's immanent presence in the upper room gatherings. Christ has transformed life from slavery to freedom, but this emancipation also carries with it a warning: "For freedom Christ has set us free. Stand firm, therefore, and do not submit again to a yoke of slavery. . . . For you were called to freedom, brothers and sisters; only do not use your freedom as an opportunity for self-indulgence, but through love become slaves to one another" (Gal. 5:1, 13).[7]

Important as these biblical perspectives are, what can we learn from them about alcoholism? While it always involves alcohol abuse (of which the scriptures speak), the addiction has moved beyond the realm of conscious, voluntary action. To move further into the wisdom of Scripture and tradition, we need to incorporate contemporary understandings of the experience of alcohol addiction itself. Let us turn to that.

How Alcoholics Describe Their Problem

Recovering people typically describe their alcoholic drinking days by listing the wrongs they committed and harmful attitudes they carried. That focus on specifics is predictable. After all, in our society morality is usually equated with *morals*, and in most common religious pieties sin means *sins*. In some measure, the Twelve-Step program seems to concur, with various steps speaking of our wrongs, shortcomings, defects of character, and need for a moral inventory. One of the recovery movement's most widely used daily reading books, *Twenty-Four Hours a Day*, contains an intimidating list of these: ". . . fears, resentments, inferiority complexes, negative points of view, self-centeredness, criticism of others, over-sensitiveness, inner conflicts, the habits of procrastination, undisciplined sex, wasting money, boredom, false perfectionism, jealousy, and envy of others."[8]

But what lies beneath all this multiplicity? The well-known Fifth Step of A.A.—confession to God, to oneself, and to another human being— does not ask the alcoholic to list every possible iniquity. At first I did not understand this. The "searching and fearless moral inventory" called for in Step 4 took me hours and hours, writing pages and pages of items. I was still unfinished when my treatment counselor reminded me that Step 5 did not call for admission of every wrong caused by drinking, but rather "the exact *nature* of our wrongs." (I had much in common with Luther's preconversion scrupulosity: he was terrified lest he omit confessing any single wrong he had done.) What, then, was "the exact nature" of my fundamental alcoholic problem? What was my sin beneath the sins?

On reflection, I have considered several candidates, each a serious applicant. While I hear these things mentioned frequently at recovery meetings, I make no claim for their universality. We alcoholics have a great deal in common, but the dynamics that fuel our addictions will also reflect our varied histories—including gender, sexual identity, race, economic position, age, and the formative events of our unique lives. In any event, here are my candidates for the sin beneath my own alcoholic sins: *perfectionism, control, selfishness,* and *attachment*.

First, *perfectionism*.[9] I was constantly striving for the unattainable ideal. An inner voice repeatedly told me that if I were good enough or if I achieved enough others would accept me, maybe even admire and love me. But all of this came at a price. I prostituted myself, not in body but in soul. I sold myself for their acceptance. M. Scott Peck once spoke of the disquieting feeling that others assumed they owned him: write this for me, sign that, speak here, give me advice, and on and on. The disquiet is familiar.

When failure in performance, achievement, or goodness came—as it inevitably did—I had to deal with self-condemnation and feelings of rejection. However, projecting those same impossible standards on others allowed me some psychic relief: they, too, often failed, and I could judge them accordingly. In short, the incessant demands of perfectionism could make me rich in achievement but left me poor in joy, always a competitor, and welcoming alcohol as an escape.

Perfectionism has such power to inflate anxiety and to deflate self-worth. Other "character defects" (in A.A. language) such as self-pity, resentment, envy, and judgmentalism emerged in its wake. The moral wisdom of earlier centuries had it right: *corruptio optimi pessima*. The worst thing is the best gone bad; sin is always corrupted goodness. Even though Jesus counseled perfection of a sort, he was fiercely aware of the demonic results flowing from the kinds of perfectionism that the Pharisees exhibited. They were devout. They were serious. They were also unaware of how dangerous this spiritual attempt at invulnerability was.[10] Jesus took the sin of perfectionism seriously, but it was still symptomatic of something deeper.

Control was another candidate for my cardinal sin as an alcoholic. Joshing about our control needs is a staple of in-group humor among recovering people. After all, each of us had discovered that alcohol was a dependable agent to help us control many things. I could count on it to control my feelings of inadequacy. It dissolved my reticence with others. It was my escape from performance demands. With it I could change my perceptions of reality to embrace my own desires. In short, alcohol was the answer to any mood: I drank because I was happy, and I drank because I was sad; I drank to celebrate, and I drank to grieve; I drank to reward myself, and I drank to blunt the sharp edges of pain. Alcohol was there for me—to help me control my world.

As my disease progressed, I increasingly felt the need for regular drinking, and I also then needed to control my daily circumstances in order to make that possible. I tried hard to drink moderately in public, but I also needed alcohol more frequently than social situations permitted. The answer was clear enough: I simply had to plan for my private times undisturbed by well-meaning people.

At the same time, I needed to convince myself that I was *truly* in control of myself so that I need not worry about my drinking. If I seriously admitted that I had a real problem, the whole edifice of fabrications I had erected to protect and disguise my compulsive drinking would collapse. The more the disease progressed, the more I needed to control things so that I could drink. The more I drank, the more doubts crept in about the normalcy of my drinking. The more the doubts crept in, the more I needed to convince myself that I was still in control. The more I needed to convince myself, the harder I tried to control things around me. The more successful I was in controlling my environment, the better I was able to continue drinking as much as I wanted. And the more I drank the more the doubts came and the more frantic became my need to control them. It was viciously circular. And it was crazy. While all of this is clear to me in recovery, in the midst of active alcoholism it looks utterly different. It's just the way things are.

Though its main nerve may be cut with the admission of powerlessness over alcohol and surrender to God, the desire to control may not vanish immediately. Over a decade after his entry into sobriety (and after a difficult episode in the young A.A. organization), Bill Wilson saw something more clearly than ever before: "I suddenly realized the extent to which I have been trying to dominate . . . [with] everything swinging in the direction of *control* of something or somebody."[11]

From whence comes the powerful urge to control? Surely, alcoholics have no corner on the market. Control as a way of "playing God," some would say, is the primal sin of humanity. Even so, the alcoholic has a particular energy in this direction: the biological changes leading to craving, and then the need to control the surroundings in order to satisfy that craving. But if this need lies so far beyond free choice, is it not symptomatic of a deeper malady? And what if control is not really the way that even *God* "plays God"?

There is another candidate for my primal alcoholic sin: *selfishness*. I mentioned it briefly in the previous chapter, and it is the Big Book's choice for alcoholism's basic spiritual disorder: "Selfishness—self-centeredness! That, we think, is the root of our troubles . . . [which] arise out of ourselves, and the alcoholic is an extreme example of self-will run riot."[12] Indeed, my active addiction was a very selfish phenomenon. As it progressed, so did my concentration on how to satisfy my alcoholic thirst. When and where could I have my first drink of the day? How would I deal with others' intrusions into my drinking plans? Did I have an ample supply? Control is the means, but selfishness appears to be the more basic malady. It is putting one's own desires, even needs, for alcohol above all else regardless of what that does to others.

Nevertheless, A.A.'s founders recognized that selfishness is more complicated and many-sided than even this. They saw it as a given of the human condition, something that people in all great religions attempted to transcend but never would completely. Hence, its destructiveness should be minimized, but its continuing reality should be honestly acknowledged rather than dangerously denied.

Thus comes the candid admission that "A.A. is a selfish program." For those distressed by this description Bill Wilson tried to furnish clarification. He could understand their concern, he said, for "selfish" usually suggests that one is thoughtless of others, demanding, and acquisitive—surely not A.A.'s intent. However, Wilson continued, "We are of no value to anyone, including ourselves, until we find salvation from alcohol. Therefore, our own recovery and spiritual growth have to come first—a right and necessary kind of self-concern."[13] The self-care necessary for one's usefulness to others should not be confused with plain old self-centeredness. It is the latter ("curved inwardness" [*incurvatus se*], as Luther often called it) that lies at the heart of alcoholism, Wilson believed.

Like the relentless desire to control, selfishness does seem to be an accurate description of the drinking alcoholic's spiritual state. But whether this is a *sufficient* description is quite another issue. Indeed, classic Christian theology puts a question mark to selfishness as the basic human problem. It is individualistic. The focus of sin remains completely on the individual disconnected from wider relationships. The assumption is that if selfishness in individuals were cured then somehow sin would disappear. This idea is not only inadequate in principle, but it also does little to address alcoholism's complexity, arising as it does from a variety of converging causes. Further, the explanation of selfishness (unlike that of idolatry) leaves God out of the picture. But how can our relationship to the Creator and Giver of Life be incidental to our problem?

I found still another candidate for my primal alcoholic sin: *attachment*. While recovery discussions often name perfectionism, control, and selfishness as big issues, attachment is seldom spoken of directly. But the reality always seems present and underlying everything else. Heads nod when someone finally names and describes it. Attachment's pervasiveness is why the recovery slogan "Let go and let God" is so important—and so often repeated.

Psychotherapist and recovering alcoholic Christina Grof describes attachment as "clinging to other people, places, objects, or behaviors" or "clinging, craving, grasping, clutching, holding on, and wanting."[14] Admittedly, addicted folk have no monopoly on this problem, which (at least in its milder forms) seems to be another equal opportunity employer. But, says Grof, "True addicts surrender themselves completely to a substance, activity, or relationship."[15] The result is utter powerlessness and lack of control regarding the object of attachment, which, in turn, takes precedence over everything else, even life itself. Nevertheless, both addiction and the milder forms of attachment are a matter of mistakenly directing our underlying search for wholeness toward substances and activities that do not fill our spiritual emptiness.

In his analysis of addiction, Gerald May also gives attachment a central role.[16] To him attachment is any process that enslaves our desires and creates the state of addiction. Our true desires are spiritual ones, and attachment is the process of giving energy to things that are not our true desires. Addiction then is life organized obsessively and compulsively around those false desires. It sucks up our energy and leaves us with less and less available for other relationships and pursuits. I discovered alcohol to be a very jealous lover, and these accounts of attachment strike home.

But having named attachment, have we named enough? Is there something lying behind it, too? In a way similar to Buddhist teaching, Grof maintains that all suffering is caused by attachment, and the power of attachment depends on anxiety about our mortality. Our bodies will wither, our children will leave, death will separate us from our spouses, our possessions will vanish, others will take over the responsibilities of our work —everything will go. Attachments are the frenetic ways we tenaciously cling to life in the face of inevitable loss. They can give a temporary illusion of immortality, but somewhere beneath our drivenness there stirs the uneasy feeling that nothing is permanent.

Attachment now sounds akin to idolatry, the false god, and we are getting close to traditional theological perspectives on sin. So let us move directly into the theological arena. What is sin? And why might naming it and grasping its meaning be liberating for alcoholics and for those who care about us?

Alcoholism as Sin

What is sin? Theologies give diverse descriptions of the fundamental problem: missing the mark, disobedience, pride, sensuality, selfishness, inordinate self-loss, injustice—the possibilities are numerous. While I find some truth in each of these, I find sin best described as profound estrangement. It is relational brokenness, separation from everything meaningful. It is alienation from ourselves, from those around us, and from our environment. It is separation from life itself. Fundamentally, it is estrangement from God, the source and ground of all that exists.

Every drunkalogue I have heard—or I have given—is a striking illustration of an estrangement that goes beyond psychological or medical description. Granted, our stories are frequently laced with humor, and hearers' laughter in response is spontaneous and empathetic. With all of the devastations of alcoholism, a nonalcoholic might see such levity as strange and inappropriate. But the storyteller's humor conveys a clear recognition: "I now see the insanity of it all." And the group's laughter not only confirms the speaker's judgment but expresses unspoken relief: "Thank God, I wasn't the only one; somebody else understands me; we're in this together." Though in style obviously different from typical religious confessions, the drunkalogue is usually a genuine, even profound, confession of sin. With vivid illustration it says, "In my active alcoholism I was floundering in a sea of estrangement that strained, diminished, and sometimes alienated every significant relationship in my life."

The Devil as a Fallen Angel

"In the beginning . . . God saw that it was good." That is the litany in the first chapter of Genesis. Stage after stage in the cosmic creation is achieved, and then come the words "And God saw that it was good." The biblical creation stories convey with explosive power the essential goodness of all that has been brought into being, and God's intention that all creatures live in the harmony, peace, and justice, which together are *shalom.*

Augustine was fond of saying, "Whatsoever in any degree is, is good."[17] Surely, he did not mean that evil is trivial or that whatever is, is right. He did mean that goodness is fundamental and that evil is a distortion or corruption of what is essentially good. That is true of alcohol and its use. It is not demonic, but rather a good gift from God. When for some of us alcohol *became* demonic, that was still a corruption of the good. Fr. John C. Ford, an early pioneer of the church's outreach to alcoholics, put it this way: "Beverage alcohol is . . . a creature which man [sic] should make use of so far as it helps him, and withdraw from so far as it hinders him on his journey back to God."[18] Use of alcohol is a matter of free will, said Ford, but the user should remember its risks since it is extremely attractive to the senses.

However, alcohol is only one example of innumerable possibilities. Everything we experience as evil is a corruption of the good. To understand it this way does not erase its destructiveness or pain, but it does allow us to respond more creatively. Consider disease. My examination of several dictionaries brought a uniform result. Each defined disease as a distortion or loss of health: abnormality, impaired organ functioning, destructive process in the organism, etc. The image of health is presupposed. Even to grasp the notion of disease, I need some prior knowledge of an organ's healthy functioning.

There is a parallel with sin. Evil has no positive existence in and of itself. It is always a corruption of the good. Putting that into mythic imagery, our ancestors spoke of the devil as a fallen angel. According to Augustine, "[there] cannot be a nature in which there is no good. Hence not even the nature of the devil himself is evil, in so far as it is nature, but it was made evil by being perverted."[19]

It follows that the General Confession of Sin, a classic prayer of the church, is seriously wrong in one of its phrases. After describing various manifestations of our sin, that prayer continues with the words "there is no health in us." It is not so. If there were *no* health in us, we would be dead with no chance for recovery. It holds true for both physical health and moral health, both physical sickness and moral sickness.

Here then is one way a theology of sin can bring hope instead of condemnation to the alcoholic. Alcoholism is a disease, and a life-threatening one at that. Untreated and unarrested, it leads to death in one way or another. But short of death, *there is still health* in the active alcoholic, and that health is the foundation on which recovery can be built. Were I given the privilege of rewording the General Confession of Sin, following the list of our commissions and omissions I would put these words: "And, thanks to God, there is still health in us!"

Original Sin?

Embracing the mythic story of Adam and Eve as conveying profound truth, classic theology suggests that this estrangement and corruption of our goodness is not entirely of our own choosing. We can thus understand our own culpability only to a point. Beyond that there is a mystery about it.

I believe this is true of my alcoholism. On the one hand, had I chosen never to drink, I would obviously not have become alcoholic. But I made that choice and believe there was nothing wrong in it. Moderate drinking can be a life-enhancing good, and when I began drinking I was not really aware of my genetic vulnerability. On the other hand, after a time I began to sense that I was not drinking the way "normal" people were. However, even that recognition was so dim for so long and the alcoholic process so gradual and insidious that I am not sure where or when I should have stopped it. Or whether I could have.

The attempt to decipher and faithfully respond to similar questions about human experience gave rise to the doctrine of original sin in the early church. Centuries later Puritan women cross-stitched this maxim on their samplers: "In Adam's fall we sinned all." That little statement implied two important claims. First, there is *a fallenness that somehow exists prior to our own fall*. The sin we experience did not begin with us. And, second, *sin is universal*. No one escapes.

Augustine shaped this doctrine in a particular way that influenced centuries of Christians: he located sin's transmission from one generation to the next in the act of sexual intercourse. In spite of his enormously important contributions in other areas of theology, when it came to sex Augustine fumbled (in personal life as well as in theology). Nevertheless, it was the universality of sin and the need for divine grace that he rightly wanted to articulate—and the notion that sin is "inevitable but not necessary." In other words, none of us escapes it, yet we cannot blame it simply on blind fate.[20]

Centuries later, the Social Gospel movement fashioned an understanding of original sin that substituted *social* transmission for biological and sexual. In 1917 the great theologian of that movement Walter Rauschenbusch wrote these words—significantly, following a lengthy discussion of alcohol abuse:

> [T]heology has done considerable harm in concentrating the attention of religious minds on the biological transmission of evil. It has diverted our minds from the power of social transmission, from the authority of the social group in justifying, urging, and idealizing wrong, and from the decisive influence of economic profit in the defense and propagation of evil.[21]

Perceiving original sin as estrangement that is conveyed by social means was an important new perspective in the early twentieth century. It is no less relevant to a twenty-first-century culture where instant gratification is taken almost as a right, and where one corporate slogan, "Better living through chemistry," has become emblematic for society as a whole. It is present in an alcohol-saturated society wherein messages that urge responsible drinking are drowned out by voices announcing that a certain beer will cement one's manliness and a certain vodka is the mark of real class. This social context impinges on us all, but some of the oppressed are particularly vulnerable. The high alcoholism rates for gay people and for Native Americans provide chilling reminders.

Nevertheless, the handing on of our estrangement need not be construed as an either/or—either biological *or* social. Both elements seem present in alcoholism. We need not adopt Augustine's dark suspicion of all things sexual (a wrong-headed, unfortunate part of his legacy) to embrace the notion that *something* is passed biologically from one generation. That fits with what we know about genetically based vulnerability to alcoholism. I inherited much through my family blood line, both for good and ill. As part of my inheritance it strongly appears that I received a predisposition to alcoholism. By itself this inherited factor was not a sufficient reason for the disease. Yet it placed me at risk and was part of the mix that gave rise to the addiction. And it was a "something" quite beyond my voluntary choosing.

Nevertheless, the disease theory could tell me that much. Why add theology and, in particular, the notion of original sin? My answer is that this theology adds critical elements beyond those provided by medical and psychological interpretations. For one thing, theology adds *mystery* to the equation—and science does not suffer mystery gladly. By its very nature science presses for answers, not for living the questions. But theology reminds me that now I must live into the questions, accepting the fact that more facts will never be enough. Theology reminds me that the *why* of it all leads into the arena of faithful response to what *is*.

Why did this happen to me? I don't ask that question feeling like a victim, for I am quite aware of two things. One is that, along with the pain for others and for me, a great deal of good has come from it all (which I will speak about in later chapters). I am also aware that even while my free choices did not bring on this disease in any simple cause-and-effect manner, I am still more than a pawn of fate. My responsibility is not erased.

So I approach the *why* question expecting neither neat answers nor the erasing of all mystery. I approach it wanting to respond to my addiction as creatively as I can. What is the meaning of this fact that I am an alcoholic? How can my response make life larger and richer instead of diminished and poorer? Knowledge of what happened to my brain's neurotransmitters is helpful, but it does not answer these questions.

Quite obviously, the challenge of living with unanswered questions is a human predicament in no way unique to the alcoholic. It is there for anyone dealing with any major disease or difficult, life-changing event. To all such persons the Christian tradition of original sin replies, something beyond our own individual choices and actions has gone askew in the scheme of things. We don't fully understand why. Blaming our mythic ancestors in Eden's garden will not particularly help. Nor will blaming God or fate. But it does help to know that we are caught up in a mystery with which we must live as creatively and as responsibly as we can. And it helps to know that we cannot live this question by ourselves. God's grace and human companions are utterly necessary.

I have been suggesting that some key features in the experience of alcoholism *parallel* the experience of original sin as understood in the Christian tradition. I also want to say more than that. Alcoholism is not just *like* original sin. It *is* original sin in one manifestation, and it is helpful for persons of faith to see it in that light. This does not mean, however, that original sin and addiction can be equated. Sin is a larger reality of which addiction is only one manifestation. The concept of addiction is not large enough to encompass all we mean by sin.

In his otherwise insightful book, psychiatrist Gerald G. May errs in virtually equating sin and addiction. Reflecting on his work with addicted people, he observes "that all people are addicts, and that addictions to alcohol and other drugs are simply more obvious and tragic addictions than others have. To be alive is to be addicted, and to be alive and addicted is to stand in need of grace."[22] It is one thing to say that everyone is involved in sin. It is another, however, to say that everyone is addicted. This stretches the addiction net too far.

A similar tendency is evident in the spread of the addiction explanation to ever-increasing patterns of human behavior. A.A. has unintentionally contributed to this through the usefulness of its Twelve Step program to many nonalcoholics. What often happens, however, is that addiction then becomes the key interpretation of the human problem. It becomes a quasi-religious replacement for the classic understanding of sin.[23]

What's wrong with that picture? Several things. For one, while sin is universal, addiction is not. Everyone suffers from the fundamental alienation that theology calls sin, and it has widely varied behavioral manifestations. Not everyone is addicted. Addiction is characterized by uncontrollable, compulsive behaviors; it is one serious expression of alienation, but only one. Nor are all addictions the same—for example, as in the matter of organic brain changes. The brain of a typical alcoholic and that of a typical nonalcoholic compulsive gambler are significantly different.

Further, there are expressions of sin for which the recovery model is of little relevance. War is one example. While certain elements of the Twelve Steps might be applicable, to say that this recovery program affords a sufficient, appropriate response to international violence stretches it far beyond its limits.

So, addiction and sin are not the same, just as one country and the inhabited earth are not the same. To equate them muddies the waters. But, having recognized this fact, I want to underscore the major emphasis of this chapter: alcoholism is one manifestation of the larger phenomenon of sin, and it is extremely helpful to see it in this light.

Sin and Alcoholism as Idolatries

An active alcoholic deprived too long of alcohol is, as the Big Book says, restless, irritable, and discontent. It echoes St. Augustine's famous prayer: "Our hearts are restless until they find their rest in thee." Except now, the "thee" refers to alcohol—the new god. While the psychological concept of attachment comes close, I find it important to name this *idolatry*. It is the worship of a false god. It is placing one's trust in some golden calf that does not merit that kind of trust. It is making absolute something that is not absolute. It is substituting something finite for the Infinite. It is giving ultimate significance to something that is not truly ultimate, and allowing nothing else to take priority over that loyalty. Common religious knowledge knows that idolatry is not only sinful; it is the number one sin, the state-fair, grand-prize sin.

As an active alcoholic I did not label my situation idolatrous, but my failure to do so did not change the reality. Here I was, an ordained minister, a seminary professor, sincere (I was convinced) in my Christian faith, but sliding slowly, imperceptibly into a powerful idolatry. And as I depended more and more on the spiritual powers of alcohol, patterns were being etched on my brain by physical and chemical changes—a fact that makes recovery such an endless process. Regrettably, Christina Grof's brutally frank description fit me well: "Our vision is fiercely concentrated on the object of our addiction. . . . Swaddled in layers of complex denials, rationalizations, and illusions, we alternate between a monumental well of shame, self-degradation, and self pity and a prodigious stream of grandiosity."[24]

As the slide gathered momentum, my new god insisted on more and more allegiance. The apostle Paul urged Christians to be constant in prayer, and we alcoholics know what such spiritual constancy is all about. Even when not drinking, an active alcoholic is "thinking drinking." This did not mean I was always consciously thinking *about* drinking. It was more like the avid skier whose bumper sticker says, "Think Snow!", or, better, like the young lover saturated with thoughts of the beloved. Always in the back of my mind, there was a certain presence. It was a presence to anticipate, around which to plan one's day, a presence that guaranteed one would truly come alive when drinking time arrived, for that was sacramental. And, let this discipleship take second place to none other, for alcohol is a jealous god whose first commandment is exactly the same as the one in the original decalogue: "Thou shalt have no other gods before me."

Even when doubts about my growing allegiance to alcohol assailed me, my denial vigorously did its work. I was so entangled in the pretenses I had developed to serve my addiction that I could not see how to extricate myself, yet it seemed that practicing my addiction was an assertion of my freedom. The more I used, the less free I was, but the freer I thought I was.

I have no doubt whatever that my time of active alcoholism involved the deepest experience of sin I have had. I am not saying that I was a moral failure or a bad person. I mean that I was immersed in spiritual bondage—"sinking deep in sin, far from the peaceful shore," as the gospel hymn puts it. For sin, remember, is not fundamentally an act, but a condition. It is not essentially something we do, but a state of being. It is the situation of being cut off, disconnected, in a real sense homeless. The alcohol that originally had promised a bit more of life's goodness had become life itself to me. I was learning that false gods not only disappoint; they also destroy.

In sin, everything becomes contradictory—not paradoxical, but truly contradictory. It is a contradiction that I earnestly wanted God to be central in my life, but I was a practicing idolater. It is a contradiction that I tried never to lie about my drinking, but daily I camouflaged the amount I was consuming. It is a contradiction that at times I saw alcohol threatening everything I held dear in life, and I still wanted desperately to keep drinking. The apostle Paul says it all: "I do not do the good I want, but the evil I do not want is what I do. . . . Wretched man that I am! Who will rescue me from this body of death?" (Rom. 7:19, 24). That is more than a medical condition. It is alienation from life, and that is what sin is about.

Classic Christian understandings of sin are far different from the shallow moralism inflicted on so many alcoholics. Sin is not to be found *basically* in specific acts we commit, character defects we have, or our failures of willpower. It is to be found in our deep alienation or estrangement. And, note well, one is not a sinner because one commits various sins. It is the other way around. We act in ways that injure others, ourselves, and our environment precisely *because of* the prior disorder and alienation within us.

I find the alcoholic experience a striking illustration of these things. Just as I did not become a sinner by committing sins, so also I did not become an alcoholic because I drank too much. It was the other way around: I drank too much because I was alcoholic. Nor did I become an alcoholic because I couldn't control my use of alcohol. It was the other way around: I consistently abused alcohol because I was an alcoholic literally incapable of using alcohol moderately.

"Sin presupposes sin," says the Christian tradition. And consistent alcohol abuse is preceded by alcoholism. Addiction is not a matter of better living through chemistry. It is the self-destructive location of divinity in alcohol.

Total Depravity?

The experience of *totality* in alcoholism is well-documented, and recovering alcoholics provide ample illustration of it. Everything in one's life is affected by the addiction. Nothing in body, mind, or spirit is left untouched. Nothing.

In a way strangely parallel, the sixteenth-century Protestant Reformers were trying to describe the totality of sin. In our fallen state, they maintained, no dimension of life is unaffected. Sin is pervasive, total in its reach. They were reacting to the medieval theologians for whom sin or "the fall" was limited to only part of our humanity. According to these medievalists, sin disabled or perhaps even destroyed our "supernatural" endowment (our destiny for salvation). However, the fall into sin left our "natural" capacities relatively undistorted. Our capacity to reason was still intact, as was our basic goodness.

In contrast, the Reformers spoke of *total depravity*. Admittedly, the term feels offensive. It seems to mean utter perversion, complete moral corruption. Our negative reaction is understandable. However, by this grim-sounding term the Reformers did not mean that we were totally evil or that there was no health left in us. They were simply insisting that sin affected every part and parcel of our lives. When we used our reason, we were using a reason distorted by self-centeredness. We did morally good things, but we did so with mixed motives. The alienation of our lives did not eradicate our goodness but left its distorting shadow over *everything* —our thinking, our feelings, our actions, our bodies, our spirituality. As with astigmatism in the eyes, everything—regardless of the object, re-gardless of the distance, regardless of the light—is out of focus.

Alcoholism is that way. It is a total phenomenon affecting the entire person: body, mind, spirit, every relationship. Everything suffers distor-tion because of it. In the midst of active alcoholism my brain suffered or-ganic changes, but the rest of my body was affected as well. I smoked more heavily, exercised less regularly, and watched my diet less faithfully. My drinking increased my lactic acid, my uric acid, and the fat content of my liver. Though more measurable in some parts of my body than in oth-ers, alcohol affected every cell.

Alcoholism affected my reasoning. No one thinks clearly when drunk. Even when I was able to abstain for several days or even weeks, my mind was still distorted by the disease. Though my thought processes seemed clear, always in the background of my mind I was thinking drinking, de-siring alcohol's release, waiting impatiently and planning for the time when a good drink would once more bring relief. Increasingly I became aware of constant anxiety, and once again the body spoke its mind: my anxiety levels, I learned later, were directly related to the increase in lac-tic acid brought about by my alcohol consumption.

The addiction also impeded my emotional growth. It is well-known that active alcoholism brings positive psychological development to a vir-tual standstill. The person who becomes alcoholic at age fifteen (as some do) and later enters into sobriety at age forty will be an emotional teenager with a middle-aged body. Fortunately, I escaped that pattern. Since I was abstinent for twenty years after college, I had a good period of time for adult emotional development unfettered by the substance. My arrested development, however, came later.

My father died quite suddenly when I was twenty-one and at an army base half a continent away. For the next twenty-five years I did not shed a tear about his dying, nor did I acknowledge my anger about his cruelty. I lived for a quarter century with a mountain of unresolved grief and anger until it all surfaced during an experiential seminar at California's Esalen Institute.

On returning home from Esalen, I was finally ready to face those issues. I agonized through them in countless conversations with my wife. I laid the issues out before my men's support group. I sought help from therapists. For several years I seemed to be making modest progress, and then I got stuck. At the time I did not understand why. Now I do. I got stuck because of—no surprise—alcohol. It would take sobriety to do the hard, necessary emotional work that I needed, but by that time I was in the early stages of alcoholism.

Spirituality also suffers with the addiction. My prayer life became truncated, as did my relationships with other persons. I could be fully open, spontaneous, and honest with no one including God, for I was living with a dreadful secret. Alcoholism is a total phenomenon that leaves nothing untouched. It is not just *like* total depravity. It *is* a vivid expression of that reality.

The term *addiction* has a significant derivation.[25] Coming from the Latin, it literally means to say or pronounce "toward" something. In Roman law it was a technical term meaning delivering or giving over by court order, and the addict was the person who, by official court action, was formally spoken over (surrendered) to a master. Addicts, after such action, were no longer free for other relationships or responsibilities. They had already been spoken for. They were enslaved.

And what is slavery? It is not just that certain choices are taken away. That would limit one's freedom, but it would not constitute slavery. No, a slave is deprived of far more than certain choices. A slave is deprived of his or her very being. One is deprived of the fundamental right *to live* as one chooses—and as one believes one ought to live.

In terms of the self, addiction is slavery. In relation to God, addiction is idolatry. And the effects pervade the totality of the person's world.

Surely these effects were the result of *disease*. But the experience cries out for another language as well: it is *sin*. The words are ominous: "the wages of sin is death" (Rom. 6:23). But this death is not punishment by an angry God as some Bible-thumping evangelists would have us believe. What we experience is simply the consequences of our addiction—the physical, spiritual, emotional, and intellectual processes of disintegration. As one of the standard A.A. handbooks puts it: "Under the lash of alcoholism, we are driven to A.A. and there we discover the fatal nature of our situation. Then, and only then, do we become as open-minded to conviction and as willing to listen as the dying can be."[26]

Using Two Languages

Complex realities call for multiple languages and perspectives. I live in commitment to a woman named Wilys Claire. She is a marvelously complex person. I have known that for over fifty years. I need many perspectives to describe her: wife, lover, soul mate, partner, significant other, best friend. All of those descriptive terms are true, and no single one of them does her justice. Yet each expresses a different facet of our relationship and of my experience of her.

In a very different sense, addiction is a complex reality. As I reflect back on my active alcoholism, here too I need more than one language for description. I find both the language of disease and the language of sin useful and necessary. At times the distinctions between these terms and modes of discourse get fuzzy, but they are not finally the same. Disease is based on a medical model; sin, on a religious one. Disease cries out for healing while sin cries out for grace.

The psalmist found reason to use both images:

> Bless the LORD, O my soul,
> . . . .
> who forgives all your iniquity,
>   who heals all your diseases,
> who redeems your life from the Pit.
>   (Ps. 103:1a, 3–4a)

Disease language, relying on medical metaphor, suggests the need for treatment and therapy. Sin language cries out for grace, forgiveness, and liberation. Therapy aims at healing. Grace aims at rebirth. As an alcoholic I have urgently needed both, and I honestly do not know where one leaves off and the other begins.

Neither moralism nor medicalism will do. If moralism is a judgmental, superficial understanding of sin, medicalism is a one-factor analysis that fails to see the depth of the alcoholic's estrangement *and* the spiritual resources possible in recovery.

Languages and word definitions are social constructions. We find terms that will meet our needs, and even when they are imprecise they can have great power. Addiction historian William L. White observes, "What is most remarkable about the 'disease concept' of alcoholism . . . is the concept's sheer survivability. This concept has survived more than 200 years of attacks from theologians, philosophers, reformers, psychiatrists, psychologists, and sociologists, and yet continues." To White, the durability of this disease concept suggests our individual and collective need for it to be "true" even though its scientific status is sometimes challenged. There are different kinds of truth.[27]

If the disease concept is bound to remain with us, we can also count on the ancient and durable notion of sin to stay around, too. The staying power of both for alcoholism lies in the light they shed on its painful realities and in the doors of hope they open for recovery.

In chapter 1 I spoke of the distinction between *disease* and *illness*. Disease refers to the organic reality as described and categorized by the medical profession, while illness refers to the experienced, existential reality—how the sick person and those around him or her interpret and respond to the symptoms and the disabilities. Interestingly, the Big Book of A.A. characteristically uses neither "disease" nor "sin," but it does use "illness" in describing alcoholism. Indeed, the Big Book is "an illness narrative"—an account of the *meanings* of the disease to a group of people. They are meanings that have transformed lives. So also, the pages of this book (beside being a personal theological account) are an illness narrative.

In my narrative I see the meanings of both addiction and recovery coming in paradoxes—like disease and sin. Each term needs the other, even though some people have considered them mutually contradictory. But when only one is chosen and the other negated, both descriptive adequacy about alcoholism and hopefulness for the alcoholic suffer.

When I was in treatment I needed to apply to myself the theology I knew in my head—that sin is always deeper than moralism. Furthermore, I needed to understand that the mystery of this paralyzing alienation was also a disease. When I could begin to grasp these things then I could, like the disabled one pictured by the Gospel writers, begin to hear Jesus say, "'Which is easier, to say to the paralytic, "Your sins are forgiven," or to say, "Stand up and take up your mat and walk"?'" (Mark 2:9). Jesus appears to have intended both: in the midst of your deep alienation the Holy One is accepting you with a radical love, and in the midst of your disease the Great Physician is restoring you to health. Which of these things is easier to hear? I would rather not have to choose between them. I need them both.

Chapter Five

Body and Spirit

Alcoholism and "Manhood"

This chapter is about masculinity and alcoholism.[1] It is especially about white, middle-class, straight masculinity and alcoholism. Even more specifically, it continues the reflection on my own addiction story, but now with attention to gender issues. I am quite aware that this focus reflects only one small piece of the addiction scene, and I will make occasional reference to what others of different group identities have said about themselves. But I need to concentrate on what I know from experience. Not only is it what I feel called to do, but also I am convinced that we who are men, especially men of the dominant power group in society, have been generally oblivious to the *gendered* nature of alcoholism.

When I introduce myself at a recovery meeting with "My name is Jim, and I am an alcoholic," I am pronouncing two significant words about my identity: that I am a man (with a masculine name), and that I am an alcoholic. About twenty-five years ago I began consciously trying to understand my experience as a man in Western society. In the past decade of recovery I have been searching also for the connections between my gender and my addiction. Men are almost—but not quite—infinitely variable. Not only race and sexual orientation but also ethnicity, age, social class, geography, and particular life experiences surely condition men's alcohol use and its meanings. Nevertheless, I also assume that we have certain commonalties simply because we are all men in a particular society.

It is likely that drinking has been a gendered experience in every society. In the United States, men drink almost twice as much as women, and over twice as many men are heavy drinkers compared to women.

Our intoxication rate is also twice as high, and more than 90 percent of those arrested for alcohol and drug abuse violations are men.[2] Alcoholics Anonymous meeting attendance is about two-thirds male. Men are three times more likely than women to be in chemical abuse programs, and five times more likely to be diagnosed as alcohol dependent.[3] Furthermore, there is little evidence that *genetic* factors can account for these striking gender differences.[4]

In spite of all of this, there is surprisingly little serious investigation of just why men drink that much more and why we are that much more vulnerable. My literature searches in several university libraries turned up almost nothing for "men and alcoholism" or "men and addiction." When I tried "gender and addiction" I found numerous sources—virtually all about women.

Some three decades ago feminist scholars began asking why addiction research routinely ignored gender. They discovered that while women drink significantly less and have far fewer alcohol-related law violations than men, alcoholic women are still stigmatized more severely. Like addicted men they are held culpable for moral deficiency or self-inflicted illness, but they face two additional stigma. Since women are still held to a higher moral standard than are men, there is more shame in their "fall from grace." And, most perniciously, alcohol abuse is assumed to make women sexually promiscuous.[5]

In addition to these stigmas, physical and sexual violence and clinical depression frequently are involved. Moreover, signs of women's alcoholism are more frequently ignored or dismissed, and hence they are underrepresented in treatment programs. They wait longer to seek help and are more likely than men to turn to mental health services than to alcohol and drug treatment programs. Physiological factors also enter in: women typically become more intoxicated than men when drinking identical amounts of alcohol; alcohol and certain other drugs disrupt menstrual cycles, inhibit ovulation, affect fertility, and sometimes lead to early menopause.[6]

Obviously, drinking is not always the same experience for men and for women. In my focus on men in this chapter, I do not minimize for one moment the varied and serious issues women face, but I am not trying to compare men's and women's experiences. Feminist scholars and recovering women have done significant work on addiction in women, and I am simply trying to stay close to my own experience and to what I have learned about other men.

Why have we largely overlooked the masculinity issues in alcoholism? Perhaps men's alcohol abuse is so obvious that it is simply taken for granted. We men have always had more access to alcohol, and greater access means more abuse. For gay men the access factor is the same as with other men, but alcohol abuse is even higher because of social oppression and the dominance of gay bars as gathering places.[7]

In addition, in spite of the abundance of feminist gender work, the fact remains that those doing most of the addiction research are men. And in patriarchy men still too often remain invisible to themselves, invisible in their distinctive experience *as men*. Those who take themselves to be normative humanity, as men are taught to do, seldom look critically at their own experience. In more ways than one, the ruler doesn't measure the ruler. All of this is particularly true if men are straight, white, and economically secure—in other words, "hegemonic men." Thus, for those of us with dominant power in the system, it is not only our gendered *privileges* that become invisible to us, it is also the gendered nature of our *problems*—including addiction—that remains invisible.

In my earlier discussion of the difference between disease and illness, I observed that the patient's reconstruction of the disease into an illness narrative, a reconstruction that evoked creative responses to the disease, was frequently critical for healing. Surely that is true with alcoholism. And for many of us who are male alcoholics, reconstruction of our masculinity narratives will be an important part of our own healing.

Proving Manhood

I chose to drink because I liked so much what alcohol did for me. It made me feel good. And a large part of that was its paradoxical effect on things pertaining to my gender: *it both helped me feel more masculine, and it also eased the burdensome pressures of masculinity.*

In much of Western society, "Alcohol is the only drug which is part of the male sex role, the only mood altering drug which society overtly promotes as manly."[8] Here is the quintessential (and insecure) man, Ernest Hemingway, questioning the masculinity of a literary colleague: "I have never seen him drunk . . . [and] I like to see every man drunk. A man does not exist until he is drunk."[9] Parenthetically, Upton Sinclair once made a list of all the noted American writers who had been destroyed by drink, and virtually everyone on it was male. Curiously, I found Sinclair's observation a welcome reinforcement, for it was plain that if you didn't drink copiously you didn't stand a ghost of a chance of success in anything, even including manhood.[10]

So I drank for my manhood. And for many years I also smoked unfiltered Camels. Not that the gender connections were all that conscious to me at the time, but for a man uncomfortable with traditional religious piety who nevertheless felt drawn to a religious profession it made some emotional sense to do these things.

At the same time, alcohol also medicated my masculine stress. In my particular experience of middle-class, Midwestern, American Protestant culture, I had learned very well that whatever else masculinity is, it is strenuous performance and hard-won achievement. In addition, one's self-esteem *as a man* is never finally and permanently secure—one's manhood is never finished.

Today, sometimes at least, I can look back with a little more perspective and some wry amusement on my quest for male self-esteem. Indeed, as Wilfred Sheed noted, it makes one think of a Jane Austen clergyman patting his stomach. One can imagine Austen writing, "Mr. Forbush was a man of unquestioned self-esteem, to the great amusement of his friends and the mild astonishment of those parishioners who ever gave much thought to the matter."[11] But in my earlier years, my self-esteem was not a matter of amusement to me, and alcohol seemed to allay some of the anxieties.

Granted, the issue of earned masculinity is culturally relative. In both traditional Jewish and traditional Chinese cultures, boys are ascribed masculine status simply by virtue of their biological maleness. Not surprisingly, male alcohol abuse in those cultures is low.[12] On the other hand, as anthropologist David Gilmore observes, in most parts of the world manhood is something to be proved by successfully enduring distress, and alcohol helps the process. In the Balkans, "the real man" drinks excessively, fights bravely, and raises a large family. And in the Truk Islands of Micronesia, "real men" drink heavily to acquire the courage and numbed senses requisite for masculine bravado. Gilmore finds it striking about these young Micronesian men that their sense of masculinity is a deeply conflicted pose. On the one hand, it is "a mask of omnicompetence and an almost obsessive independence. . . . [Yet] the youths experience a relentless anxiety . . . that the external mask will suddenly fall away, revealing the trembling baby within."[13]

But those anxious, heavy-drinking young men of Truk were not far from one middle-aged, middle-class American man. In the decade of my fifties when I began to drink heavily, I feared nothing more than that my mask would fall away. My students and colleagues would then see me for what I really was: one with nothing left to say, no achievements worth noting, no contributions worth giving, little left in the inner bank with which to purchase self-respect, that is, manhood. I could give a decent lecture about the grace of God, yet in my heart of hearts I wasn't sure it applied to me. But drinking helped me cope with those feelings. It helped enormously.

Some other men apparently have found this to be the case, also. Another cross-cultural study concludes that men's desire to feel stronger and more powerful is the basic clue to their alcohol abuse. According to these authors, "Our main conclusion is that the alcoholic experience has a common core for men everywhere. . . . While individuals in different cultures embroider and interpret the experience in different ways, . . . the experience centers everywhere in men on increased thoughts of power."[14] But that is precisely the problem. It backfires. When we men orient ourselves to the world hierarchically, assuming that our masculine identity depends on comparison with others in status and power, we become chronically insecure and emotionally isolated. Then we are prone to turn to alcohol or other drugs to quiet our discomfort, anxiety, or sadness.[15]

This phenomenon is not limited to privileged males. Listen to the staff psychologist at a facility for indigent, hard-core alcoholic men of the street, both white men and men of color: "Over and over I heard an emphasis on the absence of fathers, both physically and emotionally, from the lives of the men. I heard a confusion about how to express love, pain, anger, and even happiness. *I heard the relentless burden of expectation for competence, for control, for prowess.*"[16]

Masculine Shame

The distinction between guilt over one's specific actions and shame over one's very being is now a familiar and a useful one. Guilt says, "I *made* a mistake." Shame says, "I *am* a mistake." While prone to both, typical alcoholics most deeply need to confront their own shame.[17] And for male alcoholics the sense of deficiency about an unfinished, inadequate masculinity is often central to that shame.

In my boyhood there were many well-intentioned attempts to shame me into manhood. Later as an adult I could tell myself that I couldn't be good at everything, and yet I operated emotionally with the opposite assumption: I *had* to be. I was not so concerned about moral goodness, at least by conventional standards. What I really feared was that I lacked competence—wasn't good enough—and that others would find out.[18] Taught early in life that men were doers and achievers, I learned that competence in doing and achieving was essential to authentic manhood. When I failed or was unsure of myself, I felt ashamed. There was some kind of judgment on my being itself. To cope with that shame I turned to the rules familiar to so many men: stay in control, be right, deny negative feelings, and if all that doesn't work, drink. For some time, drinking seemed to work particularly well.

The groundwork for my own struggle with masculine shame was laid in a typical place—my relationship with my father. He was (as we all are) quite a mix of qualities. In so many ways he was admirable, indeed, impressive. An elder son in a large immigrant family, by dint of native ability, ambition, and effort, he turned an impoverished childhood and a limited education into World War I heroism and then substantial business achievements and community leadership. He was hardworking, high-achieving, and civic-minded—a man of impeccable integrity who expected much of himself and those close to him.

As a young boy I experienced my father not only as a model of manhood but also as a demanding taskmaster, swift and cruel in meting out discipline when I failed to measure up. Any tears from me during physical punishment constituted reason for an extra dose: "Now I'll give you something you can *really* cry about!" While physical punishment was limited to earlier years, adolescence provided continuing occasions for my father's verbal abuse and emotional withdrawal. Though I achieved well enough in school—teams and offices, Eagle Scout and academic honors— his message was that it should have been better. In college being summa cum laude and runner-up for a Rhodes Scholarship were not enough; he made it painfully clear that someone else was actually first in the class, and someone else got the Rhodes.

He wanted one son to be a doctor; the other, a lawyer. My older brother had chosen medicine, so on graduation from college I entered law school. But law, I decided, was not for me, and much to my father's consternation I quit before the end of my first term. The Korean War had begun, and I volunteered for the army. Though I would not please him as a lawyer, perhaps I could as a soldier. My father died from a heart attack four months later. I returned home on emergency leave, attended his funeral in uniform, and shed no tears. Big boys don't cry, nor do good soldiers.

One need not be in the military to put armor on. Men learn how to do that in numerous ways. As a youngster I had grown a protective body layer, and by the time I was in late adolescence I was fifty pounds overweight. My body was also tight. Beginning early in grade school I developed recurring bouts of intestinal cramps that would double me up in pain for a day at a time. They faded away shortly after my father's death.

In the previous chapter I mentioned a seminar at the Esalen Institute in California. It was the 1970s, and Esalen was avant garde in exploring the edges of human development. The week's workshop I attended was an intense immersion into body awareness through breath work, yoga, massage, nudity, and encounter groups. In the midst of that experience, the dam of my grief and resentment broke. Tears never before shed now flowed. From somewhere in the depths came an excruciating longing for my father's love and blessing, a thirst repressed for a quarter century since his death. There were feelings long forgotten and some I did not know I had. The shame I had carried seemed lighter, and there was a surge of bodily aliveness almost frightening in its intensity. Even in the midst of exhaustion and confusion, the new masculine energy felt wonderful. In my drinking, now becoming heavier, I found less to escape and more to celebrate. Serenity, however, would await a later time.

Now, years later, with the gift of sobriety, serenity is more than just a hope. Most of the time I see the futility of believing that my father was responsible for how I feel. I see the futility of believing that it was possible for me to control his behavior; the futility of thinking that my self-esteem must be based on pleasing him.[19] Most of the time I now feel genuine warmth for him and gratitude for his positive legacies. Most of the time I now know that parents usually do the best they can with their children, and I know how every parent, surely myself included, needs to be judged with a full measure of grace.

I am also more aware of the dangers of unfinished masculinity, the dangers of living with shame about not measuring up. I found alcohol as my gateway to relief. Many men do. Our primal yearning is to feel fully and expansively alive, to be at home in the world, contributing to and affirmed by the goodness of life. But we are vulnerable, and some of our experiences along the way have frustrated these needs. To that extent, we contract in fear and self-defense, and when this happens we inevitably feel it bodily. Ironically, then our fearful reactions often lead us to treat our bodies as things to manipulate: to appease, to indulge, to ignore, to discipline, to shape up,—or to medicate. And, to the extent that we treat the body as an object, we further damage our own coherence and spontaneity.

All of this can be true without one's using alcohol to cope, but when heavy drinking is in the picture we shrink far more. It shrinks our imaginations, our willpower, our judgment, our bodyselves. When the self's primal needs are unsatisfied, the self too often becomes untrue to itself. It is bought off by substitute satisfactions and ephemeral ecstasies, and since these are ephemeral they must be repeated addictively.[20]

Men, Disembodiment, and Addiction

One of the oldest and most lethal tricks we play on ourselves is believing that our bodies are mere appendages or instruments of our *real* selves. Since the late classical period in the pre-Christian era, to Descartes ("I think, therefore I am") in the seventeenth century, to the present, both sophisticated and simple-minded philosophies and theologies have proclaimed the body-spirit split.

Whatever the form of this dualism, it has two predictable features. One is that the human being is a stitched-together composite of two fundamentally different essences—one spiritual and mental, the other bodily and material. The second assumption is that one of these realities is of greater value and should control the other. Almost always this means that the spirit or mind should control the body. And since, in most cultures throughout history, men have claimed that they are essentially more rational and spiritual than women, and women more emotional and bodily than they, this means that they, the men, should control women and, if they choose, denigrate all things feminine.

There is one more result of the body-spirit split that is seldom recognized: the nourishing of chemical addiction. When men are taught (as most are) that their masculinity is based on achievement and is never complete, when men fail (as they repeatedly do) in securing that masculinity once and for all, and when in their failures men know they must always stay in control of their emotions (which emerge from the body), some men—some of *us*—will find alcohol a splendid help. It is the substance, par excellence, for controlling our worlds.

Indeed, as my alcohol dependence grew, I, who had studied so much theory about the body-spirit unity, believed that I was finally beginning to experience it. But the split within me was being more firmly established. My drinking could drown out my body's true thirst for authentic emotions and for good physical care, and my drinking could silence the true promptings of my spirit.

In a strange way, however, alcoholism is proof that spirit and body can never finally divorce. Gerald May reminds us that our brains never forget what they have learned. "[The addiction memory] stands ready to come back to us with only the slightest encouragement. . . . Years after a major addiction has been conquered, the smallest association, the tiniest taste, can fire up old cellular patterns once again."[21] Yes, the body speaks its mind.

In chapter 3 I proposed that deeply rooted religious and cultural suspicions of body pleasure were a barrier to accepting a disease-understanding of alcoholism. I challenged the notion that because drinking is done for pleasure, alcoholism should be understood primarily as a moral issue. Now I want to add another piece to the puzzle: body distrust and alienation can be major factors in the addiction itself. I know it was true for me.

Philosopher Bruce Wilshire writes, "No attempt to divide us up into mind and body—or into mind and body and spirit—and then to add it all up to get our wholeness can succeed. . . . [W]e *are* our bodies, *are* body-selves meant to be ecstatically involved in this world."[22] Wilshire maintains that "ecstasy deprivation" is strongly linked with addiction, and I find that argument compelling.

While ecstasy—the feeling of enormous joy and delight—is emotional, mental, and spiritual, it is also fundamentally and sensuously grounded in the body. In this sleep-deprived society filled with excessive stimuli around the clock, regeneration by a good night's sleep is one example of body ecstasy. The human brain evolved over millions of years and developed its own "uppers"—analgesics and endorphins. "These are," Wilshire observes, "natural opiates needed for survival in wilderness—rewards for meeting the demands of Nature and satisfying basic periodic needs. Lacking a minimal level of these opiates—no less now than then—we fall into 'ecstasy deprivation.'"[23]

In addition to our basic physical and survival needs, body ecstasy also depends on the satisfaction of our distinctively human and spiritual needs. These include steady affection and support in early life, confirming initiations into various developmental stages, induction into respected roles in our communities, and the encouragement to explore the meanings of life in groups that share our concerns. These satisfactions are typically sensuous, full of feeling, often playful. When these needs are met we feel significant and vital as persons. Indeed, the drive to find our lives significant is so powerful that we can sacrifice virtually everything else to find a feeling of belonging and worth.

However, if our primal needs have not been adequately satisfied at an early age, the void can gradually appear quite normal, receding into "the hazy margins of consciousness." Even so, an awareness—like a ringing alarm bell we cannot locate—tells us something is missing. Though its bell is muffled and its location puzzling, the alarm tells us that something threatening is going to happen, and it creates in us a vague and pervasive restlessness. When the restlessness becomes too much, addiction can move in to fill this emptiness and loss of connectedness. But the efficacy of substitute gratifications is a fleeting pleasure. They are compulsively repeated efforts to keep the emptiness at bay, though in the end they drain the body of its regenerative capacities. Even so, when we are addicted we do not recognize this. We cannot. In fact, when we are addicted we crave the very thing that damages us. It seems to promise the ecstasy for which we deeply thirst.[24]

Was such ecstasy deprivation responsible for my addiction? Not without the conjunction of other factors. But I am convinced that it was a significant factor in that constellation. I am also persuaded that the much higher incidence of the disease in men can be understood only when we take this factor seriously. After all, we men too typically don't know very well what we are feeling, and we will go to extraordinary (often self-destructive) lengths to prove we are alive.

African American Masculinity and Alcoholism

The connection between masculinity issues and alcohol abuse is, of course, not limited to privileged, straight white males, this society's hegemonic men. The gender and body-spirit issues surface in different ways for different men, and African American males currently provide one striking illustration of the masculinity-addiction connection.

Cornel West argues that body issues still lie at the very core of white racism today: "[M]uch of black self-hatred and self-contempt has to do with the refusal of many black Americans to love their own black bodies —especially their black noses, hips, lips, and hair. . . . White supremacist ideology is based first and foremost on the degradation of black bodies in order to control them."[25] At the same time that whites demean black bodies, their fear of and fascination with black sexuality are basic ingredients of the racist dynamic.

Fueled by centuries of white racism, this dynamic takes its toll on African American masculinity. Black male heterosexuality plays on "the dominant myth of black male sexual prowess [which] makes black men desirable sexual partners in a culture obsessed with sex."[26] Furthermore, young black males (in spite of the fact that they are murdered and imprisoned in record numbers) have found ways of capitalizing on white myths about them. Helped by the prominence of black male athletes and the cultural weight of black male pop artists, these young men have stylized their bodies in ways that exaggerate the perception of sexual power and control. It is a way of coping with a hostile culture through a heightened machismo identity.

If there is a correlation between the exaggeration of masculinity styles and increased alcohol abuse, it should show up in statistics for African American men. This appears to be true. Those who use alcohol show higher rates of heavy drinking, more adverse consequences of drinking, and increased morbidity from alcohol-related illnesses and injuries than do white men. While one might suspect that the heavier drinking is caused by race-based economic discrimination and poverty, this does not seem to be the case. The pattern persists even after statistics are adjusted for income, occupation, and employment status.[27] The most significant factor for heterosexual black men seems to be the larger effects of racism on their perception of their own masculinity. In short, the more "masculine" a man's self-image and way of being in the world, the more vulnerable he is to alcoholism.

African American gay men are in a still more vulnerable position. Many reject the stylistic option of black machismo, yet as a consequence black America penalizes them and white America further marginalizes them. West observes, "In their efforts to be themselves, they are told they are not really 'black men,' not machismo-identified."[28] They are subject to the same heterosexist oppression as their white gay counterparts, and to that is added their rejection as inadequate representations of black manhood. The alarming incidence of alcoholism among African American gay men is, sadly enough, not surprising.

Masculinity and Recovery: Denial and Living into Paradox

Reinhold Niebuhr reminded us that we do not actually break the laws of God; in fact, we break *ourselves* upon the laws of God. Part of God's desire—indeed, God's law for us—is our wholeness, our integration as bodyselves. When we violate the law of wholeness succumbing to the divided self, we break ourselves. One striking illustration of this is the way sexism makes men more vulnerable to alcoholism. Another is the way in which our recoveries are made more difficult by the dynamics of traditional masculinity. Controlling, emotionally invulnerable, competitive loners can be tough prospects for continuing sobriety.

In the chapters to follow I will deal with some of the issues that I as a man found especially difficult, such as powerlessness and surrender, admitting my brokenness and need of healing, learning to ask for help, accepting grace, and depending on community. Aspects of my masculinity complicated these basic recovery matters for me—I know that beyond any doubt. At this point, some observations on denial and the paradoxical might illustrate the gender complications.

In a health newsletter I recently came across a self-test for spotting drinking problems. While I would never have taken that test during the last year of my drinking, I was curious now, and I answered the test questions as I would have if I could have been totally honest during that last year before treatment and sobriety. The scoring instructions said that 9 or more points indicated a possible drinking problem and the need for a thorough assessment. My score was 28. Yet until the very end of my drinking I strongly resisted any admission that I had a serious problem. Indeed, at one level I simply did not believe I did. Denial, as they say, is not just a river in Egypt.

As a practicing alcoholic, of course I needed to hide my excessive drinking from others. But even more, I needed to blind myself to the reality of my progressive condition. While denial is no respecter of gender, we men seem to have particular training and gifts for it. In our masculine initiation rites we learned to say, "It's OK, coach, just a broken arm, doesn't hurt, I'll finish the game." When alcoholism enters the picture, our considerable denial capacities seem to escalate. F. Scott Fitzgerald (who knew something about it) could say of his character Dick Diver, "The facade can remain intact after the interior has crumbled—and . . . a clear eye and a steady voice can stand guard over a seriously disintegrating personality."[29]

It is a mistake, however, to confuse alcoholic denial with lying or conscious fabrication. As a practicing alcoholic I *actually believed* there was no serious problem. To admit otherwise would have threatened the whole edifice of my alcoholic world. But the same thing is true (even if in a less exaggerated way) of most men who are in denial about their feelings. It is not typically conscious deception, but rather the unconscious defense of a whole psychic edifice under threat.

Leslie H. Farber has identified these dynamics. As a boy gradually becomes aware that he must manipulate his self-presentation to get the attention and approval he craves from others, he finds this both painful and corrupting. He is ashamed of hiding a secret, illegitimate self. He is ashamed of appearing to be someone different than he really is. This painful spiritual burden is so intolerable that he commands his private self to conform to the public one. However, Farber says, "There are some things it is impossible both to do and at the same time to impersonate oneself doing. Speaking truthfully is one of them."[30]

Thus, at some point, some bottom, some moment of truth, there begins the breakthrough of alcoholic denial. When that came for me I had to recognize the vast difference between relaxation and numbness, between falling asleep and falling into a stupor, between the warmth of genuine relationships and boozed-up euphoria.[31] The movement to reality was possible because of both hopelessness and intimations of grace. Without the jolt of hopelessness my denial would have persisted. Without the sense that nonjudgmental help was waiting for me, I could not have moved into reality. The old hymn has it right: "And grace shall lead me home."

The central wisdom of both Western religion and philosophy is on the side of paradox, and "home" for recovering people is full of it. Long ago I had accepted and affirmed the significant role of paradox in my theology, but believing with the mind and embracing with the totality of one's being can be different things. Paradox was viscerally difficult for me because I was still too immersed in aspects of a traditional masculinity that preferred contrast and contradiction.

One clue to this typical masculine preference comes from the body psychologists who tell us that the more persons distance "themselves" from their bodies, the more they are inclined to populate their perceptual worlds with sharp contrasts and either/or's. Then people are either good or bad—not both. They are either right or wrong, male or female, gay or straight, black or white, healthy or sick, them or us. A man who has learned to distance himself from body feeling and emotion, who has learned that his body is essentially an instrument, likely wants clear-cut answers in an either/or world.[32]

But new friendship with the bodyself is an important mark of recovery. So also is the willingness to live with paradox. Indeed, the two feed each other, as I have learned in recovery. Blaise Pascal reminds us that the one who would be an angel is also a beast. I drank attempting to be one or the other. Luther reminds us that we live justified by grace and at the same time are still sinners. I drank to experience one or the other. My sobriety depends on my acceptance that I am always both justified and sinful; always both angel and beast.

Recovery means living into a host of paradoxes. Here are a few more:

> It is paradoxical that alcoholism is both a disease and a manifestation of that basic alienation called sin.
> It is paradoxical that those who have been deepest into denial can become most vulnerable to the truth about themselves.
> It is paradoxical that out of limitation comes freedom: "I cannot drink" (limitation) becomes "I can *not*-drink" (freedom).
> It is paradoxical that in facing our powerlessness we find power; that in facing our imperfection we find wholeness.
> It is paradoxical that since grace is both justification and sanctification, recovery is both a gift and hard work.

The clear-cut world of either/ors and of linear power is the world of traditional phallic masculinity. Elsewhere I have argued for the importance of a both/and revelation in the male body. Such wisdom can be grounded bodily in the male genital experience of *both* the erect phallus and the flaccid penis, even though cultural masculinity almost exclusively emphasizes the former and denigrates the latter. In the power, hardness, and size of erection men can find the physical representation of a certain kind of strength, assertiveness, determination. It is, if you will, the active (or "doing") spirituality of the *via positiva*. These qualities can be very good, and they are typically what we think of as masculine—as phallic masculinity.

By themselves, however, these qualities are not enough. Half-truths become demonic. Power, hardness, and size become violent and oppressive if they are not balanced. But in the softness, smallness, and vulnerability of the flaccid penis, men can also find the embodiment of receptivity, of quiet generativity, of an undemanding male gentleness. It is, if you will, the *via negativa* of sinking into God more than rising to the heights. It is the way of gentle darkness more than light. It is the spirituality of "being" more than doing, and that side is just as important. Not only the hard phallus but also the soft penis is truly masculine. Not only thrusting but also receiving. Not only the courage to act but also the vulnerability of being. Not only rising to God but also sinking into God. Always we need both.[33]

In recovery I have seen this more clearly than ever. The paradoxes of my own sexual body furnish important metaphors for my spirituality. They are also good guides for sobriety.

God's Good Pleasure

Years ago John Dewey recognized the peril of living dualistically: "Oppositions of mind and body, soul and matter, spirit and flesh all have their origin fundamentally in fear of what life may bring forth. They are marks of contradiction and withdrawal."[34]

Though it might surprise many, the apostle Paul would largely agree. His Hebraic heritage, with its clarity about the unity of the bodyself, was a stronger element in his thought than the dualistic influence of the classical world. Paul's perorations against "the mind of the flesh" and his warlike speech pitting spirit against flesh have all too often been misunderstood as sheer attacks on an inherently sinful human body.[35] New Testament scholars are in considerable agreement: in these instances Paul did not mean by "flesh" the human body as such but rather the whole self in alienation from God. His Greek word for this was *sarx*. When he spoke of the human body he used the word *soma*. For this latter kind of bodyflesh he had genuine gratitude. It was God's gift to be treated as a temple of the Spirit. The *soma*-body metaphor was actually the key metaphor for Paul's entire theology. God's incarnation in the bodyself of the Nazarene was the divine embrace of fleshly humanity—not a blessing on disembodied spirits.[36]

"It was God's good pleasure to take on our human flesh." So says a venerable prayer of the church. "It was the pleasure of God to dwell in Christ fully." So says one of the church's ancient confessions. The embodiment of God in human flesh is, according to biblical story, greeted by shepherds rejoicing, magi bearing gifts, and angels bursting into song—pure ecstatic pleasure.

Were Christians less skittish about affirming body pleasure, we might be more familiar with a Hungarian named Sandor Ferenczi. Far less well known than Sigmund Freud but nevertheless an important colleague, Ferenczi believed that each of our various body organs has its own life and finds pleasure in what it does. He used the term "organ eroticism," suggesting that "the body's parts not only function, they also take pleasure in what they do. One asks, not is the organ *working*, but is it enjoying itself." The effect of this is "to shift the mythic base of our ideas about body organs from performance to pleasure."[37] Similarly, Thomas Moore suggests that in a context of the cultural numbing of our bodies, "We could imagine disease as not just a physical phenomenon but as a condition of the person and world, as the failure of the body to find its pleasure."[38] In the same vein, Deepak Chopra sees addiction as the quest for a pleasure that will both help us transcend our ordinary and often painful experience, and in addition convince us we are alive.[39]

I became alcoholic thirsting for release from performance. I sought release in alcohol, but the enjoyment became shallow and short-lived. I now know that *both* alcoholism and recovery have to do with our body-selves and their ability (or inability) to find pleasure. But the pleasure critically at stake in recovery is not a shallow gratification of senses. It is the deeper body ecstasy of knowing one's connectedness. It is connectedness to one's own bodyself, to others, to affirming and supportive social groups and institutions, to the natural world, and to the very Ground of Being and Source of Love beneath and beyond all of this.

Early in May 1993 I had been in the treatment center for about two weeks. Though my emotions were still shaky, the alcohol was now largely gone from my system. Steadiness was gradually returning to my body, and my eyes were once again clear. One day I saw something that had eluded me for several years: *spring*. The trees were leafing out; crocus and narcissus were blooming; the grass was freshly verdant after a long Minnesota winter. It was almost overpowering. I had missed truly seeing spring's advent for the past several years of my drinking. But now I saw it, and e. e. cummings's lines came rushing back to me as he thanked God "for most this amazing day," and for "the leaping greenly spirits of trees and a blue true dream of sky." The poet knew about having died and now being alive once more, about the resurrection of life and love, about tasting and touching, hearing, seeing, and breathing the unimaginable God in all of this.[40] Now I knew, also.

For several years Wilys Claire and I have lived in Tucson, where the desert edges up to our back patio and the mountains rise just a few miles away. Though a child of Minnesota's lakes and forests, I have now also fallen in love with the Santa Catalina Mountains and the Sonoran Desert. Such latter phenomena have formed archetypal images in Western spirituality, with seekers for centuries finding transcendence of ordinary experience through the mountain and deeper entrance into ordinary life through the desert.

Belden Lane interprets the way of the mountain as that of ecstasy, vision, and prophetic insight. The mountain is where the spirit soars. The mountain bestows gifts of clarity and patterns for life's details. The desert, however, is like the cave or the vale. It is where the soul descends into the depths of the ordinary and the earthy, even into the dark night. The mountain gives us flight even as the desert anchors us. Says Lane, "The two, of course, ultimately feed each other. . . . Both journeys are necessary."[41]

During my alcoholic drinking, I would have found such thoughts interesting but quite unreal. Preoccupied with my addiction, I would have felt no intense connection to mountains or desert. In recovery I find their power. It is not a power based on my intellectual assent to a metaphor ("Oh yes, the mountain is *like* my spirit's need to soar and reminds me of that.") No, it comes from a visceral identification. When I gaze on a particular mountain in the morning, I can feel it. Its carbon *is* the carbon of my own bones, and the mountain spirit bears my spirit aloft. So also I feel bodily the desert's hard dryness, yet my soul knows that its own dryness, like that of the desert, is teeming with hidden life and that there will be remarkable greening after a monsoon shower.

On such occasions I *know* with the sensuous knowing of the Hebrew verb—"the man knew his wife Eve and she conceived" (Gen. 4:1). My bodyself knows intercourse with mountain and desert, and I feel the consummate pleasure, even when craggy, mysterious mountains elicit a shudder and the parched desert cries out in thirst. Even then it is pleasure, the joy of being sensuously alive and part of it all. With the Apostles' Creed, "I believe in the resurrection of the body." It is a different way that a man can experience his body—not as a thing to be controlled, an instrument to be used, much less an appendage devoid of feeling. Resurrection of the body is also another way of describing recovery from a numbing addiction.

The Recovering Alcoholic and His Masculinity

Each major movement of the recovery experience—such as the shifts from control to surrender, from denial to reality, from contradiction to paradox, and from separation to community—mark changes in a person's identity. The founders of Alcoholics Anonymous believed a spiritual conversion process to be essential to finding real sobriety. But that is true of any major illness. A health crisis assaults one's identity, forcing the person to decide who and how to be. So also, healing requires a conversion narrative—the construction of a new identity with an interpretive story.

For some of us this new identity is that of a recovering alcoholic. But for some of us alcoholics who are men it is also a changed masculinity. While most alcoholic men do not enter the recovery process looking for transformations in their masculinity, such do occur. As one man said, "I got into recovery to save my ass, and I discovered my soul was attached."

Both of these identities—as a man and as a recovering alcoholic—are socially constructed. They are not given from on high but are learned in particular communities. Each has its particular language and symbols. Each involves certain ways of looking at the self in the world. And, importantly, each identity has a significant impact on the other. But the image of recovering alcoholic often carries more weight, reshaping some of the individual's previous masculine self-understandings. The reason is not hard to find. I hear it given voice frequently in recovery meetings and have said it myself: "Without this program I'd be dead right now—I have no doubt of that whatsoever." That is a strong motivation for giving priority to the recovering alcoholic identity.

Traditional masculinity has forbidden most emotional expression, deeming it weak and feminine; the recovering man finds emotional expression critical to his sobriety. Traditional masculinity has led men to see other men as competitors; in sobriety a man seeks other recovering men as sources of support. One of the pillars of traditional masculinity is homophobia; the recovering heterosexual man finds that gay men can be his mentors because living in a homophobic society has made them intimately familiar with vulnerability, risk taking, and powerlessness—all qualities critical for any alcoholic's sobriety.

In spite of society's increasing enlightenment about chemical addiction, most alcoholics still experience some judgment and marginalization. But a little marginalization can be good for the masculine soul. Now that we have admitted we are alcoholics, somehow there seems less to lose in dropping our other masks. Over the years we learned manhood by wearing masks, too often hiding our real faces from those around us. We hid our insecurities and fears because we wanted so badly to be accepted. Now we see the costs of these charades.

A decade ago in treatment one of our lecturers said, "You may think I'm crazy, but some day you will be grateful for your alcoholism." I remember my reaction well: "You *are* crazy, mister. I'm grateful for the help and the hope, yes, but *not* for the alcoholism. I'd just as soon have passed on that one, thank you."

And yet, amazing grace. "Once I was blind, but now I see." We—and here I make bold to speak for other recovering male alcoholics I know— we are grateful for all that has helped us move a little bit closer to becoming, as a friend describes it, "the men we long to be."[42] And in the process, at least modestly, becoming a little bit more human. I think Rabbi Abraham Heschel was right: "Being human is difficult. Becoming human is a lifelong process. To be truly human is a gift."[43]

Chapter Six

Power and Powerlessness

The day before my admission to the treatment center, in great embarrassment I called a good friend. She was a law school professor in whose class I had agreed to lecture the previous day. I had anticipated that event for several months, but because I was drunk that afternoon I had completely missed it. She received my labored but candid apology. She also heard me report my decision to enter treatment immediately. Then she said two wise, unforgettable things based on her own experience of years in recovery: "Jim, you won't believe how much power you will discover by going deeply into your powerlessness. And you'll never believe the energy you will have when you are no longer struggling to control your drinking."

I heard her words but did not understand them. They went counter to all of my masculine conditioning. What I needed was *more power*, not less. What I needed was *more control* over my drinking, not giving up. Gradually I have absorbed her truth.

The Hazelden Center shapes its treatment approach around the philosophy and steps of Alcoholics Anonymous. Thus, at the very beginning of my month there I was confronted with the challenge of Step 1: "We admitted we were powerless over alcohol—that our lives had become unmanageable." I found that enormously difficult.

For one thing, in its better days at least, alcohol had done wonderful things for me. It seemed to expand and unify the self—a power well-known to most alcoholics. William James, the renowned nineteenth-century psychologist who had a profound effect on Bill Wilson, described it this way: "Sobriety diminishes, discriminates, and says no; drunkenness expands, unites, and says yes. It is in fact the great exciter of the *Yes* function in man. It brings its votary from the chill periphery of things to the radiant core."[1]

Giving in to powerlessness felt like capitulation, quitting the struggle, admitting utter defeat. In retrospect I know that is exactly what I needed to do: to surrender utterly. I did not realize it at the time, but the old gospel hymn had it right: "Make me a captive, Lord, and then I shall be free; force me to render up my sword, and I shall conqueror be."[2]

Powerlessness and the Oppressed

Though the challenge to confront my powerlessness over alcohol was precisely what I needed, these things frequently look very different to many other people. Praises to the virtue of powerlessness are more easily sung by those who have had social power bestowed upon them and have not had it preempted for biological, historical, or economic reasons. Countless women, sexual minorities, people of color, and persons with disabilities doubtless see this issue differently than I do—and with good reason.

Feminists have reminded us that, like sin, powerlessness is a gendered issue. Just as male theologians often identified pride as the central dynamic of sin without considering women's different experience (not too much pride but too little), so also middle-class male pioneers of A.A. spoke out of *their own* experience: alcoholics seemed characteristically self-centered and ego-driven. "Self-will run riot" was how they described it in the Big Book. It may not have looked quite the same to women alcoholics.

One alternative approach agrees with A.A. that a thoroughgoing admission of powerlessness *over the addiction* is a necessary and critical step in recovery, but it rejects the general insistence on ego deflation. Stephanie S. Covington speaks out of a woman's experience, and Douglas J. Federhart, from that of a gay man.

"It can be difficult to acknowledge we are powerless over our addictions because we already feel powerless in so many other areas of our lives," writes Covington.[3] Not only are alcoholic women stigmatized as slovenly, promiscuous, and immoral; they are also impeded in their recovery by the expectation that women should always be selfless, concerned about the needs of others and oblivious to their own. Women traditionally have not had access to direct power and prestige. As a result, Covington observes, "many of us have perfected the art of manipulation. . . . When we begin recovery, we begin to . . . *consider if this is the kind of power we want to keep.*[4]

Covington agrees with A.A. that even those who traditionally have been disempowered need to admit their powerlessness *over their addiction*. However, the image of power as "power over" (winning and losing, control and dominance) needs to be replaced by "power *with*" and "power *to*." "The idea is to share power so that we can create more of it."[5]

From his experience as a gay man and a recovering alcoholic, Douglas Federhart similarly observes that ego deflation, when seen as a necessary recovery step,

> runs contrary to the instincts of nearly anyone whose primary lived experience is one of low (or no) self-esteem. . . . Women have pointed this out, and I think it is likely to hold true for the majority of gay and lesbian people, too. . . . Much of *our* recovery involves *gaining* a healthy sense of self and *building* ego strength. And yet, if we are to get our lives back, we have to make peace with this idea of surrendering.[6]

What kind of surrender is necessary? Federhart responds, "I am not being asked to relinquish my identity, but simply to acknowledge the basic fact that addiction has hijacked that identity."[7] In his understanding, what recovery asks of the gay, lesbian, bisexual, or transgendered person is the admission of powerlessness *over alcohol* and, because of that, the admission that life had become unmanageable. This is not a negation of personal power. Federhart realizes, however, that prior to surrender "it has been my denial and rationalizations that have perpetuated my habit of misnaming my predicament and assuming that I am in control of the situation."[8]

Covington and Federhart both have stayed squarely with the A.A. movement, but they have done so through a reinterpretation of Step 1 appropriate to those who have known social oppression. Charlotte Davis Kasl offers a somewhat different path to recovery, an alternative for women and minority men whose problem is not inflated egos but, quite the opposite, lack of ego strength.[9] She has created "Sixteen Steps for Discovery and Empowerment." While there are many overlaps with the traditional twelve, Kasl's plan is distinguished by several different emphases: ego strength instead of ego deflation, inclusive language, acknowledgment of the social roots of addiction, and movement from "chronic recovery" to "discovery." Regarding the issue of power and powerlessness, here is her Step 1: "We affirm we have the power to take charge of our lives and stop being dependent on substances or other people for our self-esteem and security."[10]

I don't wish to argue for one approach over another—the traditional Twelve Steps or an alternative. In matters of recovery, I do believe (with the title of one of Kasl's books) that there are "many roads, one journey." My concern is to reflect on powerlessness and power as I have experienced them while recognizing that others have had different experiences. Among those others is Linda A. Mercadante, whose work I mentioned in chapter 4. She has given us a thoroughgoing feminist theological reassessment of sin and its relation to recovery—an essential issue for our understanding of power.

However, to grasp Mercadante's argument, we first need to revisit the way that the Christian tradition typically has understood sin. It goes like this: sin predictably arises out of the discovery of our human limitations and our finitude. Since our humanity is composed of both spirit and "nature" (or "body" as I termed it in the previous chapter), we have two major paths to escape that basic anxiety—through our spirits or through our bodies. The *sin of pride* takes the spirit route. Thus, pride of power, moral pride, intellectual pride, and spiritual pride are all ways in which we have tried to convince ourselves that we are not fated with finitude and death. The other path, says this tradition, is the *sin of sensuality*. Here is our attempt to escape anxiety through immersing ourselves into the bodily world of the senses (in gluttony, drunkenness, material extravagance, sexual irresponsibility, and the like).

Now, however, we must remember the gendered understanding of these things. In a patriarchal culture men have identified themselves as more spirit and intellect, and men have identified women as more constituted by their bodies and their emotions. And if one assumes that men are the more significant sex, it is a short step to seeing pride as the more serious and more fundamental dynamic of sin. The male founders of A.A. followed the same path of mainstream Christian thought: While drunkenness *seemed* to be a bodily and sensual sin, its real cause lay in the more fundamental realm of the spirit. It was pride: "self-will run riot."

So much for background. Mercadante's critique begins by acknowledging that traditional gendered understandings of sin have labeled sensuality as the "secondary" form of sin and have identified it as typically of women. However, she responds, the sin called "sensuality" can be just as grave as that called "pride." Sensuality is usually thought to include mediocrity, sluggishness, inertia—in a word, sloth. This kind of sin is just as alienating because the self fails to make the effort or take the risk to be a true self.

A better term than sensuality, Mercadante suggests, is "inordinate self-loss." If women are more susceptible to it than men, it is not because they are more bodily and sensual, nor because they chafe more at human finitude. It is "the panic of disconnection." Women simply have been socialized to place high value on relationships and interdependence. As a consequence they fear being without connection and acquiesce too quickly to poor relationships. So, concludes Mercadante, "self-will run riot" is not the only way to turn from God. When we say that it is, we inadvertently reinforce self-loss as a virtue—to the detriment of over half of the human race.[11]

The issues raised by Covington, Federhart, Kasl, and Mercadante are significant ones. As I hear them, none of these critics doubts the enslaving power of addiction. Nor have they disputed that alcoholics are powerless over *alcohol*. However, they rightly protest other generalizations about power and powerlessness that purport to be to true of all alcoholic people regardless of sex, sexual orientation, physical condition, race, or economic state.

Powerlessness and Freedom of the Will

Though in a myriad of ways power looks different in different life stories, *powerlessness over alcohol* is the defining condition of alcoholics and their common denominator. Finally coming to grips with that fact about myself, I began to grasp the paradox experienced by countless predecessors on this journey: only by acknowledging fully my powerlessness over alcohol was I able to begin the empowering process of recovery.

First, I needed to hit bottom. For me that came on the morning of April 20, 1993, after five and a half days in that hotel room two miles from my home. The night before I had run out of vodka and it was too late to order more. Morning had come, and there was no morning drink to continue my escape. I looked into the mirror and saw defeat. The strange disease had me, and my efforts to conquer it had only wrapped the web more tightly around me.

It would be some time before I realized what a gift the bottom experience was. At the time it seemed anything but that. It felt like the tumult before the end of time depicted in the New Testament—earthquake, famine, and war. Years later, I can say with Luke, "Now when these things begin to take place, stand up and raise your heads, because your redemption is drawing near" (Luke 21:28). In April of 1993, however, it was not a foretaste of heaven. It was just hell.

This kind of powerlessness may well be difficult to imagine unless one has experienced it. It is all very contradictory. During much of my active disease, the more I used alcohol the less free I became, but the freer I thought I was. Toward the end of my drinking, however, the illusion of freedom was beginning to erode. Like most alcoholics, I tried a host of methods to get my drinking under control. The Big Book describes such strategies well: "limiting the number of drinks, never drinking alone, never drinking in the morning, drinking only at home, never having it in the house, never drinking during business hours, drinking only at parties, . . . taking more physical exercise, reading inspirational books . . . we could increase the list ad infinitum."[12] I tried most of these, plus others. But if any strategy of mine worked for a time, its efficacy soon evaporated like the dew under an Arizona sun.

A psychiatrist specializing in alcoholism treatment describes the slavery of the addiction as total and absolute: "Everything in life becomes subordinate to complying with the demands of the addiction."[13] The sense of our own history begins to fade; our strong connections with others weaken; we begin to doubt the connection with any power greater than ourselves. And then when we are almost overcome by shame and embarrassment for what our lives are becoming, alcohol is there to salve the wound. The relief it gives is both predictable and remarkable. Yet its price is high. It demands from us yet more of our freedom and takes away, along with our other emotions, our capacity to feel the loss.[14]

It is a slave-making disease, and the rebirth of freedom seems to require our hitting bottom. But if the bottom is to be a turning point, we also need enough freedom precisely when we are at that low place to call for help. Even that is paradoxical.

Late in my active alcoholism, how free was I? In one sense, even in the last stages I had the freedom to drink or not, for every time I drank I made that choice. There was not some inevitability about it, as if an external force were mechanically causing me to reach for the bottle. When I chose to drink it was because that seemed to be the most desirable choice in that situation; it was what (for whatever reason) I wanted to do. As another recovering alcoholic said, "In all my years of drinking, I never once took a drink unless I had decided that *it was the right thing to do at the time.*"[15] Indeed, A.A. recovery philosophy is firmly grounded on the assumption that at least *some* freedom remains to the active alcoholic. "One day at a time" assumes that person can choose *not* to drink for at least a short span of time. The great paradoxical insight permeating A.A.'s approach is that though alcoholism is a paralyzing disease for which the individual ought not be blamed, it is not an excuse for anything. It is not an excuse for the damage done to others and oneself, nor is it an excuse for failing to do something about the disease.

On the other hand, was I all that free? Let me return for a moment to the way I experienced the progression of alcoholism.[16] As the disease gradually worsened, I felt increasingly alienated from my feelings. I did not want to share the pain of my sense of strangeness with anyone else— I couldn't find words for it, and were I to talk about it I would feel even more different. The very fact that I was unable to express these things increased my sense of being out of control. However, alcohol (though it was causing this progression) came to my rescue. It seemed to return my life to manageability and my world to normalcy. When I used it, the feeling of being connected with others and comfortable in my own skin returned. Once more I could be free and creative and loving. I felt larger, more adequate, more like everyone else—so it seemed.

Yet all was not as it seemed. While apparently restoring my connections, in fact alcohol was eroding my real desire to connect, and increasingly I sought isolation in which to drink. While I sought normalcy, in fact alcohol was making me feel increasingly different. At times, I would wonder whether it was playing tricks on me. But I was loath to give it up, for it had always worked so well. So I counted on it all the more.

So how much freedom did I have? Though in one sense I drank only when I chose to, I drank much more and far more frequently than was in my best interests. In other words, I drank more, and more often, than I *intended*. My power to bring about my intentions was being eroded. What had happened gradually over a period of time (for both genetic and experiential reasons) was that my brain had been hijacked. I *thought* I was choosing for my best interests, but I was making choices that ran exactly contrary to them. I could choose to take that first drink, but I had lost my freedom about the second, third, and fourth. On most occasions, once I started drinking, I could not choose to stop—a phenomenon all too familiar to any alcoholic, and one that must seem wildly improbable to nonalcoholics.

Progressively, my addiction was disowning me. Increasingly when drinking, in a profound way I was not myself. Increasingly I was unable to make the choices that would affirm my best self. Seeburger asks why alcoholics, time after time, make such mistaken choices. His response: "The answer is that it is no longer the alcoholics *themselves* that are making that choice. It is their addiction choosing. And what the addiction chooses is to disinherit alcoholics of the right of disposal over their own lives."[17]

Nevertheless, when it comes to recovery A.A. maintains that most alcoholics will be able to find enough willpower to make the initial decision of surrender necessary for the process to begin. As we have seen earlier, the Big Book is unclear to what extent the individual is responsible for *being* an alcoholic.[18] However, regardless of the causation, the person is expected to make those decisions that will begin and sustain the recovery process. Though disabled in other respects, the alcoholic is still able to decide.

There is a caveat, however. The Big Book contains this hard recognition: "Those who do not recover are people who cannot or will not completely give themselves to this simple program, usually men and women who are constitutionally incapable of being honest with themselves. There are such unfortunates."[19] Yet such people likely were born that way and ought not to be held responsible.

Enslaving though the addiction is, A.A. assumes that alcoholics—with the exception of these "unfortunates"—will have sufficient capacity to make the admission of powerlessness (Step 1) and then to surrender their lives to the God of their understanding (Steps 2 and 3). This emphasis on responsibility clearly answers the charge that A.A. promotes irresponsibility through its use of a disease model. Blaming someone else or blaming fate for one's alcoholism is beside the point. Even in the middle of their powerlessness, alcoholics must take responsibility and make the decision to surrender. It is a testimony to the conviction that in the human being the image of God may be defaced but it is never totally destroyed.[20]

To be sure, some folk testify that they didn't have much freedom at all about beginning recovery. There were divorce threats from a spouse, threats from an employer, court orders threatening incarceration—these and other pressures have nudged or shoved some into treatment and recovery programs. Though at the time it seemed that there was not much of a choice, the person still chose what appeared as the lesser of evils. The person could have accepted divorce, job loss, or jail but chose otherwise. The options were limited, but there was still freedom to choose between them.

I was not one of the "unfortunates" mentioned in the Big Book. I was capable of giving myself to a recovery program. How much freedom I had to make that necessary surrender is still a mystery to me. Immanuel Kant confessed that along with the questions of God and immortality, the issue of freedom of the human will was one of the three great problems lying beyond the powers of our intellects.[21] He was right: over the centuries, philosophers have been stymied in the attempt to prove once and for all that free choice is a reality or an illusion.

But the case for freedom of the will (even the alcoholic's impaired free-dom) does not finally rest on a philosophical argument. It rests, as Kant himself concluded, on the fact that *without* presupposing it our everyday thinking and acting would make no sense to us. It is an experiential veri-fication. That is the case for alcoholics. We know from experience that our recovery would not be possible without our decisions to accept the reality of our powerlessness and to turn our lives over to the care of God in a new way. It is circular, to be sure: the decision is proof of the ability to decide. Though the argument is circular, the fundamental change in one's life is very, very persuasive.

The paradoxical combination of helplessness and responsibility is not always easy to accept, however. Addiction researcher Dr. Steven Hyman acknowledges that it is hard to say to someone, "Yes, things are terrible, yes getting to your present condition involved what was done *to* you, and it even has . . . to do with the body with which you were born, but . . . you have to be involved in the solution."[22]

Nevertheless, the compatibility of powerlessness and responsibility is not foreign to the Christian tradition. The great eighteenth-century American theologian Jonathan Edwards was convinced that we do not wait until we have resolved the theoretical issues of freedom or deter-minism before we act. Nor do we shrink from holding ourselves and oth-ers responsible for dealing with something when the causes of that situation are disputable. Edwards comments, "In order to form their no-tion of faultiness or blameworthiness, [people] don't wait till they have decided . . . what first determines the will."[23] To Edwards it was clear that people do not wait to decide the question of responsibility until they have first solved the underlying philosophical problem. No, it is just a matter of common sense. Out of his experience of recovery Bill Wilson was con-vinced of the same thing—"that 'what first determines the will' to drink has nothing to do with the question of who bears responsibility for the consequences of drinking."[24]

At this point the distinction between our *intentions* and the *consequences* of our actions may be helpful. Imagine a crowded city bus. I am one of many who are standing in the aisle. The driver suddenly brakes to avoid a child who has run into the street, and I am thrown against another pas-senger, causing her considerable discomfort. Even though I did not in-tend the action, I quickly apologize. Instinctively it seems right to do so. I do not explain that the child or the child's parents really ought to apol-ogize to her, possibly the bus driver as well. Nor do I try to explain how the child's action impaired the driver's freedom and subsequently mine so that my bumping her was not really "my" action at all. I simply apologize, knowing that, regardless of my intent and regardless of my impaired freedom, I hurt her. Similarly, as an alcoholic I could try to explain to the "passengers" on life's journey who have been wounded by my drinking, "I'm sorry, but I didn't intend to—the disease made me do it." Far better, I can simply say, "I am very sorry that I hurt you."

One last matter about freedom seems important: *where does it come from?* Though Kant's issue was whether there was freedom at all, in their controversy many centuries earlier Augustine and Pelagius assumed that freedom was real. Their question was its *source*: was freedom a permanent part of the human equipment, or was freedom a gift of divine grace in each critical moment that it was needed?[25]

Pelagius argued the former side: in our creation God has given us a fully autonomous freedom that remains ours regardless of our sin. In contrast, Augustine maintained that while human freedom is real, it is a highly paradoxical reality: the will is so disabled by sin that it cannot choose the good *except* through the gift of divine grace enabling it to do so.[26]

Through the ages, the mainstream of the church has typically settled for something of a compromise between the two, and I find my own situation illuminated by that compromise. It is a both/and matter, not either/or. I have no doubt that my freedom was alcoholically impaired. I kept making bad choices about drinking, and then my drinking contributed to additional bad choices. These choices were "out of character" for me—not evidence of my freedom, but precisely the opposite. I have experienced what Augustine was arguing for. However, in spite of the power of my denial, there remained in me something of an awareness of my increasing dependency on alcohol and my bad choices about drinking. That awareness itself meant that I was not "totally disabled." There is the truth in Pelagius.

But at the end of the day, Augustine was right about grace. I needed God's grace to take the first steps to recovery. This grace was not irresistible. God did not thrust "it" on me in such a way that I became a puppet of the divine will. Nor was it a miraculous "something" from beyond that suddenly infused me with power to choose. Not an impersonal "it," the grace empowering me to make that surrender was, simply and amazingly, *embodied love.*

It was Wilys Claire's love—the love of a spouse stretched almost to a breaking point by my addiction, but a love that refused to break. It was the love of my adult children living far away, puzzled and hurting with the reports of their father's drinking. It was the love of friends, colleagues, students, members of my church community—some of whom worried about me, many of whom were unaware—love that I counted on and that counted on me. And it was, almost unbelievably, the remnant of love for myself as I looked painfully in the mirror on the sixth morning after five solitary drunken days. I cannot imagine the capacity to make the decision I made that morning without that web of love surrounding me. That was and is amazing grace. That was and is the heart of God welcoming me back home.

I grieve for those who cannot report such grace in their own experiences. I do not blame God for withholding anything. God does not withhold. Nor do I blame God for refusing to create and arrange a world in which empowering love is equally distributed. Such a preordained world without meaningful freedom would quite literally be senseless and hardly worth living in. So, with Augustine I have discovered that I needed empowering grace if I were even to ask for help out of my bondage. And with Kant I find understanding that gracious freedom quite beyond the powers of human intellect. I can only respond with deep gratitude.

A Disease of Control

Long ago Lord Acton observed that power tends to corrupt and absolute power tends to corrupt absolutely. Perhaps, as Bill Moyers commented more recently, it is not power as such that corrupts but rather *the fear of loss of power*. Dictators order the death of those who threaten their power; gang leaders kill their opponents in drive-by shootings; husbands batter wives—all fearing loss of power and control.

In our own ways, we alcoholics have a particular insight into this. We were corrupted by the need to control others in order to serve our addictions. Control is hanging tightly onto power to manage and steer things to one's own ends. With good reason addiction specialist Barbara S. Cole declares, "Control is truly the master addiction."[27]

The dynamic of addictive control is not a simple thing. It can wear many different faces. In my case an obvious one was the assurance of supply. Any active addiction requires enormous control if its thirsts are to be quenched. To be able to drink when one feels the need requires constant vigilance and attentiveness to detail. People, places, and things must be manipulated so that the delivery system runs smoothly.[28]

I realized that another facet of my alcoholic control stemmed from my masculine gender identity. The admission of powerlessness was a huge step for me not only because I was alcoholic but also because I was a *male* alcoholic. In fact, treatment professionals agree that men's resistance to surrender is most often their greatest barrier to recovery.[29] Indeed, that resistance may be the chief reason why men's rehabilitation rate is low: two-thirds will relapse within their first year of treatment, and only twenty percent will stay sober five years.[30]

Before recovery I had not thought of myself as a particularly controlling person, but now I see myself differently. It was part of my self-understanding as a man that I *should* be in control—if not of other people, then surely of myself. As a seminary professor I should be in control of my academic discipline. I should be in control of my schedule and energies so that I might be a good husband, father, citizen, and teacher. As one committed to Christian faith, I should have the discipline (read "control") necessary for a faithful life. Control was not only something I wanted, it was something I *ought* to exercise throughout my life. It was simply the way things should be.

The notion that I was powerless over something that I should have within my control simply did not make sense. Surrender meant defeat. So the more I lost control over my drinking the more I struggled to stay in control, and the more the disease affected other parts of my life the harder I fought for control in those arenas. I struggled mightily to stay in control for surrender meant the loss of everything—my self-respect, my willpower, my chances to overcome the demons.

A third facet of my control dynamic was simply the burning desire to regain control of my own life. From that imperceptible time—exactly when I will never know—when my drinking became a disease and the disease inexorably began its progression, I found it impossible to share my sense of strangeness with anyone. The inability to express something critically important about oneself is profoundly alienating, but with more alcohol that alienation seemed to dissolve. When drinking I felt more connected and no longer crazy, back in control of my life.

Thus, the classic contradiction: I drank to get in control of myself, yet my drinking was out of control. When I suspected that I was losing control over alcohol, I continued to drink to *prove* my self-control. Then, each time I failed to control my drinking furnished another occasion to drink in order to prove that I still had self-control.[31] Admittedly, this kind of thinking makes sense only to active alcoholics.

As my alcoholism progressed, still another face of control appeared. It was my attempt to control the uncontrollable. Psychotherapist Leslie Farber notes that our will (our ability to choose) operates in two different kinds of areas. The first involves those things we can directly choose ("objects"). The second realm includes those realities we cannot directly grasp or choose ("directions" or "goals"). For example, we can directly will going to bed, but we cannot in the same way will going to sleep. Likewise, we can will pleasure but not happiness, reading but not understanding, knowledge but not wisdom. When we confuse the two realms, we are doomed to failure, says Farber, and the split between the will and the impossible goal that I am trying to will gets wider with each futile attempt—the harder I try to go to sleep, the more awake I am.

Addiction enters the picture, Farber maintains, because alcohol or other drugs appear to heal that split. I know that alcohol gave me the illusion that I could control even directions and goals in my life. But, as Ernest Kurtz and Katherine Ketcham observe, "The problem with 'willing what cannot be willed' is that we step into a territory that is not ours—we stake the claim to *be* God. . . . We try to command those aspects of our lives that cannot be commanded . . . and in doing so, we ironically destroy the very thing we crave."[32]

The unwitting claim to be God can stem also from the previous facet of control I mentioned—the desire to regain control over one's own life when that is slipping. Denial, the creative mother of invention, came to my rescue with the creation of a certain kind of self-image. It was the image of an unshakably responsible person. As an addiction psychiatrist describes it, "It is impossible for me to be out of control *because I wouldn't allow any such thing to happen*."[33] Indeed, the loss of control is incompatible with omnipotence.

Thus, self-deification comes in strange ways. For the alcoholic it is often subtle and indirect. Two of Jesus' disciples were at least candid about their desires:

> James and John, the sons of Zebedee, came forward to him and said to him, "Teacher, we want you to do for us whatever we ask of you." And [Jesus] said to them, 'What is it you want me to do for you?" And they said to him, "Grant us to sit, one at your right hand and one at your left, in your glory." But Jesus said to them, "You do not know what you are asking." (Mark 10:35–38a)

Neither did I know what I was asking in my various ways of trying to control. But the paradox of addiction is that the more we struggle to control it, the more attached we become to it.

It is like the fly struggling vainly to extricate itself from the spider's web—the struggle only entraps it more securely.[34] Then it becomes a vicious circle. Practicing alcoholics think they are in control of their drinking, even if it is crystal clear to others that they are not. Then those close to the alcoholic get caught in their own illusions—thinking that they are controlling the drinker's ways, constantly working on new methods to do so in spite of the fact that every previous attempt has failed. For both the alcoholic drinker and the codependent, the break in the cycle comes only with giving up control. It is called surrender.

Surrender

The repeated declaration "My name is Jim, and I am an alcoholic" is a critical symbol of surrender. But how extraordinarily difficult it was at first. It would have been one thing to say, "My name is Jim, and I have a problem with alcohol." But "I am *an alcoholic*" made me choke. I felt like a pariah—morally defective, weak-willed, and sinful in a particularly shameful way. Far different from a problem to be conquered, "alcoholic" threatened to become a permanent part of my identity. It was a scarlet letter "A" for "alcoholic," an ugly, indelible tattoo on my forehead forever there for everyone to see.

It felt shameful for many reasons, not the least of which was that it implied essential limitation. As an alcoholic I am one who simply cannot drink. I am limited.[35] But my father had always taught his sons never to accept limits. "The sky's the limit," he would say. "A man knows there's always room at the top." To me his words were just as loud and clear a half century later, for I had made them my own. So, the assaults on my sense of self-worth were mounting. The fear that I was losing my mind and the dread that my life was out of control were now joined by the shame that I was essentially limited.

It was not only shameful; it was also frightening. I was being asked to confess my utter and complete powerlessness over alcohol in every dimension of life. I was being asked to admit that physically I could not handle it any more, that it had become a poison to me. I was being asked to admit that mentally I would become either nonfunctional or falsely functional not only when I drank the stuff but *even when I thought about it.* I was being asked to admit that spiritually I could not handle alcohol, that the spirits were disconnecting me from the Spirit and from everything that made me truly alive. Indeed, on hearing this demand for the confession of powerlessness, at first I simply could not comprehend it. It was far too radical. I was being asked to admit my powerlessness over life, over myself—over everything.[36]

Not only frightening, it was numbing. I was told to let my Higher Power take over my life. That should have been a relief, but it was not. I had shouldered that responsibility for such a long time I was no longer aware of how heavy and destructive it was. And now I, who had been a religious professional for decades, was being told by these recovering drunks on the treatment center staff to surrender not only my drinking but *myself* to God!

But I knew they were right. I knew it beyond a doubt. I needed to make a more radical surrender than I had ever known. For years I had been like the rich ruler who went to Jesus, asking about eternal life. Like him, for many years I had done what I thought the faith required of me. But as with him, the radical demand had escaped me, or I had refused it sadly because I was rich in things I did not want to give up.[37]

Nevertheless, if recovery were ever to occur, the moment had to come when I could say without reservation or qualification, *I am an alcoholic.* When that unqualified admission finally came, it was a spiritual surrender more total than I had ever known.

Losing and Winning

If alcoholism is a disease of control, it is also a disease of *perception*. We alcoholics know there is a major difference between us and those without this addiction: alcohol's power to change our very perception of reality. "Normal people" who use alcohol report that it is relaxing, warming, and conducive to sociability. But they do not report changes in their perceptions of reality. Alcoholics do. That is why we wanted alcohol, wanted it regularly, and increasingly depended on it. It made us feel larger, more confident. It made our environments less threatening. With it we saw the world as a place where we could live with greater comfort.

One important change of perception I found is from *winning to win* to *winning because of losing*. Some readers, I suspect, may be uncomfortable with "win/lose" language and may wish to abandon such terms altogether. These concepts seem to be products of a competitive, up/down, dualistic, and closed worldview that we need to leave behind. However, we live between the times. We do need to transform our perceptions and language from the old era; we also have to recognize that the new age is not yet completely ours. Along with many other alcoholics, I was shaped by win/lose language, and I must acknowledge that. But in its transformation is my healing.

How does that transformation look?[38] I entered the treatment center certain about two things. First, while I was still loath to say I was alcoholic, I knew I was in real trouble with my drinking. Second, I was convinced that I needed to find the strength I was lacking in order to conquer alcohol. I left the treatment center a month later knowing I was alcoholic. I also left convinced that I had struggled hard against alcohol, *and I had lost*. The struggle was over. That recognition was absolutely necessary for recovery to begin. I began to hear echoes of Jesus' well-known paradox: "For those who want to save their life will lose it, and those who lose their life for my sake will save it" (Luke 9:24).

But the impetus to try to save my own life did not vanish quickly. In the early days of treatment I vowed to do this recovery thing right, perfectionist that I was. So I tried hard to surrender—fully. What I had not grasped was that *I needed to quit trying*. Before treatment I was trying to control my alcohol use; now I was trying hard to surrender. I finally realized that I did not need to struggle harder—about anything—but simply stop struggling altogether. If I threw in the towel, there could be no more fight.

Cole says it well: "If we are hell-bent on winning the fight against our addiction, we have already lost. The disease wins 100 percent of the time with this method. . . . The uncanny reason why we lose each and every time is that *the disease uses our own strengths to conquer us*. We are fighting ourselves with the best parts of ourselves."[39] One of the best parts of myself, or so I had thought, was my discipline to succeed, my determination to win. Now I was determined to surrender and to do it successfully, believing that this was the key to winning the battle over alcohol. I had yet to learn that it simply was not winnable. Furthermore, I had to learn that losing was not just a strategy for winning; it was truly losing.

Losing is really losing. Dead is really dead. The difference between Hellenistic Greek perceptions and Hebraic ones about life and death makes the point. Dualism in Greek thought affirmed the immortality of the spirit or soul and the mortality of the body, so the flesh was mortal but the spirit was eternal. ("John Brown's body lies a'molderin' in the grave, but his soul goes marching on.") Hebrew convictions about the unity of the bodyself allowed no such split. When death came, the total person died—body, spirit, mind, soul, everything. Early Christians shared this belief and that is what made their belief in resurrection so radical.

Whether they use this language or not, recovering alcoholics know about death and resurrection. Hitting bottom, finally admitting total defeat—this is the death of the old life. It is frightening but enormously promising for the new life yet to come. And, whatever words they give to it, most recovering people convey the sense that their new life feels much more like resurrection than immortality of the soul. "I was dead, and now I'm alive again!" They know that a whole person disease calls for more than Band-Aids. It calls for a transformation so fundamental that words like "resurrection" and "new birth" seem utterly right.

And it truly feels more given than earned. It comes only when we are willing to accept our limits. It is our recognition with philosopher Alasdair MacIntyre, that "we are never more than the co-authors of our own stories."[40] So, while we can *will* some things in our lives, in this matter it is truer to say that we must *be willing*—be willing that a Power that is in us and yet beyond us will change our lives in a fundamental way. The wisdom of the Twelve Steps, repeated several times over, recognizes that *becoming willing* is the prerequisite to any meaningful change.[41]

Letting Go

St. Francis of Assisi, a patron saint of alcoholics, emphasized the snare of attachment and the need for detachment in true spirituality. In recovery circles the synonyms often used for attachment are clinging, holding on, craving, and grasping, while the key phrase for detachment is letting go. As seen in St. Francis, spiritual poverty is also a persistent theme. It is not simply letting go of material wealth, but, more deeply, surrendering self-will and becoming genuinely indifferent to anything that would claim ultimacy or would claim to be an essential part of the self.[42]

Detachment, such a positive virtue in monastic spirituality, has a negative ring to it for most moderns. It suggests withdrawal from healthy engagement with others and with the world. It implies aloofness, remoteness, and indifference. To the contrary, the monastic interpretation "means not allowing either worldly values or self-centeredness to distract us from what is most essential in our relationship with God, and with each other."[43] Detachment, then, is not so much the freedom *from* desire as it is the freedom *of* desire. It is not the abandonment of all desire or passion, but rather letting go of any anxious grasping that has the desire to possess. It is not letting go of relationships, but rather letting go of the attempt to *possess* the other person in a relationship. It is not letting go of material objects or satisfying experiences, but rather letting go of everything I have deemed essential to my well-being.

As an addicted person, my central attachment was to alcohol and to what the substance did for me. But, typical for addicted people, I had companion attachments. Chief among those was performance. I majored in that form of works righteousness. Though intellectually conscious of its perils and theologically convinced of its futility, I lived as if I were forever called upon to earn my worth and security. In one form or another it is an attachment familiar to many alcoholics, as Bill Wilson's words to a friend indicate. He wrote of his "craving to depend absolutely upon the instinctual rewards of a place in society, material and emotional security, also the right romance. Consciously and unconsciously, I had always demanded these things as a condition of happiness."[44] Yet after some years of leadership in A.A. and practicing the detachment he had come to believe was essential, Wilson declined an honorary doctorate offered by Yale, explaining that he needed to avoid "the dread neurotic germ" of pursuing such rewards.[45]

It is sobering to hear Thomas Merton name the sort of performance to which I was attached a form of violence: "To allow oneself to be carried away by a multitude of conflicting concerns, to surrender to too many demands, to commit oneself to too many projects, to want to help everyone in everything is to succumb to violence."[46]

Mine was a need to be needed, thus a bondage to the Yes. Merton is right about its destructiveness. I became increasingly violent toward myself, pressing myself to the edge of exhaustion to accommodate the requests of others. I dreaded the accusation (whether it was actually made or not) of selfishness and lack of concern. When someone would ask for a commitment from me and the date book was already full, I was in a quandary. But rather than say "No," I would try to squeeze it in, and the whole thing had as much integrity and grace as one of Cinderella's homely sisters attempting to get her foot into the glass slipper.[47]

And it became a vicious cycle. My overcommitment made me angry—angry at myself for my overflowing date book, angry that I had to say "Yes" in order to be accepted and appreciated, angry that I had no life of my own. Beyond the confusion about my boundaries lurked my confusion about the meanings of life and death. Saying "Yes" to the requests seemed to mean life and actualization, new experiences, relationships, and opportunities. "No" meant renunciation, relinquishment, passing things up. "No," in short, meant finitude—fearful boundaries, restricted space and time, the final limits of death itself.

What eluded me was the paradox of it all: in truth, accepting limitation meant life and refusing limitation actually invited death. So, when the tyranny of my Yes's became too oppressive and exhausting, I turned to more and more alcohol to alleviate the pressures. But progressively as I made that turn, I was turning not toward the life I yearned for but toward the very death I feared. How true it is, as the philosopher says, "Addictions are acts of violence directed at our own insignificance."[48]

Release, Relief, and Freedom

In certain situations mental effort is futile, as it often is, according to William James, in the attempt to remember a forgotten name. Typically you work hard at trying to remember, reviewing all of the places and other persons that might be connected with the name. When this effort fails and you try all the harder, success recedes even farther. "And then the opposite expedient often succeeds. Give up the effort entirely, . . . and in half an hour the lost name comes sauntering into your mind, as Emerson says, as carelessly as if it had never been invited."[49] Reading James's *The Varieties of Religious Experience* while in Towns Hospital, Bill Wilson found the noted psychologist ratifying the value of giving up instead of pulling oneself together. It was to be a strange turnabout for a hard-driving entrepreneur, but when Wilson read that "something must give way, a native hardness must break down and liquify," he recognized his own experience.[50]

At the Hazelden Center, when I was able to surrender my futile attachment to power and embrace my powerlessness, a strong sense of release flooded over me. It did not instantly erase my sadness over the hurt my alcoholism had caused, nor the embarrassment and anger for having this damnable disease. Yet the release was genuine. The prisoner was allowed to walk free. I was unsure of my steps, I was wobbly, and I was blinking because of the sunlight, but I was free.

Release was also relief. It was a relief to admit my powerlessness not only over alcohol but also over much else. It was a relief toward the end of the treatment month to take the Fifth Step: confessing to God, to myself, and to another person the exact nature of my wrongs. The chains were falling away. I had not broken them, but some gracious power had unlocked them. Finally I had surrendered *without an agenda*. I did not let go in order to experience release; that would have been simply another form of control and manipulation. I simply gave up.

Release from every desire to drink did not come immediately—that has been gradual—but I knew that its obsessive hold on me was broken. Release began to come also from the denial and self-deception that had been so much a part of the last years of my drinking. In each of these ways I knew that the war was over even if sporadic fighting continued.

It was a release that came in the realization that any and all absolute attempts to control my own destiny were doomed, for I had come up against something that was completely out of my control. It was the discovery that *powerlessness was not helplessness*. It was not a surrender to passivity, but rather a willingness to let go of my useless and destructive efforts to control life. "It is," wrote William James, "but giving your little private convulsive self a rest, and finding that a greater Self is there."[51]

One of the most-cited passages in the Big Book is "The Promises." I find it a stirring panorama of changes one can anticipate in sobriety. *Freedom* is the first. "We are going to know a new freedom and a new happiness."[52] There is a wonderful logic to this, as Cole observes: "[T]he first thing one gets back after breaking through the denial about addiction is freedom. The first thing taken by the disease is the first thing given back once we choose to surrender our war with it."[53]

Early in recovery I found my new freedoms astonishing. Actually, they were very simple consequences of my not drinking. For one thing, I was now free from the exhausting attempt to control everyone and everything around me in order to drink. The fact is, of course, that the lengths I went to protect my freedom to drink only resulted in quite the opposite of freedom. As one recovering person put it, "The more you try to control another person, the more you're under that person's control. If what you do next depends on whether they do or don't do whatever it is you are trying to get them to do or not do, then you are under that person's control."[54] When these machinations are no longer necessary, freedom is very real.

I also began to discover freedom from the need to be right and to look good. While drinking, I always had to keep my guard up, preventing those important to me from looking very deep inside for fear of what they might see. Moments of freedom when I could now relax and lower my defenses were a breath of spring. I discovered this was linked to control. When I was trying to stay in control of things, I had to justify my controlling actions as right, good, and necessary; otherwise to deprive others of their freedom would not be justified. When I could give up control, my need to be right eased its grip. Such changes in me have neither come overnight nor in full measure, but they are freeing—and humility is a work in progress.

Anne Lamott relates an experience reported by a friend. An alcoholic man kept passing out on his front lawn night after night. His frazzled, desperate wife repeatedly dragged him into the house before the morning light came so that the neighbors wouldn't see him. Then, "finally an old black woman from the South came up to her one day after a meeting and said, 'Honey? Leave him lay where Jesus flang him.'"[55]

One of the places "where Jesus flang me" was an extra three days in the treatment center. The standard length of treatment was twenty-eight days. As that time drew toward its close, I approached my counselor puzzled and with some consternation. There must have been some mistake, I told him. Beside my name on the bulletin board's discharge schedule was the date May 21 instead of May 18. If I stayed until May 21, that would be thirty-one days instead of twenty-eight. I explained that I had conscientiously finished my last assignment work. Furthermore, I argued, the delay would come at considerable financial sacrifice. Since my health insurance did not cover any of my costs, those extra three days would add almost a thousand dollars to my bill at a time when the savings account was already sorely taxed. Could he see that this mistake was rectified and that I be discharged on the twenty-eighth day? No, he responded, the staff had decided that three extra days "would be about right" for me. My subsequent appeal of his decision produced the same result: a thousand dollar humility lesson. I was still trying to control things—managing the process, trying to do recovery right, attempting to have everything come out the way I thought it should. Here was one more lesson that freedom does not come instantaneously nor is it cheap.

Surrender also inaugurates *freedom from fear*. Though addiction magnifies, intensifies, and adds to our fears, fear itself is a common thread of humanity. Peter Gomes recognizes this: "Everybody is fearful, terrified of some public or private demon, some terrible unnamed fear that gnaws away even in the midst of our joy."[56] We are fearful that we will be recognized as frauds, fearful that we will fail in a worthy cause or succeed in an unworthy one, fearful that time will run out, fearful that we will hurt others or be hurt ourselves, fearful that we will not know love, fearful that we are untrustworthy, fearful that our most cherished beliefs cannot be trusted. I knew each of those fears and as an active alcoholic knew them with magnified intensity.

I also knew fears that were more particular to my disease. I feared that I would be unable to drink when and as much as I needed and that the amount I was drinking would be discovered. I feared that I was hurting others; that I might kill someone while driving drunk; that I would alienate all those whom I loved. I also feared that I would let down those who were counting on me professionally. Then there was the fear that I had nothing left to offer my students and that they would see me as a fraud; fear that I would never feel normal again; fear that I was going crazy; fear that my faith in God would evaporate once and for all; fear that inadvertently or deliberately I would kill myself; fear that I would finally lose everything. I was not conscious of each of these all the time. Some of them lingered just at the edges of awareness. Some I resisted mightily, for an admission would threaten my denial system. Other fears would just come and go. But none was very far beneath the surface.

I believe Easter is all about freedom from fear. The biblical stories we associate with Easter are not subtle; they are confrontational. They do not creep up on us; they hit us in the face. The terror of an unbelievably cruel death, the loss of hope, and an earthquake all get our attention. Only then do we hear Easter's empowering words: Don't be afraid, you have nothing to fear. Gomes says it well: "Freedom from fear is the achievement of the resurrection—not freedom from death but freedom from fear. We do not fear death; death is the incarnation of our fears. Thus to defeat fear is to defeat death."[57] When those fears are diminished, we have a taste of eternity.

Recovery is an Easter event or, better, an Easter *process*. Resurrection is all about freedom from fear. Alcohol was my answer not to the fear of death but to the fear of life. Now comes the resurrection with the message that by God's strange power we can have life and have it more abundantly than we have ever known.

The events leading to Easter were confrontational. So is addiction. For many of us it was the elephant in the living room—obvious but studiously avoided. Then came the day it got our attention, and the elephant turned into a dog hanging onto the leg with a bite that would not let go. Only then could God inaugurate resurrection.

The great paradox followed: in freedom, we discovered, there is a new bondage. The Christ who liberates, who gives life abundantly and without preconditions, is the same one who says, "Follow me." Now. Immediately. Without reservations. So also, we learned, sobriety is sheer gift, and it is also the road to be walked daily. Now. Immediately. Without reservations. It seems to be the only way that recovery comes.[58]

God's Own Powerlessness and Power

"First of all we had to quit playing God. It didn't work. Next, we decided that hereafter in this drama of life, God was going to be our Director. He is the Principal; we are His agents. He is the Father, and we are His children."[59] These Big Book statements echo the Hebrew *shema:* "Hear, O Israel: The LORD is our God, the LORD alone" (Deut. 6:4). Here is the firm rejection of idolatry, the challenge to all alcoholic pretensions about our being in ultimate control of our lives and our surroundings. We cannot know everything, do everything, control everything. Those illusions have almost killed us. That is the truth of "we had to quit playing God."

As they are worded, however, these Big Book statements give a one-sided picture of God, not particularly helpful to some of us. In their masculine language and imagery they convey an unflinchingly patriarchal image of a benevolent autocrat, a sovereign power jealous of "His" prerogatives asking only submission from "His" subjects. What is missing is the startling New Testament paradox: *Even God has quit playing God.*

Indeed, the paradox of powerlessness and power applies to God as well as to recovering alcoholics. In fact, it is true about us precisely because it is true about God. In the chapters to come I will probe further some issues about God's nature and activity of particular relevance to alcoholics. Here, however, I want to begin the discussion because this matter of powerlessness and power is so integral to the New Testament experience of the divine.

The paradox is abundantly present in the "kenotic Christology" of Philippians 2. *Kenosis* is the Greek term for "emptying out." In alcoholic language it could mean hitting bottom and surrendering. But now it is God (as we see the Holy One in and through Jesus) who hits bottom, who surrenders. The apostle Paul, writing what may have been his last letter from a Roman prison to the congregation at Philippi, uses an early Christian hymn to celebrate this divine *kenosis:*

> Let the same mind be in you that was in Christ Jesus,
>   who, though he was in the form of God,
>   did not count equality with God
>   as something to be exploited,
>   but emptied himself,
>   taking the form of a slave, . . .
>   Therefore God also highly exalted him
>   and gave him the name that is above every other name.
>   (Phil. 2.5–9)

Radical love means that God is at the bottom with us, sharing our slavery. And it is precisely in that pit of powerlessness that we meet God's empowering support. A similar picture of Christ appears in the Apostles'

Creed: "He descended into hell. The third day he arose. . . ." And an earlier Hebraic image of God on which later Christian imagery depended said strikingly the same thing:

> Where can I go from your spirit?
>   Or where can I flee from your presence?
> If I ascend to heaven, you are there.
>   if I make my bed in Sheol, you are there.
> If I take the wings of the morning
>   and settle at the farthest limits of the sea,
> even there your hand shall lead me,
>   and your right hand shall hold me fast.
>   (Ps. 139:7–10)

What would it look like if God really "played God" in a conventional sense of those words? God would remain pure and "on high," commanding our obedience from afar, removed from the ambiguities and sufferings of human life. But divinity looks different when perceived by the Hebrew poet or seen through Christic lenses. Holiness is met in lowliness. Grandeur comes through a bed in Sheol (the place of the dead) or a cradle in a stable. Strength is shown by hanging in there with folks who try to run away to the ends of the earth. Power is revealed hanging on an execution cross and riding the monsters all the way down. Indeed, the Holy One who for us descends into hell is not only our Higher Power but also our Lower Power, the very Ground of our being.

Our alcoholic experience has taught us something about these strange things. Along with those close to us, we have suffered from our disease. But "to suffer" means more than to experience pain or distress. Fundamentally it means "to undergo." "The reality of that lack of control, the sheer truth of our powerlessness in the face of it, makes available the fundamental spiritual insight that insists on the necessity of *kenosis*."[60]

The cross is the Christian focal symbol of *kenosis*. It is the emblem of God's "crossing over" into vulnerability and neediness.[61] The symbol was born out of a terrible reality of life in the enemy-occupied territory that was first-century Palestine. The sight of condemned criminals, bloody and naked, dragging their cross bars to the execution place was unsettlingly common. Part of the Roman repression, this hideous torture was reserved for humanity's dregs. It was especially repulsive to the Jews because their divine law placed a special curse on these victims. As the condemned ones dragged their crosses through the streets, the populace could strengthen their own sense of righteousness by further disowning the victims with jeers and pelting them with filth.

Though the comparison seems extreme, in one way or another most alcoholics have known disownment by those whose moralistic judgment seems to strengthen their own sense of decency and virtue. But here is the New Testament portrait of Jesus who intended to cross over the gulf, leaving the company of the upright and identifying with those under the sentence of death. It is a picture we see clearly in the final events of his life, but also a pattern that Jesus consistently acted and taught throughout his entire public ministry. It is there in his teachings about all those who would not let go of their own self-images of self-sufficiency and decency. It is there in the one who ate with "publicans and sinners," finding them closer to God than those who were sure of their own virtue. It is in his story of the proud Pharisee and the repentant tax collector praying in the temple, with the Pharisee on the wrong side of the divide while God identifies with the impotence and sorrow of the tax collector. All in all, both the life and death of Jesus give us the picture of a radically self-emptying holiness. It is *kenosis*, a power surprisingly found in powerlessness.

For years I missed the main point about "taking up the cross." For a long time I thought it meant a determined, unflinching, self-sacrificial kind of discipleship. Now I believe that its primary meaning is crossing over to the place of neediness and vulnerability, to the place of failure and poverty. "It is," as Martin Smith says, "an invitation, a beckoning, not a threat. 'Do you want life?' . . . But the rendezvous where he promises to meet us is where we are so reluctant to be—the place of failure."[62]

It is a counterculture picture. Most of what is sold as virtue in our society is self-sufficiency, self-satisfaction, appearance, independence, and power over others. The gospel, however, sees these not as virtues but as marks of our estrangement. Jesus' good news is different from society's. Jesus' version is that those of us who haven't got it all together, those of us who have failed to get control of our lives, those of us whose flaws are bigger than our virtues, those of us whose love was not deep enough nor integrity strong enough—we are permitted to be poor and stretch out our empty hands to God. And in doing so we meet a holy presence who has been in hell with us. We meet a love that will not let us go. We receive an invitation to the serenity and peace we have been craving for a long, long time.

When I was at the treatment center I received an unforgettable card from a close colleague. On the front of the card was a painting of the moon, delicately rendered in an Oriental style. The inscription read, "My barn having burned to the ground, I can now see the moon."

Chapter Seven

Grace and Brokenness

By the grace of God I am in recovery." That is an extraordinarily common confession among recovering people and doubtless the reason that one of the most quoted sentences in the Big Book says, "God is doing for us what we could not do for ourselves."[1] It *is* amazing grace.

What is grace? In a nonreligious sense the word suggests charm, thoughtfulness, beauty, and effortlessness. In Hebrew and Christian usage it means a great deal more. It is a countercultural reality, dramatically different from the world's common currency of debtor-creditor relationships, where giving and receiving what is deserved is the expectation. Grace is the unearned love of God given freely to us and to all creation. It is a healing, life-changing love that forgives and affirms, empowers and liberates. It is the lavish generosity of the Heart of the universe, the arms of God welcoming us back home. It is, according to the New Testament writers, divine love definitively embodied in the life, death, and resurrection of Jesus.[2]

The four Gospels give us no formal definition of grace. Instead, they tell stories. Grace is the woman lavishing expensive ointment on Jesus' feet (Mark 14:3ff.). Grace is Jesus inviting himself to lunch with the despised Zacchaeus (Luke 19:1ff.). Grace is hosting the poor, crippled, lame, and blind at the banquet instead of those who could repay the invitation (Luke 14:12ff.).

In the most memorable story, grace is "prodigality," in a twofold sense of that word. First it is the prodigality of recklessness, carelessness, and wastefulness. It is the prodigal son who ran off, squandered his money, binged out, hit bottom living among the pigs (an anathema to Jews), then "came to himself" and began the journey home. Now comes the second meaning. Even before the son could make apologies, his father came running to meet him with a prodigality of love—extravagant, exuberant, lavish. He did not

123

condemn or demand an explanation. There was simply a long, wordless embrace and then a call for celebration. "For this son of mine was dead and is alive again; he was lost and is found!" (Luke 15:24).

In our own stories, we meet grace embodied, enfleshed, and incarnate. I have already described some of the grace-bearing people who gave life back to me. And there were others. Grace was in the holy arms that held me on that men's treatment unit—tattooed arms, needle-marked arms, God's arms. While the voices on that men's unit would have struck many as simply crude (reminiscent of the army barracks I had known forty years earlier), they were the sounds of prodigal sons being welcomed home, and it was gracious, holy ground.

Grace is absolutely fundamental to my recovery, of that I have no doubt. Paul was writing not only to the Romans but also to me when he said, "Wretched man that I am! Who will deliver me from this body of death?" (Rom. 7:24). He was also writing to me in his words that followed: "There is therefore now no condemnation for those who are in Christ Jesus" (Rom. 8:1). No condemnation! I read those words time and again during that month in the treatment center. Each time I was moved to tears.

Grace as "Justification"

There are not different "kinds" of grace. God's love is not divisible into independently existing categories. However, Christian history is replete with various descriptive terms for grace that can helpfully point to different ways we experience the richness of that cosmic love. One of those terms is *justification*, and recovering people know its reality.

Justification was the watchword of the Protestant Reformation. In religious usage the term means being made just or righteous, put into a right relationship with God. Over against any suggestion that we can merit God's love by anything we do or possess, the Reformers insisted that God's love for us depends entirely on the divine initiative. Paul typically used the cross to express this: "While we were still weak, at the right time Christ died for the ungodly. . . . God shows love for us in that while we were yet sinners Christ died for us" (Rom. 5:6, 8).[3] In alcoholic experience, it is precisely when we have hit bottom that we know that only a Power greater than ourselves can restore us to sanity.

Furthermore, precisely when we have nothing of our own merit to offer, we realize that the Power greater than ourselves is truly gracious. Reflecting the centrality of grace to A.A. Bill Wilson wrote, "There is no religious or spiritual requirement for membership. No demands are made on anyone. An experience is offered which members may accept or reject. That is up to them."[4] Indeed, the only requirement for membership is the desire to stop drinking.

That is exactly what I needed to embark on recovery: the invitation to a hopeful experience rather than a demand that I produce change in my life. I needed the reality of "Amazing grace, how sweet the sound that saved a wretch like me." They are honest words. Grace *is* amazing, never to be taken for granted. And it saves. It saves not just a *soul* like me, as some tidied up versions would have it, but even a *wretch* like me. If that sounds too harsh, remember that the core meaning of wretch is not a vile, despicable person but one who is in the deep distress of being homeless, lost, in exile. Gregory Baum describes it this way: "The ground of being is not far away, hostile or indifferent to us. . . . Despite the suffering and evil . . . we are summoned to believe that the ultimate principle of reality is love itself."[5]

Perhaps we can remember a time when everything in the world seemed to be just right. Though it may have been momentary, we knew intuitively that the world was as it should be, and we fit. It may have been a childhood happiness or the first time we fell in love. But it was a joy so encompassing that it felt as though it were not just something inside us, but we were inside it. The gospel tells us that this joyful perception of the world is not an illusion. It is not too good to be true. It *is* true, more real than we had ever dared hope, more intimate than we can see or touch, yet more vast than we can imagine. And the more we can trust it, the more real it all becomes.[6]

Closely related to justification, grace is also *prevenient* according to classic Christian theology. God's gracious movement toward us precedes or goes before any movement on our part toward God. In many Christian traditions prevenient grace is symbolized most powerfully in infant baptism, where the ritual proclaims divine action toward a baby who has no awareness that God even exists.

Alcoholics know the reality of prevenient grace. Many of us arrived at a treatment center scared and still hung over. We had nothing to offer, nothing to prove we were capable of sobriety—or even worth it. But there we were welcomed by those who dared to believe in us when we could not believe in ourselves. Similarly, many of us attended our first recovery meeting with trepidation. Perhaps we were still drinking and felt duplicitous even being there. Yet we were made to feel that we were the most important persons in the room. We who had nothing to show for our efforts to control our drinking now discovered to our great relief that there was only one requirement for membership: the desire to quit. No achievements, no proof, just the desire—and that is grace.

Grace and the Grotesque

While cultural images often suggest that grace is whatever makes us feel more comfortable and in control, this is far from the biblical picture. The descriptions in Flannery O'Connor's powerful short stories are closer to the biblical images, filled as they are with "lonely, twisted people running from their brokenness, denying their sinfulness, terrified of death and change."[7] To these folk grace does not appear in ways they would like, but rather it demands that they abandon all the defenses and securities to which they have clung. Only after accepting their vulnerability are they invited into wholeness.

Doubtless, some of O'Connor's insights into the shadow side of human life stemmed from her own prolonged struggle with the disease of lupus, from which she died at thirty-nine. She found, she once commented, that illness can instruct one more deeply and fully than a long trip to Europe. O'Connor found grace in the grotesque—in the painful and bizarre twists of life that she would not have chosen, but that shattered her security and demanded her vulnerability. She echoed Dostoyevsky who, in *The Brothers Karamazov*, wrote about love not as romantic weekends with satin sheets, but as "a harsh and dreadful thing."

The art of the grotesque has long fascinated Christianity because it points to the healing that is possible when the depths of brokenness are honestly faced. Jesus' own suffering and crucifixion followed by the exultant joy of Easter set the stage for this kind of art as spiritual resource. The grotesque departs from what is usually considered normal, deviating in often exaggerated ways. It is, wrote James Luther Adams, "a depiction of the absurd, the ridiculous, the distorted, the monstrous. It is a mirror of aberration."[8] As an art form the grotesque faces the coexistence of the beautiful and the repulsive, the sublime and the gross, the violent and the healing.[9] It is in the strange gargoyles who leer at us from the columns of stately cathedrals. It is in the medieval custom of dressing skeletons of saints in bright clothes seen in carnivals, fools, and clowns, and in Mexico's Day of the Dead. It is present in the paintings of Hieronymus Bosch, Peter Brueghel, and Francisco Goya. It appears in the pages of Edgar Allen Poe, Franz Kafka, and Flannery O'Connor.

Every alcoholic knows the reality of the grotesque firsthand. Just as art sometimes depicts an estranged world, a universe that is no longer reliable, a life gone out of control, an encounter with the absurd and the demonic, this is also the alcoholic's experience. The second of A.A.'s Twelve Steps speaks of sobriety as restoration to *sanity*. The implication is obvious: an active alcoholic does not think, feel, behave, or relate to the world sanely.

Recovery involves telling and hearing, again and again, our stories of insanity. These drunkalogues are our art of the grotesque. These alcoholic stories break open the experience of the absurd in vivid, painful, and humorous ways. Here are our accounts of wounding those we love most, of our deceptions, of hiding our booze, of our blackouts, of our infidelities, of our failures at work, of exposing ourselves and others to physical dangers. No less than the stories of Kafka, O'Connor, or Poe, our tales break open the realities of the demonic and the insane.

But how does this experience of the grotesque participate in grace? There may be several ways.[10] For one, facing the grotesque as a spirituality leads us to discover the divine presence in weakness, brokenness, and despair. God's invitations to change our lives seldom come in the gentle wrappings of a nice Hallmark card. More frequently they come in confrontations with our own deformities, assaults from which we recoil and want to run. But it is only when we face them honestly that we recognize the open arms of the wounded Holy One. Then grace comes through our wounds, through our inarticulate groans, when our own resources are exhausted and when we are no longer in control of our lives and destinies. Then we discover the ironic truth that the gospel becomes "good news" only when we have honestly faced the bad news of our experience.

The grotesque can become grace also when it helps us recognize what is truly human. Flannery O'Connor reminds us that we cannot recognize a "freak" without some conception of the whole person. Thankfully, the carnival side show is fading, but when I was a youth it had a forbidden allure. Nervous laughter inside the tent thinly covered our own vulnerability and our strange encounter with human wholeness, for perhaps the image of God was silently staring back at us from the disfigured one. We were looking at humanity stripped of its pretenses, at a mortality and vulnerability to which we are all subject.

In recovery meetings I find myself regularly confronted with my shadow side, a necessary piece of the journey into grace. It usually happens through another's story. A newcomer tells her own with halting speech. After many years of total abstinence she joined a friend for lunch in a bar. Intrigued by the conversation about a new low-alcohol beer, she was confident that she could handle just a taste. She accepted a sip. And then a glass. That was all, and she had proved herself right: impressive self-control. But then came the next day and the next. There were more glasses. Low-alcohol beer turned into strong beer and hard liquor, then three years of descent into the alcoholic hell she had known two decades earlier, three years culminating in a suicide attempt that left her with a permanent, gun-inflicted brain injury. Today she is once more sober, celebrating life with limitations, having encountered grace in the harsh and dreadful.[11]

I heard that woman's story long ago, but I cannot forget it. There was no humor in it, just horror—though through the horror a strange hope. It was something like the graphic art of the brilliant British atheist Francis Bacon, who painted religious subject matter in ways that evoked the disturbing and the shocking. Wilson Yates has described Bacon's power as his ability to carry us into the land of despair, invite us to take it in and explore it—and by doing so to answer it. "He speaks to us about where we are, not where we should be or might be. In telling us where we are, he shakes us violently and, having shaken us, invites us to begin our journey."[12] Similarly, the woman's story shook me violently but with "an exhilarating despair" that pressed me more deeply into what recovery was all about—and what grace was all about.

In all of this, however, we need to hear a clear warning. The fact that grace can come in facing our vulnerability and brokenness *ought never justify or romanticize pain.* In recent decades feminist, womanist, and third-world theologians have relentlessly deconstructed theologies of the cross that have idealized crucifixions and suffering. They have turned their searchlights of outrage on atonement theories that, in the words of Christine Smith, have served to "rationalize, spiritualize, romanticize and raise to religious saintly status the concrete reality of suffering and the specific reality of Jesus' murderous conviction."[13] The distortions projected on both God and humanity by such atonement theories have been legion, and any appreciation of the art of the grotesque as an avenue of grace must make utterly clear that the cross calls us into solidarity with the suffering and into unceasing work to prevent more crucifixions. The cross calls us "to hold humanity more accountable for the unspeakable violence we are capable of doing to one another."[14]

As I listen to the grotesque stories of my recovering companions and reflect on my own, I have no desire to justify our alcoholic suffering and the pain that we caused others. It is not good because it led us more deeply into the experience of God's grace. Nor does biblical faith allow a celebration of brokenness as an end in itself. Rather, such faith is an invitation to share in the groaning of all creation for a redemption yet to come (Rom. 8:19–21).

I want to say that emphatically. I also want to point to the strange, paradoxical grace of the grotesque. When I was in anxious denial of the pain caused by my alcoholism, God remained distant and unreal. The good news got through only when I was broken open, when groans and tears became the doorway to God. Such grace dwells in paradox where surrendering means victory, where entering the darkness is illumination, where embracing wounds is healing, where dying is life.

Grace, Guilt, and Forgiveness

I have never met recovering people who did not confess to acute feelings of guilt about things they had done and failed to do during their alcoholic drinking. Nor have my recovering companions been free from shame about who they had become as active alcoholics. Such guilt and shame were surely mine.

Let us focus for the moment on guilt. Though the amount of freedom an active alcoholic has is always limited, neither freedom nor accountability are erased. Indeed, guilt can be a positive sign of our humanity and of the image of God within us that is never destroyed.

Though feel-good pop psychology treats guilt as totally negative and simply an impediment to self-realization, who would want to live in a world without it? Murderers, rapists, and embezzling CEOs who feel no guilt are pathological, and their guilt-free condition augments their danger to others. Nevertheless, there *are* inappropriate experiences of guilt, sometimes called "superego guilt."

There is, for example, guilt that arises from neurosis. If performing certain repetitive rituals is part of my neurosis and if one day I miss doing them, I will feel guilty. But, like the red light flashing on the dashboard when the car is actually functioning well, neurotic guilt is a false alarm. Sometimes guilt stems from violating cultural taboos wherein something is deemed wrong simply because it has been declared a taboo. Thus, over the patriarchal centuries women have been made to feel guilty for their menstruation. Taboo guilt also needs to be recognized for what it is—a mistaken, unfair alarm. Egoistic guilt is another possibility: scrupulosity arising from an antiseptic concern for my own purity. Egoistic guilt, too, needs to be recognized for what it is: an alarm set off by an internal dynamic that has essentially nothing to do with the real world of relationships.

But the guilt I feel for my failures when I was alcoholically drinking is different from these. It is truly *moral* guilt. It lives in a pained conscience and arises out of the wounds of real relationships. Whatever the complex causes of my alcoholism, I did wound others and myself, and my guilt for that cannot be explained away. W. H. Auden's satirical character can say that he likes committing sins, that God likes forgiving sins, and that the world is really admirably arranged—but cheap grace is no answer.[15]

A.A. has a response. It is a process described in seven of the twelve steps: a fearless moral inventory, confession to God and to another human being, readiness and prayer for God's transforming power, acknowledging and making amends to those we've harmed, and continuing self-inventory and confession. It is an ongoing, never-ending process of willingness to engage in confession, receive forgiveness, and make restitution.

Here it is important to recognize the difference between *remorse* and *contrition*.[16] Remorse is directed inward, while contrition is directed outward. In remorse I have a torturing sense of guilt, but I suffer not primarily because of the harm I caused others but because of my self-pity. In contrition, however, I am truly sorry for what I have done to others, and I am willing to confess and make whatever amends are possible. Remorse is an invitation to drink, but contrition an invitation to sobriety.

Alcoholics typically have much to be forgiven for, and when we experience forgiveness, we know grace. The day is brighter and our steps are lighter. Given and received, forgiveness cannot be earned and dispensed. It is vital to recovery, for living with a load of unforgiven guilt only makes one want to escape, and alcoholics know all too well how to do that.

But we alcoholics also need *to* forgive, for we have wounded others out of wounds that we ourselves have received.[17] Our ability to let go of resentments hangs on our capacity to forgive, and festering resentments are invitations to alcoholic relapse. They drain our energy and make us destructively dependent on others. There is truth in the saying "Harboring resentments is letting someone you don't like live inside your head rent-free."

Truly forgiving another seems to be an event of grace more than of willpower. Some research on forgiveness has focused on people who harbored no resentments against those who had victimized them. They were less aware of specific acts of forgiving their offenders than of just discovering that they *had* forgiven. In fact, they reported that their direct efforts to forgive frequently failed, but when they stopped trying and let go, sooner or later they made the astounding discovery that somehow they had already forgiven and the resentment had been replaced by serenity. Ernest Kurtz and Katherine Ketcham comment that this research confirms "that forgiveness is not a willed act . . . but a profound internal transformation involving two discoveries. The first discovery is that we *have been* forgiven, which somehow makes possible the second discovery that we already *have* forgiven."[18]

I found the process of forgiving my father's abusive behavior long and difficult. Because I had buried so much consciousness of this abuse for so many years, the Esalen experience in my mid-forties had been a soul-shaking event. I began work with a therapist soon thereafter. One day he gave me an assignment due at our next session: I was to write a letter to my father expressing everything that I wanted to say but had been unable to before his death a quarter century earlier. For most of that week I put off the assignment, and then the evening before the appointment I spent several emotional hours at the typewriter.

I recounted a day on our lake vacation when I was about four. I had fallen into deep water fully clothed, and I panicked and couldn't get to the surface for air. My father purposely delayed in pulling me out, then added physical punishment to my desperate fright. Writing to him now, I asked why. I wrote about the swift and startling physical blows on other occasions when his anger erupted. I recounted his ridicules of me to his friends and my humiliation. I described other incidents when I had so feared his anger and longed for signs of his love.

I turned in my assignment at the beginning of our session the next day. The therapist began to read my pages while I waited in silence. After a seemingly endless time he was only halfway finished but suddenly threw all of my pages on the floor in disgust and literally shouted, "He was a sadistic son-of-a-bitch, wasn't he?" Taken aback, I went to my father's defense. He had, I said, doubtless done the best he knew how—my grandfather had been demanding, punitive, and cruel, too. But the therapist would have none of it. Your father, he insisted, had no right to treat you this way. He had no right to do those things to you. You didn't deserve it. When are you going to get angry?

Slow in coming, my anger finally came. Garret Keizer wisely writes, "Before asking God for the grace to forgive, a person might think to give thanks for the grace to be angry. Anger in the face of injury is a mechanism for survival, no less than the clotting of our blood. Forgiveness is the scar, and it comes later."[19] The therapist's permission expressed a divine grace I badly needed.

However important for survival and dignity though it is, anger is never enough. Several years later another therapist asked me, "When will you be ready to forgive your father?" I had tried, and I knew that the time for forgiveness was long overdue, but my efforts were not working. I was still aware of a cloud of resentment.

Trying to forgive I had acted like a good, rational academic. As the French say, *Tout comprendre c'est tout pardonner*—"To understand all is to forgive all." I had been trying to understand what had made my father the way he was, then to excuse him. But it was only partly working. My anger was dulled, but the resentment lingered. By now I was drinking more regularly and more heavily. I found that alcohol also could blunt my anger, but it did not remove the resentment. In fact, it entrenched it even more.

Forgiveness came, but less consciously, less dramatically than I could have predicted. It came when I stopped trying to forgive. It came when I was able to admit my own failure in this process and let go. Then something began to happen. A sense of peacefulness about my father gradually replaced the resentment, anger, and self-pity. My willpower seemed to have little to do with it. It was grace. It was invited by my willingness, but it was not the result of my effort. Furthermore, I became aware that I, too, was forgiven, forgiven for my resentments and for nursing them so long. Not surprisingly, this process happened only *after* my sobriety began.

My efforts to give my father a peaceful burial gave me a vivid appreciation for a particular text in the Gospels. Jesus was asking for radical discipleship: "Come, follow me!" But one would-be follower entreated him, "Lord, first let me go and bury my father." Jesus responded (rather harshly, it seems), "Follow me, and let the dead bury their own dead" (Matt. 8:22; Luke 9:60). In retrospect I can see how I had been deadening myself in the attempt to bury my father. Only when I could trust enough to let that effort go did healing come.

The New Testament suggests intriguing connections between forgiveness and resurrection.[20] In John's Gospel, for example, in order to save his own skin on the evening before the crucifixion, three times Peter denied knowing Jesus. Then in a postresurrection account the risen Christ asked Peter the same question three times: "Simon, son of John, do you love me?" It was a gracious offer: three opportunities to undo the three denials.

It appears from this account that just as resurrection is a symbol of God's gift of new life, so also is the capacity to forgive. Forgiveness does not arise naturally anymore than the dead rise naturally from their graves. It did not come naturally to me. It did not fully materialize even when I wanted to forgive and worked hard at it. Only when I could recognize my failure and let it go did forgiveness come. It was like resurrection. Indeed, it *was* a resurrection.

There is another compelling symbolism in these stories. The risen Christ is portrayed as one now transcending the laws of the physical universe. Yet he is still pictured having the crucifixion holes in his body. And he does not hesitate to show them when that seems called for. My capacity to forgive—my resurrection, if you will—did not materialize as long as I denied my own hurt and hid my wounds. For years, in good masculinist (and Scandinavian) style I persuaded myself that this stuff didn't hurt that much. Furthermore, I should be over it, and it was bad form to talk about it. But, as long as I hid my wounds from the significant people in my life and from myself as well, I was a smiling face with the smell of death. Neither forgiveness nor resurrection itself demand that Christ hide the evidence of his woundedness. Honest candor and vulnerability about such things seems to be a necessary part of the process.

Finally, the resurrection-forgiveness connection strongly suggests that forgiveness is a reality belonging to the realm of faith. Forgiveness is not, for example, a result of understanding. It did not become a reality for me through my attempts to understand my father, his own background, his psyche. As Keizer says, "Comprehending everything can never lead to pardoning everything, for the simple reason that we will never comprehend everything. To forgive requires faith no less than to believe that 'the strife is o'er, the battle done. The victory of life is won.'"[21]

Festering resentments are poison for recovering alcoholics and lead the list as causes of relapse. Whenever alcoholics are liberated from resentments they are carrying, they know well the relief: "The strife is o'er, the battle done." And when, instead of relapse, sobriety is the gift for another day, the victory of life is real indeed.

Grace, Shame, and Acceptance

As we have seen, guilt usually involves painful feelings related to our *doing* (our actions, what we have done or left undone), while shame arises from a perceived attack on our very *being* (who we *are*). Guilt is a *violation*; its fault lies in my exercise of power or control. Shame is a *failure*, a falling short; its problem lies in my lack of power and control. Guilt results in feelings of wrongdoing, of wickedness, of being *not* good. Shame results in feelings of inadequacy, of worthlessness, of being *no* good.[22]

As important as guilt is in the typical alcoholic experience, shame appears even more significant. Frequently, I hear alcoholics say two things about their past: "I never felt very good about myself," and "I always felt different from other people." The summary word for that combination is shame. The core problem of active alcoholics is not that they are wicked but that they feel worthless.

Furthermore, our responses to guilt and shame are very different. I can do something about the pain of guilt by asking forgiveness and making amends. Similarly, when another has wronged me, my willingness to let go can gradually release resentments and accomplish forgiveness. But shame is different. There seems to be no action on my part to remove it. I can only cover it up, hide it, or find some escape. Because I see myself not good enough to be accepted and loved as I am, and since I am convinced that others would judge and withdraw if they really knew me, I must bury the deeper, chaotic parts of myself from view.[23]

Since it is an attack on one's very being, shame would seem devoid of any positive functions, but I believe there may be some. Our use of the words themselves gives a clue. To be "guiltless" is to be praiseworthy, innocent, blameless. On the other hand, to be called "shameless" is an epithet. "Shameless" means that one is brazen, impudent, without a sense of decency, insensitive to one's best self. At its best, shame is our acute discomfort when aware that we are not who we want to be. A passage in the Talmud expresses this idea: "Whoever has a sense of shame will not sin so quickly; but whoever shows no sense of shame in his visage, his father surely never stood on Mount Sinai."[24]

When we have the capacity to assess the meanings of our shame, we can sort out the appropriate from the inappropriate ones, do something about the former and let go of the latter. But sometimes our capacities to do that are incapacitated, and when that happens our shameful feelings get stuck deep within us with crippling results.

In my experience, there are two particularly powerful agents of shame: *gender* and *alcohol*. Both are particularly skilled at producing shame, and both incapacitate us in our efforts to cope with the shame we feel. When gender and alcohol join together as a team, they are dynamite.

In a patriarchal society (which ours still largely is), women and men must deal with different kinds of shame. Women's shame comes from having been pronounced inherently deficient by men. Men's shame stems from their never-completed sense of earned masculinity. Both forms of gender shame are insidious, painful, dehumanizing, and unfair. Without making comparisons, let me simply try to speak once more to my own experience.[25]

Since the masculine identity typically depends on comparison with others in matters of success, achievement, status, and power, a chronic sense of emotional insecurity and isolation often results. One's masculinity seems never complete, and failure at its requirements is shameful. Then, because the experience of shame *itself* is shameful, it goes underground and becomes disguised as other feelings—discouragement, embarrassment, shyness, self-consciousness, inferiority, and the like. Such things were not foreign to my experience.

When my alcoholism began to take hold, I had another powerful reason for shame: *moral* failure. Though at the time I had some knowledge about the disease factor, I remained viscerally convinced that alcoholism was basically an issue of willpower and character. While one could say that I felt guilty in discovering my powerlessness over alcohol, the more accurate description is shame. It was not primarily guilt over my actions, even the repeated actions of excessive drinking. More accusingly still, it was shame about my defective *being*. In my very being I was powerless and alcoholic.

Shame is particularly difficult to deal with. Guilt feels as though I am carrying a burden, weighed down and oppressed by it, but shame is a void. I feel off-balance, without center, and emotionally uncertain. I am usually sure of what I feel guilty about, but my shame is indeterminate, unspecifiable, and encompassing. Guilt is difficult enough for a person; confessing and making amends take courage. But shame seems almost impossible to deal with because it has no specific referent or form. It just seems to persist as a crippling and toxic feeling, a feeling that can engender paralysis or anger turned against the self or others.

I am not suggesting that shame is the special province of men or of addicted people (or of addicted men for that matter!). Most people know the experience. While much evidence suggests that the shame with which we alcoholics deal comes less from adult experiences than from childhood, many nonaddicted folk also have had to deal with painful childhood experiences of deficiency and abandonment. None of us had perfect families or parenting—nor have we who are parents done justice to our own children.[26]

Nevertheless, there is reason to understand addiction as a particularly shame-based phenomenon. Simply put, *compulsive behavior typically stems from trying to avoid shame*.[27] Often the cycle begins when we are young and experienced abuse or abandonment in some way. As children we felt the shame, decided that it hurt too much, and learned to avoid the feeling. As adults we still looked outside ourselves for something—alcohol, for example—that would make us feel better. But our compulsive behavior with that outside "something" only led to more shame. We alcoholics learned to medicate our shame. And it seemed to work, sometimes for years, until finally it didn't work any more.

If grace as forgiveness is God's fundamental answer to our guilt, grace as acceptance is the divine response to our shame. Paul Tillich writes an unforgettable description of the experience:

> It strikes us when our disgust for our own being, our indifference, our weakness, our hostility, and our lack of direction and composure have become intolerable to us. It strikes us when, year after year, the longed-for perfection of life does not appear, when the old compulsions reign within us as they have for decades, when despair destroys all joy and courage. Sometimes at that moment a wave of light breaks into our darkness, and it is as though a voice were saying: 'You are accepted. *You are accepted*, accepted by that which is greater than you, and the name of which you do not know. Do not ask for the name now; perhaps you will find it later. Do not try to do anything now; perhaps later you will do much. Do not seek for anything; do not perform anything; do not intend anything. *Simply accept the fact that you are accepted!*' If that happens to us, we experience grace.[28]

Addiction is a misdirected search for God, and my alcoholism was an obsessive and misplaced thirst for grace. I often thought my thirst was simply for alcohol, but it was not. It was for *what alcohol did for me*. It had the power to change my self-perception and my perception of the world. It made me feel bigger, more confident, more desirable—indeed, more lovable. It made the world a friendlier, less hostile place. The high I got from alcohol was chemically induced, but it was a spiritual high.

Yet after a while it took more and more alcohol to produce that spiritual state. Then it came rarely if at all, and I was using alcohol just to get through the day. Finally I had to admit that I was powerless to bring about that for which I most deeply thirsted. It was then that justification by grace, grace as a deep sense of acceptance, began to become more real than it had ever been.

Some alcoholics seem to experience divine grace directly, intuitively, mystically. Bill Wilson's transforming "white light" event in Towns Hospital apparently was such. But most alcoholics dealing with shame seem to need something more concrete and enfleshed. Many of us have found a crucial incarnation of grace in recovery groups.

The experience often begins in the newcomer's first meeting. The person may have come willingly or under duress, neatly dressed and appearing self-confident or dirty, discouraged, and reeking of alcohol. The welcome is always the same: *you are accepted*. You are the most important person in this room not only because you are particularly needy but also because you put everyone else back in touch with their own beginnings on the sobriety journey. You are accepted because there is only one requirement for membership in this group, and it has nothing to do with your achievements or your character. It is simply the desire to stop drinking. You are not even asked to prove that desire. The point is simply that you are accepted. It is gracious, it is authentic, and it is powerful.

The therapeutic power in A.A. seems to come from the combination of the program's steps *and* the experience of the fellowship itself. It is neither one nor the other by itself, but the combination of the program and the remarkably accepting group experience. Ernest Kurtz underscores A.A.'s impressive success as "a therapy for shame": "Other therapies fail, especially over time, because unfaced shame proves much more dangerous to the alcoholic, especially in recovery, than does unresolved guilt."[29]

Perfectionism and Sanctification

Perfectionism, as I noted in chapter 4, if not universal among alcoholics, is an exceedingly common malady. And it has much to do with shame. Simply put, it is a common form of works righteousness: the attempt to justify (or save) oneself by means of achievement. The sought-for achievement may be moral goodness. It may be worldly success with its constant anxiety about performance. It may be the need to be the most needed. Whatever the form, the dynamic is the same. It is still self-centered and prone to be alternately self-inflating and self-deflating.

My perfectionism as an alcoholic was not a pretty picture. It amounted to selling myself to others for their approval, but because my perception of their acceptance was so unreliable and vacillating, wild swings of mood and self-perception emerged. With some ease I could move from grandiosity to self-degradation and back again: "I am the greatest" and "I am a worm." At other times it was an ingenious combination: "I may be a worm, but I am the *greatest* worm."[30]

With alcoholic inventiveness, at still other times it was like listening to a stereo with the two loudspeakers each playing an utterly different song. One side sang to me about what a great person I was, so gifted, dedicated, and esteemed. But the melody from the other speaker loudly proclaimed that people could see right through me, and I was a failure and a fraud. When my self-worth was dependent on constant striving to meet unattainable ideals, I was always at the mercy of inflated anxiety and deflated self-worth. The net result was the reinforcement of my shame—and the desire to medicate it.

Even in recovery perfectionism can be stubborn, as is apparent in Bill Wilson's candid words:

> My basic flaw had always been dependence on people or circumstances to supply me with prestige, security, and confidence. Failing to get these things according to my perfectionistic dreams and specifications, I fought for them. And when defeat came, so did my depression.[31]

Perfectionism is exhausting. As more than one alcoholic friend has said in exasperation, "I did it all. I busted my butt for them and what did I get? They kept moving the damn goal posts!" Here are echoes of Elijah. The prophet was standing at the mouth of the cave. God appeared to him and asked what he was doing there (though God clearly knew). Elijah had done all the right things: "I have been very zealous for the Lord, the God of hosts. . . ." But now he was feeling deserted, rewarded only by more demands and more threats, and very sorry for himself: "I alone am left, and they are seeking my life, to take it away" (1 Kgs. 19:10). It is not a story of failure, but one of success. Yet the prophet has no sense of vindication or even achievement. Here, as Peter Gomes observes, is the irony of it all: "Elijah was tired, very tired of success and tired of the fear of failure. He was exhausted by all of his days."[32]

In perfectionism the oppressive superego exhausts us with its demands. The loss or deficiency of love from significant figures in early life is usually at its roots, and the fear that love once again will be lost is its powerful dynamic. What I yearned for was freedom from the constant need to appear competent and compassionate. One addiction therapist notes, "When perfectionism is used to hide shame and guilt, the addict/alcoholic feels like a 'fake.'"[33] Indeed, there were years in my active alcoholism when I often felt transparent in my incompetence. Compared to my peers, my professional capacities were superficial, and I was letting everyone down.

The irony was that during those same years I was receiving abundant affirmations: various awards, an honorary doctorate, full classes, published books, and a crowded off-campus lecture schedule. At the same time I alternated between grandiosity and despair—on top of the world, then knowing myself a fake.

I knew I was searching for grace, thirsting for it. Because of my alcohol abuse I was feeling increasing shame and yearning for God's embrace—"just as I am, without one plea" as the gospel hymn puts it. But my alcoholic mind could add a creative twist, as it did many evenings. As I worked at the desk I often sipped alcohol. Then would come a point mid-evening when I realized that I had had so much to drink that I could no longer work effectively. *Voilà*! My drinking had suddenly become a courageous act. It had counteracted my excessive concern for sanctification; it had undermined my works righteousness; and it had thrown me into the arms of divine grace! In such conclusions the alcoholic mind rejoices.

Literally, *sanctification* means "the process of becoming a saint." More generally it refers to that growth in holiness or wholeness of life made possible by divine grace.[34] Traditional Catholic theology spoke of sanctifying grace as a supernatural quality added to the soul, uniting it to Christ, infusing virtues into it, and making the soul acceptable to God. Similarly, evangelical and Pentecostal Christians often speak of sanctifying grace as something given by the Holy Spirit at the moment of conversion or later at a "second blessing," and producing growth toward the purity and sinlessness that God desires of us. Both of these views suggest that sanctifying grace is "something"—even a substance—which is given to make one more acceptable to God.

Curiously, this is close to the way I actually viewed alcohol when practicing my addiction. I depended on something, a substance (the term is common addiction parlance) I could take into myself to make me more acceptable, and I became convinced I needed that kind of "grace" for my well-being.

Other Christians are less optimistic about the achievement of perfection in this life. While growth in holiness or wholeness can be real, the power of sin remains. Among mainstream Protestants, those shaped by Martin Luther are particularly leery of sanctifying grace, leaning much more strongly toward justification: *simil justus et peccator* (though justified by grace we are still sinners). Methodists and others in John Wesley's footsteps lean more hopefully on sanctification. Even though we will not attain perfection in our actual conduct, Christlikeness in attitudes and motives is both a gift of the Spirit and a goal we should seek. The Calvinist tradition in which I was reared tried to steer something of a middle course.

Whatever the specific religious traditions have said, American culture seems permeated by a concern for secular sanctification. From the plethora of volumes on the bookstores' "Self Help" shelves, to the self-realization promised by popular psychology, to the slick magazines' ubiquitous counsels for improving one's physique, beauty, love life, and financial affairs, we Americans—for a cluster of reasons in our history—are inclined to be a perfectionist people endlessly in search of sanctification.

However, sanctification can be a difficult notion for recovering people as was evident early in A.A.'s history. Though A.A. was born in the Oxford Group, a strongly sanctificationist "house church" movement, Bill Wilson, Dr. Bob Smith, and other early leaders soon discovered that the high Oxford expectations were far too much for recovering alcoholics. Wilson interpreted the break in this way:

> When first contacted, most alcoholics just wanted to find sobriety, nothing else. They clung to their other defects, letting go only little by little. They simply did not want to get "too good too soon." The Oxford Group's absolute concepts . . . were frequently too much for the drunks.[35]

It all sounded too much like the perfectionism with which so many alcoholics struggle. Thus, the Big Book wisely insists that we are interested in progress, not perfection.

To add to the confusion, Western spirituality has been plagued by misinterpretations of Jesus' Sermon on the Mount statement "Be perfect, therefore, as your heavenly Father is perfect" (Matt. 5:48). When those words are placed in the larger context of that "sermon," clearly the injunction is not a command for moral perfection, as if that were even possible. Nor does it counsel some state of invulnerability in which we are safe from not sinning. Jesus was fully conscious of the demonic ways in which the devout can make the religious life a dangerous business through their passionate moral seriousness. Furthermore, his reference to being like God sounds ominously like the serpent's words to Adam and Eve—"You will be like God . . . ," words that were bad news with sad consequences. No, in the Sermon on the Mount, Jesus' teaching is best understood as "Be compassionate and just as God is compassionate and just." Marcus Borg puts it this way: "As one who knew God, Jesus knew God as the compassionate one, not as the God of requirements and boundaries. The life to which he invited his hearers was the life in the Spirit that he himself had experienced. The narrow way, the road less traveled, is life centered in the Spirit of God."[36]

In the Hebrew scriptures Job is another figure instructive about perfection. His was the familiar story of tragedy following calamity following disaster. Job's friends came to comfort him, unaware of his true circumstances and taking for granted that (because trouble naturally follows sin, doesn't it?) Job was getting what he deserved. In fact, however, Job was "blameless and upright, one who feared God and turned away from evil," innocent of what his friends had assumed (Job 1:1).

Nevertheless, Job's relevance for us is not about *his* perfection (which did not exist anyway in spite of his admirable character), but about his sturdy and persistent faith in *God's* perfection, which he knew he would see in another day. "Job is a study in faithfulness, in steadfastness, in the hope of glory in the face of despair; but he is also a study, a portrait, of the ambiguity of perfection and the reality of life lived in the midst of imperfection."[37]

The problems with perfectionism are multiple. For one thing, it simply is in the nature of things that perfection cannot be directly achieved. Moreover, the attempt turns us in on ourselves and away from the neighbor. Father Ed Dowling, confidant of Bill Wilson, spoke to his fellow priests who seemed afraid to dirty their hands with alcoholics: "The trouble with you priests is, you all have 'digno-sclerosis,' hardening of the dignity. If you weren't afraid to make a mistake, you'd be out curing people of these things."[38]

Accepting our limitations is a more promising route. If we are to come to terms with our shame, we must deal with the reality that we are essentially limited people. This should be obvious to alcoholics. As one with this disease, I cannot drink *any* alcohol safely. That is limitation. I have already described how enormously difficult it was for me to accept my powerlessness over alcohol. But the point here is that alcohol per se, was not the fundamental issue. To be sure, it was hard to give it up, for I had an obsession with drinking. But the greatest difficulty of all was accepting my essential limitation. It was shameful. Kurtz has it right: "These are narrowing, choking, tightening experiences. We feel these sensations in our innards, and we struggle against their implications with all our might."[39] In recovery I gradually grasped the paradoxical message that I should have long known from my study of theology: there is wholeness in accepting one's limitation.

We are human. We are neither gods nor animals, though (as the writer of Psalm 8 wisely observed) we participate in both the divine and the animal and our true humanity lies in gratefully accepting that created position. But we are tempted to deceive ourselves into thinking we are one *or* the other. Alcoholics may have particular temptations in this regard, as Bill Wilson regularly reminded us: "the alcoholic is an all-or-nothing person."[40]

So, as an active alcoholic I often drank to be a god—reaching for absolute control over my feelings and over my environment. Just as often I drank to escape my humanity into animality, like Walt Whitman envying the cows who just enjoy their grazing without endlessly lamenting their sin or fretting about their mortality. Now I am grateful for the ironic laughter that regularly permeates the recovery group rooms, laughter that punctures again and again the absurdity of thinking I can lose myself in the perfection of the divine or in the sure instincts of the animal. I am not either/or, I am both/and.

I have learned that recovery does not require renouncing all control, but rather giving up the pretension of controlling anything (including my feelings) *absolutely*. Recovery does not demand that I give up all dependence, but rather that I abandon dependence on *alcohol*. I am learning how to live with more humility about my true station in life—neither angel nor animal—and I am discovering freshly how to live with creativity and gratitude for that station.

In learning my limitations, I have discovered things about my willpower. My early shame about being an alcoholic stemmed from a combination of things. Part of it, I am sure, came from the sense that my worth was being adversely judged in this still-moralistic society. But my shame also came from the limitations I was experiencing in my willpower—my inability to restrict my drinking. It felt shameful that I was far less than I should be and truly wanted to be. I asked myself time after time, "Why do I drink when I don't want to and when I have actually decided not to?"

Later the answer came. It was disarmingly simple. "You didn't want to drink, but you did, and you did simply because you are an alcoholic. That's what alcoholics do. They drink when they don't want to." It was strangely gracious to learn that.

Grace has a way of changing one's perceptions about things. It has changed my perceptions about childhood experience, about anger, about emptiness, about shame itself. Perhaps the most striking change in perspective has been about drinking itself. Early in my sobriety a recovering friend told me, "I don't think of it as *giving up* alcohol. I think of it as *getting rid of* alcohol." That became a surprisingly useful change to my perception, too.

Even more has been a movement from law to gospel. Most of the time I now know that I am not living under prohibition or law, as one who *cannot* drink. I am living with freedom and joy, for today "I *can* not-drink." That shift from prohibition to permission, from the negative to the positive, from law to gospel involves far more than a clever wordplay. It is a fundamental shift of perception that has made a world of difference.

"Do You Want to Be Made Well?"

At some point early in the first century, a man disabled for thirty-eight years lay beside a crowded Jerusalem pool known for its healing waters. Around him were a host of others with severe disabilities—the blind, the lame, the paralyzed. Passing by, Jesus for some reason noticed this particular man. Apparently aware that the man had been lying there a long time, Jesus asked, "Do you want to be made well?" The question must have struck the disabled one as presumptuous, perhaps insulting. Hadn't he been trying for a long, long time, even when repeatedly his efforts failed and he got crowded away from the water? "Sir, I have no one to put me into the pool when the water is stirred up; and while I am making my way, someone else steps down ahead of me" (John 5:2–18).

Alcoholics know something of that man's experience. We, too, have known aloneness, immobilization, and self-pity. We, too, have had the desperate desire to be well, only to be followed by repeated failures. Then grace came on the scene with some hard, demanding questions. How thirsty are you for the healing waters? Do you really want to be made well? Jesus said, "Stand up, take your mat and walk." It was a strange, even preposterous demand to be made of one so long disabled. But, according to this story, it was a healing word.

Most alcoholics seem to know that grace is very paradoxical stuff. We clearly recognize that recovery—not just abstinence from alcohol but also emotional sobriety—is truly the gift of a power beyond ourselves, *and also* that it means picking up our mats and walking. Grace *and* work.

Recovery takes effort, discipline, and work. It means making sobriety a priority. It means continuous self-examination and a commitment to be as honest as humanly possible. It takes daily meditation and reading, going to countless meetings, reaching out to alcoholics who are still suffering. Speaking of the work of salvation, in words that might well have been about alcoholic recovery, Jonathan Edwards said this:

> [The work of salvation must be] not only . . . the business of Sabbath days, or certain extraordinary times, or the business of a month, or a year, or of seven years . . . but the business of [one's] life . . . which [one] perseveres in through all changes, and under all trials, as long as [one] lives.[41]

Grace and work. Though the work of recovery is demanding, I have found the work part of the paradox easier to understand than the grace part. I was one of those reared on a sturdy belief in the salvific efficacy of honest work, that Puritan legacy that Edwards represented so well. So, upon entering recovery, I thought serenity would come if I worked hard enough at it.

Not only did the paradox of grace and work elude me, but also this basic contradiction: if my search for serenity was so important, I would have to stay *un*-serene so that I could continue to search for it. It was the same contradiction involved in trying so hard to stay sober. Therapist Barbara Cole recognizes the self-defeating contradiction in trying to will sobriety directly: "As long as you try to stay sober you've got to stay drunk so that you can continue to try to stay sober."[42]

Work and grace, grace and work—it was a paradox very familiar to the apostle Paul: "Therefore, my beloved, . . . work out your own salvation with fear and trembling; for it is God who is at work in you, enabling you both to will and to work for [God's own] good pleasure." (Phil. 2:12–13). The point is, however, that work *follows* grace. It neither precedes grace nor is a condition for receiving it. The apostle urged the early Christians to work at their own healing ("healing" and "salvation" are from the same root word) knowing that God was already graciously at work within them. The long-disabled man at the Jerusalem pool heard Jesus' words urging effort only after he had experienced the healing presence coming graciously and unexpectedly into his life.

My parents, in their different ways, embodied the paradox of grace and work for me. My mother was forever busy in doing good for people. True, at times she seemed unduly concerned about approval, but most often she was just spontaneously loving. Though sometimes her concern for my moral goodness felt suffocating, most of the time she loved me just about as unconditionally as one person can love another.

My father, as I have said, was usually suspicious of grace and had a no-nonsense approach to earning salvation, at least in this life. For years I struggled with this attitude—both in him and in myself. Only belatedly have I recognized his unexpected and gracious gift. Thomas Moore calls it "a deep father figure that settles into the soul to provide a sense of authority, the feeling that you are the author of your own life, that you are the head of the household in your own affairs."[43]

In death both of my parents grace me in my recovery. From my mother it is the glimpses of unconditional love, not always consistent, but remarkably there. From my father, it is the strange gift of self-possession that comes not apart from struggle but in it and through it.

"You are the author of your own life." Interpreted one-dimensionally the statement suggests a self-defeating self-sufficiency. Understood paradoxically, however, it is healing for an alcoholic. The Fourth Gospel's portrait of Jesus is instructive in this regard.[44] Here Jesus displays a strong sense of centeredness. This Gospel is full of "I am" statements. He can say, "I am the way," "I am the vine," "I am the good shepherd" so confidently because he knows himself utterly known and utterly loved by God. If that happens to my life, then I *am*. Because I mean everything to God, my life has meaning and center. So, to an extent surpassing the other three Gospels, in the Fourth Gospel Jesus radiates self-confidence. His words keep emphasizing his own authority and responsibility, and the Gospel ends with Jesus emphatically repudiating the role of an impotent victim.[45]

One of the delights of recovery meetings is feeling the energy so palpably present. Impotent victims are largely bygone memories. Soulful lives are present now, people who are living from their depths. They know themselves weak and broken, poor and humble. They speak openly of their troubled pasts. They have learned that God comes through the wound. Facing their own darkness and giving up their pretenses to innocence, they are finding their lives much more passionate and robust than they had ever known before.[46]

As recovering people we know that we are in the process of being healed *and also* that we continue in our brokenness. We are not recover*ed* alcoholics, we are recover*ing*. We continue to live with the disease, but our sobriety is, by the grace of God, a reality for us today.

There is a sense, somewhat parallel, in which I find this true of Jesus also. Typical understandings of his sinlessness do not serve us very well. Rather than understanding his "perfection" as a quality of life that he had fully achieved and possessed, we might see it as the perfection of his *faith*. This was radical: his devotion to God's cause, his honest recognition of his own needs as a human being, and his willingness to trust utterly in God for meeting those needs and the needs of the world.[47]

So we live with imperfection, and our thirst continues. But that, too, is a strange gift. With perfection we would have no spiritual life, for our spirituality is grounded in our thirst for completion. When such thirst is not present, there is no spirituality. So precisely in and through our imperfection, God gives us a continuing spiritual life. The healing waters comfort aching bodies. They also soothe parched throats, but do not remove our thirst completely.

"Progress, not perfection" is both realistic and theologically sound. So it is in an old monastic story. A young seeker approached an elderly monk asking, "What do you do in the monastery?" The veteran replied simply, "Oh, we fall down and we get up again. And we fall down and we get up again. And we fall down and we get up again."

One word should be added to that monk's story: gratitude. It is the reason that we can get up again after falling down. Gratitude is a characteristic feature of the healing stories told about Jesus, though not because he demanded it. It comes naturally, spontaneously to most people who have experienced healing. It is surely so with alcoholics, and with one difference: for us it is also a necessary attitude if recovery is to continue.[48]

An A.A. slogan that has stood the test of time is "An attitude of gratitude." I find it intriguing that Webster's first definition of "attitude" does not deal with feelings or dispositions or opinions, but rather with a position or posture of the body. Significantly, the dictionary example of this is "to kneel in an attitude of prayer." This definition suggests that gratitude as an attitude is not only something that arises spontaneously in response to a gift but also something that we can intentionally nurture.

When I assume certain body attitudes (sitting, standing, running, etc.) other things will become possible (rest, alertness, change of location, etc.) that depend on those postures. Likewise, when I assume a posture of gratitude—deliberately reminding myself to see the world through grateful eyes—other things that might not otherwise happen become possible. Resentments seem to dissolve. Self-pity becomes impossible. In fact, gratitude seems to counteract those states of mind and soul most conducive to alcoholic relapse.

I do not intend to compare recovering alcoholics—or anyone else— with Holocaust survivors. However, I find Elie Wiesel's Nobel Prize acceptance words movingly appropriate for anyone who has known rescue or healing: "No one is as capable of gratitude as one who has emerged from the kingdom of night. We know that every moment is a moment of grace, every hour an offering; not to share them would mean to betray them."[49]

Chapter Eight

God and the Self

Is God Necessary?

The ballots have been counted and the outcome is clear: without a significant spiritual transformation most people are unlikely to recover in any lasting way from chemical addiction. But that does not answer the question, Is *God* necessary for recovery? Some say no. Groups such as Secular Organizations for Sobriety and the Rational Recovery Society Network rely on cognitive-behaviorist and motivational psychology, and while agreeing that significant changes in the addicted person must happen, their answer to the theological question is direct and simple: belief in God is neither necessary nor helpful for recovery.[1]

In a negative sense, however, even the skeptics seem to agree with the premise of Alcoholics Anonymous: recovery is dependent on the addicted person's willingness to let go of *faith in destructive deities*. Such deities, of course, include the self. A fundamental teaching of the Big Book of Alcoholics Anonymous declares, "First of all, we had to quit playing God. It didn't work."[2] And of course the alcoholic has to abandon faith in alcohol itself, for that deity has been proving itself lethal.

Early in recovery I began to realize how much I had been playing God, attempting to control every aspect of my own life. Only when I could abandon that illusion could I find the serenity that alcohol had promised but failed to deliver. This experience, confirmed by many other recovering people, persuades me that, at least in a rudimentary sense, a God-belief is necessary. *Something* must displace the false gods—the notions that I am in absolute control of my life and that alcohol is worthy of trust for its saving powers. These destructive deities might be de-

148

throned by a higher power other than the God of traditional faith. The higher power might be the community of one's sober peers or a set of principles for living or both. But some constructive object of faith must displace the destructive ones.

Even among the many recovering people who do profess belief in God, the contours of those convictions vary enormously. For good historical reasons, A.A. insists on latitude for everyone in this regard. Even though some members speak of the Twelve Steps as divinely revealed in an inerrant and miraculous manner, history discloses contentious debates early in the movement, especially when it came to God. Just before the first edition of the Big Book was released in 1939, the wording about God in the Twelve Steps was still under debate and quite at the last minute the phrase "as we understood Him" was inserted into the Third and the Eleventh Steps to conciliate those who could not profess traditional forms of faith.[3]

If in the early days of this movement there was no agreement on the fundamental matter of God's nature, neither is there any consensus today. Indeed, "God has always been A.A.'s raw nerve."[4] Having said this, it is also true that there seems to be a bottom-line pragmatism about the nature of the Higher Power in A.A.: it is *whatever keeps me sober.* It is a belief that surpasses the pragmatism of Bill Wilson's major theological inspiration, William James. In fact, it is the ultimate pragmatism about God: whatever works.[5]

However, my intent is not to argue in some general way for God's essential role in recovery, which could not be proven in any event. By now it is evident that I believe God to be utterly central to my own recovery. So, here I simply want to speak of several ways in which my faith experience and my recovery experience have interacted, changing some of my perspectives and deepening others.

Webster defines "perspective" as one's specific point of view in understanding things or events, especially a viewpoint that shows their true relations to one another. It is a good reminder. When we speak of God we are speaking of certain ways of relating—the relations of God to us and ourselves to God. We are speaking of faith—again a relationship, that of trusting in a deity. We best speak of our perspectives tentatively and confessionally, believing (with our Puritan ancestor John Robinson) that God has still more light and truth that will break forth, more light and truth than we yet know. I know all too well that I am capable of being one of the blind men who feels only part of the elephant yet claims to understand the shape of the whole animal. With those cautions in mind, I want to explore some shifts in perspectives on God and the self that have come in recovery.

Paradox and Mystery

Recovery has brought me a more vivid experience of *divine sovereignty*. In some ways, the emphasis was hardly new. It was Calvin's constant theme, and that was my heritage. In that same Reformed lineage, two of my most influential theological mentors, H. Richard Niebuhr and James M. Gustafson, articulated profoundly God-centered approaches. For Niebuhr it was "radical monotheism," and for Gustafson "a theocentric perspective."[6] Process and feminist theologians have also been my teachers. They have rejected images of divine sovereignty that picture God as an omnipotent and masculinized monarch ruling the world with absolute and controlling power. Whatever sovereignty means, they insist, surely it is a power shaped by love, thus a power profoundly respecting all creatures and limited by their freedom.

For many years I had been influenced by such perspectives on God, but in recovery they have become more real. For one thing, divine sovereignty in my experience means the centrality of the thirst for God in my life, something of which I am more aware than ever before. Admirers sometimes described the Jewish philosopher Spinoza as "a God intoxicated man." While that is the only kind of intoxication I now want, I cannot claim anything like Spinoza's. But I can testify that recovery has brought forcefully an unanticipated paradox: while my thirst for God has been slaked and satisfied in ways I never dreamt, I have also experienced a more acute thirst than ever.

It is a thirst that now more frequently reduces me to silence before the sovereign One. It is a more vivid awareness that God is infinitely more than words and concepts can describe, overflowing any and all analogies. Speaking of the desert Arab's *apophatic* spirituality, T. E. Lawrence ("Lawrence of Arabia") wrote, "He found luxury in abnegation, renunciation, self restraint. He made nakedness of the mind as sensuous as nakedness of the body."[7] I now experience a bit more of a sensuous "nakedness of the mind" before God. I now know (sometimes at least) that "God is a desert to be entered and loved, never an object to be grasped or understood."[8]

This has not been the most natural spiritual emphasis for me. I have long believed that God is both transcendent and immanent, and that God is both eternal mystery and incarnate Word. But over the years I had been drawn more toward the latter poles—the immanent and incarnational. It was the *embodied* God that grasped me far more than the eternally mysterious One. It was God decisively manifest in Jesus of Nazareth, God enfleshed in all human life, the sacred in the midst of the secular, the divine known in the depths of the soul, the Holy One revealed in and through creation—to know and experience God in these ways had been my primary thirst. So I listened for speech more than for silence. I looked to see God described in words, pictured in metaphors, enfleshed in life.

I am sure part of this came from working professionally in the theological field where concepts, images, and metaphors for the divine flow freely. But now I recognize an additional reason for my leaning. My strong tilt toward one side of the paradox perhaps also had something to do with my alcoholism. Recovery brings a keen awareness of one's control problems, and I suspect that part of my shying from divine transcendence and radical monotheism was my desire to control all significant things in my life, even God. To the extent that God is embodied, the divine seems more manageable.

But the sovereign One is utterly beyond my capacity to contain in any way—ineffable, impossible to describe with any adequacy. Augustine is right: "If you have understood, then this is not God. If you were able to understand, then you understood something else instead of God."[9] When one wants to control, silence in God's presence is frightening. Words can be used to structure perspectives, and then to manipulate. The absence of words, however, means loss of control, and silence becomes surrender.[10]

In many ways, addiction is a disease of control, and now recovery has challenged my assumption that controlling everything in my life was always a good idea. In fact, recovery poses the question to alcoholics whether we in fact *can* control anyone. If this is true in relation to other human beings, how much truer in relation to the Infinite who is "a desert to be entered and loved, never an object to be grasped or understood."

Surely, I still believe (and strongly so) in the other side of the paradox—the speaking God, the embodied God. Indeed, I could not write these pages without that conviction. It is always both/and, not either/or. But recovery's insistence on letting go has invited me into more of the nameless, awesome mystery and into more of the pregnant, life-giving silence than I have ever known.

Faith and Priorities

Commitment is another changing perspective. Prior to entering recovery I thought I knew at least something about it. I had heard Jesus' words and images from the Gospels. I had learned that the realm of God was like a banquet, and the invitation must not be refused (Luke 14:15–24). I knew that God's cause called for commitment like that of that poor widow who gave her two coins, all that she had (Luke 21:1–4). I was well aware of the teaching that no one could become a disciple without willingness to give up everything else (Luke 14:33).

While I never had illusions of total commitment, I had tried to invest myself seriously in those things to which I believed God called me. Family, students, seminary, church—hadn't I given myself energetically to them all? And the larger human family? Hadn't I labored for civil rights, protested war, worked hard for sexual justice? I thought I knew something about commitment. Apparently I did—at least when it came to alcohol. My mid-life commitment to that latter cause was impressive.

Recovery has a way of changing one's perspectives. After my month of in-patient treatment came six months of outpatient "aftercare" with a focus on relapse prevention. The leader hammered home one paramount lesson week after week: recovery must come *before* everything else in your life. In A.A. slogan language it was "First things first."

It sounded like a skewed priority. How could I now give chief energies to recovery when I owed so much makeup time to my marriage? For too long Wilys Claire had taken a back seat to alcohol, and now was she to take a back seat to recovery? Gradually, the obvious broke through to both of us: if recovery were not the most important thing in my life now, nothing else, our marriage included, would matter. Without that primary commitment to sobriety, relapse was virtually guaranteed. What initially felt selfish and cold-hearted became wisdom to both of us.

Prior to that realization, this New Testament story had always struck me as rather unfeeling:

> A crowd was sitting around him; and they said to him, "Your mother and your brothers and sisters are outside, asking for you." And he replied, "Who are my mother and my brothers?" And looking at those who sat around him, he said, "Here are my mother and my brothers! Whoever does the will of God is my brother and sister and mother." (Mark 3:32–35)

Now I think I understand.

A radically monotheistic faith makes relative everyone and everything except God. Only God is worthy of absolute trust and loyalty. H. Richard Niebuhr observed that we inevitably live by our faiths. While we can deny the existence of God, it seems impossible to live with radical skepticism about the actuality of things around us, the food we eat and air we breathe. "To deny the reality of a supernatural being called God is one thing; to live without confidence in some center of value and without loyalty to a cause is another."[11]

The real problem, then, is not lack of faith. It is the wrong kind of faith, faith wrongly directed, trust in that which is less than God. There are, Niebuhr argued, two main forms of bad faith: *polytheism* (the belief in many gods) and *henotheism* (the belief in one god, but a deity that is less than ultimate, "a tribal god").

My alcoholic drinking often immersed me in polytheistic faith, though I was not aware of it. It was, in effect, faith in many gods: first this loyalty, then another claimed my primary allegiance. The obsession with alcohol seemed to scatter my focus regarding everything else. When my drinking progressively dimmed the vision of the ultimate God, it replaced it with numerous other possibilities in which I thought I could trust.

Whatever a person trusts most deeply seems to give shape to that person's identity in significant ways. For example, if my basic allegiance and trust are directed to my career, that role will dominate my self-understanding and give primary shape to the way I am in the world. If the objects of my faith are numerous and shifting, I will have too many gods to know the one true God and, inevitably, too many selves to know truly my one self. I am a husband, teacher, father, citizen, church member —butcher, baker, candlestick maker—but who, really, am I? My problem is "identity diffusion."[12]

During my active alcoholism I knew that problem well. Demands coming from various sources just seemed too much. My several selves were in constant competition, and my life seemed to have little coherence. Though I could not recognize or admit it at the time, practically speaking, I had several gods. Too many gods result in too many selves. Like the proverbial cowboy, I regularly mounted my horse and rode off in all directions. One doesn't need to be alcoholic to be caught up in this confusion, but it helps enormously.

But then came retreat into an alcoholic henotheism. I discovered escape from the many gods through a more radical allegiance to one. My newfound center of value, alcohol, was not a universal deity but rather a tribal god—deity of only the loyal band of drunks. This god was attractive at first and promised the world, but it then failed the tests of divinity miserably.

It is said that Alexander the Great went to the philosopher Diogenes, whom he greatly admired, with an offer to grant him any one favor he might name. The king found the philosopher sunbathing. Standing in front of him, the world's conqueror said, "Ask for whatever you desire and I will grant it." From out of the shadow cast by the king, Diogenes responded immediately with his single request: "Get out of the way of the sun." There is singleness of mind and heart! Perhaps it was even purity of heart, which, in Kierkegaard's words, is "to will one thing."

It is difficult to describe how living a truly monotheistic faith looks, but the great people of faith whom we admire, however different from each other, all seem characterized by a remarkable singleness of vision and integration of life. Now I was discovering that my recovery had to take precedence over everything else in my life. It was an immersion into singleness of vision and clarity about priorities unlike anything I had known.

But wasn't this just another tribal god? After all, the recovery cause is not a universal one—it pertains only to the addicted, and we are a limited tribe. Furthermore, anything good that merits our relative allegiance can be fashioned into an idol demanding total commitment. Perhaps as a warning to potential "A.A. junkies," for whom this movement would become a new absolute, Bill Wilson pointedly declared, "We took the position that A.A. was not the final word on treatment; that it might be only the first word. For us, it became perfectly safe to tell people they could experiment with our therapy in any way they liked."[13]

I have no doubt whatever that in the grand scheme of things my sobriety is small stuff, indeed. Nevertheless, the priority I give to recovery reflects the very practical recognition that I would be useless to any other commitment—my family, my community, my church, the wider world—without it. It is foundational for literally everything else. It is not the realm of God, but for this alcoholic it is surely an essential means to that end, making possible whatever commitment I can give to that blessed vision. In some strange way this necessary instrumental commitment helps me understand better Jesus' teaching: God knows we need all sorts of things, but if we seek first God's realm those other things will be given to us as well (Matt. 6:32–33).

So, it is all curiously paradoxical. My strong conviction about the urgency and foundational importance of recovery has somehow pressed me toward a more radical trust in God. That renewed faith in God, in turn, has validated the importance of my recovery commitment. And at the same time, this monotheistic faith has relativized everything else, including my sobriety and the recovery program of which I am part. "A radically monotheistic faith says [to all] claimants to 'the truth, the whole truth and nothing but the truth,' . . . 'I do not believe you. God is great!'"[14]

Interpreting God's Activity

In addition to relativizing everything that is not-God, a theocentric faith invites and even requires me to see God's presence in all events. Everything depends on interpretation. How we respond to any occurrence depends directly on our interpretation of its meaning for us. Is God in the midst of it, or not?

Again I turn to H. Richard Niebuhr, whose work persuaded me that while the Christian life has often been interpreted as either an ethics of goal-seeking or as an ethics of obedience, a more adequate perspective is that of *responsibility*. It is the call to respond fittingly and appropriately to the events of life by interpreting God's presence and activity in the very midst of them. In Niebuhr's words, "God is acting in all actions upon you. So respond to all actions upon you as to respond to [God's] action."[15]

It is crucial to understand that the divine presence and action in all events does not mean that God *causes* everything. Were that true, we would have no genuine freedom and our actions would be devoid of any moral or personal significance. Were that true, God would be the author of evil as well as good, and divine love and justice would be meaningless. Divine causation implies a God who acts with mechanistic force and coercive power, not one whose actions are truly personal. Indeed, "omnipotence" (incidentally, a nonbiblical word) is a term that I think should be laid to rest.

"God is great, and God is good"—so goes the familiar table grace. Since divine greatness is expressed through divine goodness, love works through intention and influence, not coercion and manipulation. Since God respects creation's freedom, events such as alcoholic addiction have their own finite explanations and causes. And since God cares infinitely about creation's well-being, the Holy One's presence, yearning for our fulfillment, is in the midst of everything that happens—including addiction.

I emphasize this matter of interpreting divine action because so many alcoholics report having to reject a harsh, vindictive God.[16] Some of this belief doubtless stems from moralistic judgments about their alcoholism they have felt from the church. But much of it surely comes from a common but destructive determinism about God and the world. The founders of Alcoholics Anonymous realized early on that many drunks would never get sober if they held on to a perception of God that was both judgmental and deterministic. That was part of the reason lying behind the insertion of "God *as we understood Him*" in Steps 3 and 11.

So how might we see God's presence and meaning in the midst of the events (alcoholism included) in our lives? First, we need *discernment*. The word comes from the Latin *discernere*, meaning "to separate," "to distinguish," "to determine," "to sort out." Several spiritual traditions have accented its importance. Ignatian spirituality, from Ignatius of Loyola and the Jesuits, emphasizes the discernment of spirits as a way to judge God's will in the midst of our choices.[17] Out of the Quaker tradition comes this observation: "In classical spirituality, discernment means identifying what spirit is at work in a situation; the Spirit of God or some other spirit. Discernment is 'sifting through' our interior and exterior experiences to determine their origin."[18]

How then do I discern God in the midst of my alcoholism? First, it is clear to me that God neither willed nor desired my disease. I became alcoholic through a combination of factors I have named earlier. But now I want to respond to this addiction faithfully, trusting that the Holy One is present in the midst of it with divine creativity, yearning for my healing and the healing of all those whom my disease has wounded. I want to discern how—by God's grace—this alcoholism can become the occasion for good. Can it actually be used for the reordering of life, for empowerment, for transformation, even for blessing?

The Hebrew scriptures are full of such interpretations of events. In Genesis we see Joseph interpreting and forgiving his brothers' betrayal of him (an act for which he clearly holds his brothers and not God responsible): "Even though you intended to do harm to me, God intended it for good, in order to preserve a numerous people. . . . So have no fear; I myself will provide for you and your little ones" (Gen. 50:20–21).

Here is the prophet Isaiah trying to make faithful sense of the Assyrian invasion of the faithless, corrupt people of Judah. First, Isaiah speaks as if God planned and caused the invasion: "Ah, Assyria, the rod of my anger— . . . Against a godless nation I send him" (Isa. 10:5–6). Then, however, it becomes apparent to the reader that the prophet knows Assyria has no intention whatsoever to act as Yahweh's hard word of grace to Judah: "But this is not what he [Assyria] intends, nor does he have this in mind; but it is in his heart to destroy, . . ." (Isa. 10:7). Now the question comes to the people of Judah, just as it did to Joseph: how might we respond to this destructive event, not seeing divine *causation*, but discerning divine *intention* in the midst of it all?

For Christians, of course, the supreme challenge is to interpret Jesus' terrible execution faithfully. How might we see the cross as something different from either meaningless cruelty or a divinely engineered "plan of salvation"? How can we see it as a humanly caused event, utterly vicious and dehumanizing, *and* as an event with enormous power to change human lives when it is perceived through faith in the God whose love is just and whose justice is love?

At some level I had sincerely believed these perspectives for many years. I had taught them to seminarians and preached them in pulpits. I had tried to live them with some kind of faithful interpretation and response to God's presence in the midst of life's events. But not until I became ready to deal with the crisis of my alcoholism did I realize the enormous power of interpretation—in both its faithful and unfaithful modes. Indeed, part of the reason for my illness, I now see, was my own false interpretation of my reality. I have described those invalid understandings earlier and need not repeat them here, but the fact is that they contributed heavily to my addiction.

I learned that a way to begin a more faithful interpretation was to befriend, even honor, my disease. As unwelcome and as destructive as it was, it could be "an angel unawares."[19] Though I tried to understand its various causes, I finally had to bracket those questions, set them aside, and focus on the question of God's will for me now.

I found this fascinating story in the Fourth Gospel instructive:

> As [Jesus] walked along, he saw a man blind from birth. His disciples asked him, "Rabbi, who sinned, this man or his parents, that he was born blind? Jesus answered, "Neither this man nor his parents sinned; he was born blind so that God's works might be revealed in him. . . . When he had said this, he spat on the ground and made mud with the saliva and spread the mud on the man's eyes, saying to him, "Go, wash in the pool of Siloam." . . . Then he went and washed and came back able to see. (John 9:1–7)

Since the attempt to assess responsibility was irrelevant to the larger issue, Jesus simply set the disciples' question aside. "Neither this man nor his parents sinned." Nor did he move the problem of causation from a human to a divine focus. Rather, he shifted the inquiry completely. Instead of *how did it happen?* the crucial matter was *what does it mean?* His

answer was disarmingly direct: "So that the works of God might be revealed in him." Then Jesus proceeded to assist in the man's healing, and,
since all this occurred on the Sabbath, one more controversy with the religious authorities erupted.

It is a gripping story. Just as Jesus was seen as a disreputable figure by
the religious powers, so also many of the agents in my healing have been
persons of questionable religious status: recovering drunks. Like the
man who was given sight, I too feel compelled to express gratitude and
not hide it. And after I have wrestled (as I must) with all of the causes of
my alcoholism, John's story presses me to put the focus where it finally
belongs: how can my addiction and recovery be to God's glory?

In myriad ways, our own alcoholic stories seem to leap from scripture's
pages. With blind Bartimaeus the beggar, some of us have shouted for
help and refused to be quieted (Mark 10:46ff.). With the Gerasene possessed by demons, some of us have lived in the graveyards of life, injuring
ourselves day and night, yet fearing God's healing: "Do not torment me!"
(Mark 5:7). When actively alcoholic we carried, with Lazarus, the stench
of death until someone said, "Come out! Unbind him, let him go!" Then,
with Lazarus, we began to understand Jesus' words: "This illness does not
lead to death; rather it is for God's glory" (John 11:4). Thomas Moore
has it right: "We need to feel the teeth of the god within the illness in order to be cured by the disease. In a very real sense, we do not cure diseases, they cure us, by restoring our religious participation in life."[20]

The Birth of Divine Friendship

Pregnant with the Holy Child, Mary visited Elizabeth and sang her song
of praise:

> My soul magnifies the Lord,
>   and my spirit rejoices in God my Savior,
> . . . .
> for the Mighty One has done great things for me, and holy is
> [God's] name.
>
> (Luke 1:46–47, 49)

It is a song for recovering alcoholics, a song about new birth. Let us expand that image a bit. Recovery is not only our new birth; it is also a new
birthing of God within the self. It is the birth of the Holy Child within, a
new infant born out of the old child who had long been living in our adult

body. The old one had been stuck there, denying the depth of feelings, intent on pleasing others and keeping the peace, constantly performing for approval. The old child was prone to addiction, but the Holy Child is the bearer of health. The prayer expressed in the words from a familiar Christmas carol is utterly fitting:

> O holy Child of Bethlehem,
> Descend to us, we pray;
> Cast out our sin and enter in,
> Be born in us today.[21]

In recovery, the Holy Child's birth within will likely be gradual and uneven. It surely has been so for me. But as the sacred presence grows we might find ourselves able to recognize and even move beyond some of the false dependencies that contributed to our addictions. In a revealing letter written in 1953, Bill Wilson spoke candidly of his own struggle: "Since I have begun to pray that God may release me from absolute dependence on anybody, anything, or any set of circumstances, I have begun to do so much better that it amounts to a second conversion experience."[22]

Whenever we are absolutely dependent on someone or something else other than God, we experience what Paul Tillich called *heteronomy*.[23] One of the ensuing problems, of course, is that an idol can never deliver what we ask of it. The other main difficulty is that such dependence nurtures our rebellion. We do not like depending on something external or foreign to us. The word heteronomy itself carries the clue: *hetero* is "strange" or "other," and *nomos* is "law." Our allegiance to something less than God has imposed a strange law upon us. It is a command other than the law of our own innermost beings.

So, when heteronomy becomes oppressive, we often take refuge in *autonomy*, literally, "self-law." Now, "I am the master of my fate, I am the captain of my soul." I will depend only on myself, ignoring or dominating others as seems necessary to me. While this authority (myself) is obviously not strange or foreign, it will not work. Distorted by my own estrangement, limited by my own self-interest, my autonomy finally serves no one well—including me.

I described this vacillation between heteronomy and autonomy in different terms earlier. It was between self-abasement (I'm a worm) and grandiosity (I'm the greatest). When I felt like a worm, I also felt dependent on others for my worth, my meaning, and my direction. The demands

I perceived coming from them felt strange and external—heteronomous. It felt as though I would lose their approval and love if I did not comply. That threat, in turn, aroused my resistance to their authority. I could feel this dynamic not only in my relations with others, but also with God.

So I escaped into autonomy. "The worm" became "the greatest." Now the authority for my life did not feel strange and oppressive, for it came from me. But the move to autonomy brought only short-lived relief. How could I experience myself as lovable when, as an active alcoholic, I was still alienated by guilt and shame? And how could I have true communion with others and with God if I insisted on my autonomy?

By the grace of God, however, there are times when I know that the ultimate authority for me is neither strange nor oppressive. Still I experience that authority as something far beyond myself and my own will. Such are moments of *theonomy*. It is then I discover that God's desire for me is true fulfillment—and God's law for me is exactly the same as the deepest and truest wishes of my own heart. It is the Native American's question, "Who is this who speaks to me with my own voice?" It is the apostle Paul exulting, "If God is for us, who can be against us?" (Rom. 8:31). It is the Holy Child being born within. It is Mary's experience at the tomb hearing the risen Christ: Mary, do not hold on to me. Do not cling to me. You can go now and tell the others, for the power of my resurrection is not above or beyond you, it is *in* you. *God wills our fulfillment in harmony with the whole community of creation.* Knowing that is theonomous. Indeed, as a venerable maxim from the Christian tradition puts it, "The soul rejoices in hearing what it already knows."

True recovery is not a matter of God's winning the battle of the wills. It is not God's taking control of my alcoholic life as ruler controls subject or parent controls child—"for your own good." Were that the case, the struggle would continue within me. No, the war is over. I have surrendered my false perspective. My letting go and falling into the arms of God is a profound relaxing into my true self. It is coming home.

So also, when I take A.A.'s Eleventh Step seriously—"praying only for knowledge of [God's] will for us and the power to carry that out"—the net result is not that I give up my own will by focusing on God's. It is more paradoxical than this. Once again, it is losing and finding life. In willingness to pray only for God's will and not my own, I receive myself back as a gift. I am grasped by Reality, for the harmony of our wills is what is finally real.

Then "requirements" of the recovery program lose their demanding quality and become its invitations. My continuing sobriety does not *require* that I meditate, study, go to meetings, and extend myself to struggling alcoholics—all out of a begrudging sense of duty. It *invites* me. I can do these things gladly and with gratitude, for in these opportunities are the gift of life.

Theonomy is not taming God. It is not reducing the Holy One to my little needs and purposes. Nor does A.A.'s invitation to trust in "the God of my understanding" become an invention for me to create a cozy and comfortable deity in my imagination. It is rather my grateful recognition that the Creator of all that is, the One beyond the many, the Mystery beyond all knowing, is a deeply personal Lover who passionately desires to enlarge, not diminish, my life. Theonomy is experiencing a relationship with God in which my authentic personhood and freedom are not lost— they are truly found.[24]

Love is the source of every true moral demand.[25] I had long affirmed this intellectually, but in recovery this truth grasps me more viscerally. During my active addiction I often experienced various moral obligations as external and burdensome duties. They were commanding laws that always stood outside me and over me. They almost paralyzed me with the demand that I do more, more, more. I can appreciate how Luther must have felt in his attacks of scrupulosity. Nothing he could do was good enough, even climbing all of the steps of St. Paul's in Rome on his knees.

Now I understand that my true conscience does not judge me according to my obedience to a moral law; rather, it invites me into a reality that both transcends and fulfills the law. That reality is the amazing love of God. When I know that, my conscience is not fundamentally my judge; rather, it is a gracious invitation to authentic selfhood. There is an answer to the Native American's question "Who is this who speaks to me with my own voice?" It is Love.

Frequently I hear my recovering companions speak of the oppressiveness of their pre-recovery religion. Many speak of their earlier images of the divine as a tyrant full of punitive judgment, ruling by fearsome threat. It is heteronomy with a vengeance, the impoverished kind of faith that condemns one to live in fear or abandon traditional religion altogether.

A reported statement of Jesus to his disciples seems to reflect a bit of that notion: "You are my friends if you do what I command you" (John 15:14). Friendship here appears highly conditional: if, but only if. God bestows favor only upon our successful obedience, which is a good recipe for servile existence. But in this text, Jesus continues (somewhat surprisingly) by calling his disciples *friends*, not servants. He speaks disarmingly of our intimacy with God, the One who gives whatever is needed and whose commands have but one purpose: love.

Both H. Richard Niebuhr and Alfred North Whitehead have argued that the true revolution in life comes when we experience the "transition from God the void to God the enemy, and from God the enemy to God the companion."[26] As practicing alcoholics, many of us knew well the experience of God as the great void. The divine was either irrelevant to us or, when we needed God, there was nothing there. Many of us also knew well the experience of God as enemy. After all, alcoholism was our great escape from the oppressive demands of life and of life's Creator.

In recovery we have begun to know something of the companionship —the friendship—of God. It is a relationship that no longer keeps us dependent, but instead nurtures our maturity. It is so typical of Jesus' teachings, echoing the prophets before him. What is required of us is to do justice, to love mercy, and to walk humbly with our God. Note, that is walk *with* God, not *behind*. In the realm of God the moral demand becomes the invitation of love, and what was once fearful obedience becomes the reciprocity of friends.

A friendship between two persons is instructive. Of all relationships among people—including parent to child, lover to lover, spouse to spouse —friendship seems most free. Writing from prison, Dietrich Bonhoeffer described it as the only relationship that exists outside the bounds of duty or function. Friendship exists in freedom and as such is, he said, the "rarest and most priceless treasure."[27] Similarly, examining various models of God, Sallie McFague finds the image of God as Friend particularly compelling: "Of all human loves, *philia* [that kind of love expressed in friendship] is the most free, the most reciprocal, the most adult, the most joyful, the most inclusive."[28]

On one occasion a bold questioner reportedly asked Albert Einstein what was the most important, most critical question that could be asked. Always one to drive to the heart of the matter, Einstein replied without hesitation, "Is the universe friendly, or is it not?" Without exception, every alcoholic I know testifies that in the midst of their addiction the world was a markedly unfriendly place where God was either absent or felt like an enemy. And without exception, every sober alcoholic I know testifies that in the midst of their recovery a remarkable transition has occurred. The world and the world's Creator have become friendly. In fact, there are moments when we know that the Eternal Mystery has become the Friend embodied within us and the Holy Child is born again.

Love of Self and Love of God

If the friendship of God is born within us, we have become friends to ourselves. Unfortunately, a long theological history in the West has made a certain understanding of *agape* normative for Christian spirituality. It claims that *agape* is a love that is purely selfless. Divine sacrificial love expressed in the cross provides the standard for the Christian, and hence the appropriate spiritual life is the progressive triumph of this self-giving love over every form of selfishness, egocentrism, and narcissism.[29] Even the Big Book of Alcoholics Anonymous can be interpreted as reflecting this view: "Selfishness—self-centeredness! That, we think, is the root of our troubles." The alcoholic is "an extreme example of self-will run riot."[30]

If the Big Book is speaking of the results of self-hatred, I fully concur. But excessive self-love is not the problem. When we are caught up in selfishness, self-centeredness, and narcissism, our appearance and our reality are at odds. Since we are trying so hard for attention, approval, and self-acceptance, the appearance is one of excessive self-love. The reality, however, is that we actually don't love ourselves, and the irony is that our narcissistic display of apparent self-love is itself a sure sign that we cannot find adequate ways to affirm ourselves. Indeed, the magnitude of our grandiosity is typically proportional to the intensity of our own feelings of worthlessness.

Profound self-disappointment is a predictable factor in addictions. An example of this was my tendency to believe (even though my mind knew better) that meeting my own needs was somehow illegitimate. I had so internalized certain notions of *agape* as sheer self-giving that I acted as if I had a limitless supply of energy and was capable of responding endlessly to everyone and everything. I actually believed I would take care of myself tomorrow, but tomorrow never came. What did come was exhaustion, self-pity, and resentment—all persuasive invitations to drink. Drinking, in turn, magnified each one of them. It was typical alcoholic behavior. We try to deal with that needy voice within through immersion in a substance that will silence it. But it is a doomed effort and in trying to save ourselves we almost destroy ourselves.

Healthy self-love and self-esteem are essential to lasting sobriety and emotional recovery. Indeed, those oppressed because of race, gender, sexual orientation, or disability will quickly remind others of us that self-abasement is a lethal foe of recovery. In light of this, some recovering folk maintain that when people do moral inventories of their own lives and when they list those whom they have harmed (the Fourth and Eighth Steps) they need to put *themselves* at the top of the list. Though as a gay man and recovering alcoholic he clearly understands the need of self-esteem, Douglas Federhart counters, "If we shy away from the fundamental reality of our brokenness, and give out the idea that if we are just gentler with ourselves all will be healed, then we are not helping each other face and deal with the despair that so often lurks several layers behind our initial joy of sobriety."[31]

I agree. Simply putting ourselves at the top of the list of those to whom love is due will not carry the day. No more effective is the merely *cognitive* recognition that true self-love is necessary if we would love others. I thought I had understood these things long before I became addicted. After all, I had even taught seminary courses on the nature of love! At one level, I did know these things, but at a deeper level I did not. For the real problem is not *knowing that* healthy self-love is essential. The real problem is *loving* the self. And the barrier to that is distressingly simple: the self that needs so much love is not a very lovable self.

Perhaps part of the solution lies in taking positive actions that will enhance positive self-regard. For example, some of us have struggled with the temptation to live too much by others' agendas. It was true of Bill Wilson. During a prolonged depression he began to see a psychiatrist, Dr. Frances Weeks. She helped him acknowledge that he was constantly being diverted to secondary, even useless activities by A.A. members, and she urged him to clarify his boundaries in order to leave room for his own needs. He subsequently described his new realization to a friend: "Highly satisfactory to live one's life for others, it cannot be anything but disastrous to live one's life for others as those others think it should be lived. One has, for better or worse, to choose his own life."[32]

But is humility a casualty in such apparent self-preoccupation? It is, after all, vital to recovery and foundational to the spiritual life in general. Indeed, when asked what were the four cardinal virtues, St. Bernard answered, "Humility, humility, humility and humility."[33]

Typical understandings of humility, however, are often misleading. It *seems* to mean abject meekness and self-abasement. So it did to Churchill, still smarting about losing the prime ministership to Clement Atlee after

World War II. When the suggestion was made that a bit of Mr. Atlee's humility might be appropriate to Sir Winston himself, he barked, "That man has a great deal to be humble about!"

Authentic humility is different. It is neither groveling timidity nor bland servility. Nor is it "I am the greatest worm." Humility seems to come only with genuine knowledge and love of the self. It is, as Dag Hammarskjold observed in *Markings*, "just as much the opposite of self-abasement as it is of self-exultation." It is deeply rooted in honesty about ourselves and our place in the larger picture. "To be humble is *not to make comparisons.* Secure in its reality, the self is neither better nor worse, bigger nor smaller, than anything else in the universe. It *is*—is nothing, yet at the same time one with everything."[34]

Honesty about ourselves is the key, not thinking poorly of ourselves. We need neither deny our goodness nor dwell on our lack of it. Both enterprises will lead us into making comparisons that are dangerous to sobriety. The ancient sense of humility suggests a willingness to remove ourselves from being the center of the universe.

Humility is earthiness, as in its companion word *humus*. Humus suggests being rooted in the ground of who we truly are, rooted in the Ground of Being, God, *whose* we are. Humus also means the dark organic component of the soil derived from decomposed plant and animal remains and animal excrement. It is the stuff that makes soil fertile and workable, that is vital to the growth of new life.

Once again, we are dealing with our uneasy finitude—the *both/and* that we are. As humans we are both animal and angel, both saint and sinner, and such a mix is good enough. Ernest Becker, dying of cancer at forty-nine as he finished his Pulitzer Prize book *The Denial of Death*, put it in memorable (if blunt) words: the human being is "a god who shits."[35] Seeing ourselves this way is not a matter of self-abasement. It is humble realism: both angel and animal. It is an invitation to compassion and kindness toward oneself. It invites seeing oneself with gentleness, humor, and hope—indeed, seeing oneself worthy of love and respect.

These understandings are very helpful to me. At the same time, I must confess that such honest self-appreciation does not come naturally. Working to shift my cognitive gears and to change my self-perception is important. But what I need most of all is amazing grace, the grace that can save a wretch like me. In spite of the misleading interpretations of the cross that would make it a parody of divine love, in spite of the explanations that would make the cross little more than divine child-abuse, I find in that central Christian symbol a compelling revelation of the gracious Heart of the Universe.

When Jesus took up his cross, that unspeakably cruel instrument of execution spoke of God's eternal crossing over to identify with the despised. Even dimly aware of that amazing grace, some of us have discovered that it is now time that we crossed over into those places within ourselves where love has failed and self-hatred still holds sway. I find in Martin L. Smith's words a compelling altar call that might speak even to the most sophisticated:

> There are selves within us that we despise, that we cannot forgive, that appall us with their fantasies and disgust us with their weakness. Jesus has already crossed over to them, and it is time to have compassion on these ruined and sick parts of ourselves that he is embracing with the arms of his love. He is waiting for us to accept healing of our self-hatred. It is time to cross over and meet Jesus embracing the failed and ugly selves of the heart, and healing us.[36]

That is far different from saying that if we were only gentler with ourselves all would be well. It is far different from trying to purchase self-love with a currency whose value is undermined by unacknowledged despair. It is far different from letting denial come in the back door of recovery, convincing us that our alcoholism was not so bad after all and that throughout our active alcoholic days we were really quite lovable. It is far different from blindness to a self that was, indeed, deeply estranged, sick, and hurting others. Amazing grace is far different from all of that. And how sweet is its sound.

We in the twenty-first century might find an instructive picture of grace for recovery in the desert monks of the fourth and fifth centuries. Their discipline of solitude removed them both from comparisons with others and from others' endless expectations. They discovered that only by dying to others could they really be of service to them. They learned that only when they had ceased to need people desperately and neurotically were they able to love them with genuine concreteness. Regarding their own sense of identity and well-being, they had a "holy indifference" to others. They were utterly self-dependent because they were so God-dependent. Without this spiritual detachment from others, they knew that they would simply manipulate and use the neighbor for their own needs. But with this spiritual self-dependence they could, paradoxically, be free to love with genuine connection and compassion.[37]

The same paradox seems true of the self and God. When (and only when) I have been freed from a desperate and neurotic need for God, am

I also free to be God's lover. And we deserve to be lovers of God. It is our destiny. It is a present waiting for us to accept, and we refuse that gift at our own profound loss.

Alcoholics, I believe, have the advantage of experiencing a parallel to all of this. We know that authentic recovery is more than abstinence. It is more than simply not drinking. It is *not wanting* to drink. The obsession and the craving thirst have all but disappeared, and we have experienced a wondrous sense of freedom. No matter how much we wanted it, we could not have willed that freedom. We could not have created it, no matter how strongly we desired it. It just came as a gift, and we know it is real. Perhaps self-love is something like that.

That appears true of our relation to God. When we have given up trying to climb the heights to the Eternal One, we might sink into the holy arms more deeply than we had imagined possible. In fact, now—for today—that we are free from the desperate escapism of alcohol intoxication, we might even know moments of God intoxication.

Chapter 9

Journey and Home

A Journey toward Home

Late in my active alcoholism, I was in Washington, D.C. for professional work and had some time to spend at the National Gallery of Art. I first had lunch at the museum's cafe where I drank several glasses of wine. Beginning my gallery tour, I went to the Impressionists, anticipating their usual delights. But I was not prepared for the experience of standing before Claude Monet's "The Japanese Footbridge." As its shimmering colors and light struck me, I first felt the tears running down my cheeks and then quiet sobs convulsing my gut. I was aware of only two things: the incredible cosmic harmony evoked by that canvas and the stark disharmony that I felt in every significant part of my life. I ached for home, but at that time had no idea how to start the journey—or whether I dared.

Beauty can draw us toward home, and for centuries philosophers and theologians have tried to understand that power. Thomas Aquinas believed that beautiful objects or scenes project radiance and light, and when we encounter them we are filled with a sense of connectedness to something greater than ourselves, often so overwhelming that words cannot express it. Jonathan Edwards was convinced that the beauty we encounter is a shadow of divine transcendence; it reflects God's harmony because all created beings "sweetly consent" to the Being who is their source and whose love sustains all creation.[1]

Standing before the Monet work, I had the stark feeling that, while God's radiant connectedness and love might be real, they were utterly eluding me. It should have been no surprise, for I was in the grip of an addiction that predictably convinces one that such things have vanished from the face of the earth. The integration of life conveyed by the painting left my own raw disintegration exposed for what it was.

Those who study this disease have found that the longing for, searching for, indeed the *thirst* for home is a marked characteristic of most alcoholics. Psychiatrist Edward Khantzian observes how "alcoholics seek the effects of alcohol to etablish a feeling of 'harmony'—a feeling that everything is now well between them and their environment." The addicted person's sense of incompleteness joins with "the yearning for this feeling of harmony" to become "the most important cause of alcoholism or, for that matter, any form of addiction."[2]

This acknowledgment does not nullify what I have said about alcoholism's various causes in earlier chapters. The addiction's mosaic is comprised of numerous elements likely existing simultaneously. Genetic predispositions, habit-forming body chemistry and brain cell changes, family histories, abuse patterns, and cultural influences—all of these inform the alcoholic's desire to escape reality and numb the pain. But beyond, under, and around every other element there seems to be a divine discontent, a yearning for home.

Out of her own alcoholic experience Christina Grof writes, "As far back into my childhood as I can remember, I was searching for something I could not name. Whatever I was looking for would help me to feel all right, at home, as though I belonged."[3] Most alcoholics report feeling different from other people, as though we were on the outside looking in through the windows of home. Our emptiness, loneliness, shame, or sense of inadequacy seem to keep us on the outside too much of the time. Grof describes how over the years she had fleeting glimpses of finding such home in various experiences, but nothing compared to her discovery of drinking: "I *knew* I found it in the delicious oblivion of alcohol. My boundaries melted. . . . I felt comfortable within my own skin and felt connected . . . accepted, and cherished—until alcohol turned against me."[4]

The intense desire for that larger connected sense of self, ultimately the craving for our home in God, is (though in dramatically different ways) the fundamental dynamic of both addiction and recovery. Again, it is the thirst the psalmist describes, the deer panting for the water brooks and the soul thirsting for the living God (Psalm 42). Again, it is Carl Jung's insight expressed in his famous letter to Bill Wilson: precisely because alcoholism expresses a fundamental longing for the divine, it finally takes homecoming to the Spirit to heal the alienating idolatry and wounding caused by alcoholic spirits.

But for a recovering alcoholic such homecoming is not a once and for all event. It is ongoing. In this regard alcoholics are not unique. The never-ending journey is a mark of human spiritual life as such, as witnessed in Ruth Duck's memorable hymn, "Lead On, O Cloud of Yahweh." Sung to the tune of "Lead On, O King Eternal," her words invoke the exodus metaphor with a strong sense of continuing pilgrimage. The first stanza declares, *"In wilderness and desert* our tribe shall make its home," and the second proclaims, "The *journey* is our home."[5] It is a hymn for alcoholics who know that they are *recovering*, not *recovered*, and that the journey, not arrival, is the story for the rest of their lives.

Journey is an age-old metaphor of the spiritual life that is found in many religious traditions. The exodus from slavery in Egypt toward the promised land continues to be biblical faith's supreme image of this journey, in spite of the wrenching tragedy that continues to unfold between Israelis and Palestinians.

That image is also a powerful metaphor for recovery. While they were on that seemingly endless exodus, the ancient pilgrims sometimes missed the cage and yearned to go back to slavery in Egypt. The unknown was frightening. At least bondage in Egypt had the comfort of the familiar. We alcoholics know about that. And some early pilgrims fell by the wayside. Any recovering alcoholic can readily call out the names of fallen friends. As I write I'm thinking particularly of Bill and Bobby and of cousin Barb, two suicides and one liver collapse. Recovery is not an easy stroll through the park. It is a journey through the desert with a "cunning, baffling, powerful" adversary lurking never far away. But it is a life-giving journey, and it has many dimensions. One of them is truth.

A Journey into Truth

For every sober alcoholic I know, recovery is a welcome journey into greater integrity and authenticity. T. S. Eliot once observed that people cannot take too much reality, and that is true many times over for the active alcoholic. Alcoholic denial, as I noted earlier, is violence against reality, but it is not usually willful deceit. As active alcoholics our enormous capacity for self-deception was triggered by chemical changes we did not recognize. Subconsciously we seemed to realize that denial was utterly essential to protect our disease from being discovered and to keep our drinking system intact.

In recovery we see the humor of it all. One man described himself as the kind of fellow that, if his wife locked him out of the house, he thought he had a problem with the *door*. Another said that as a practicing alcoholic he was always willing to join A.A., but the group he had in mind was "Alcoholics Alias," where he could continue drinking under an assumed name.

However, no amount of retrospective whimsy can mask all of the pain. The memories are just too vivid: If this is normal drinking, why am I hiding it? Why do I fear discovery from those I love most? So as an active alcoholic I dug my way ever deeper into the grave of deception. But there was still saving grace even in that descent. Guilt and shame kept creeping in—strange signs that the Hound of Heaven would not let me go.

Recovery is a journey into truth, but *what is truth?* It was Pontius Pilate's question as Jesus stood before him. However, that Roman governor missed the point. Pilate thought truth was a "what," an objective thing, abstract and impersonal. Jesus tried to call him into a living relationship, for truth is personal. It is embodied or it does not exist. "I am the way, and the truth, and the life" (John 14:6).

Falling into Pilate's error, we often assume that we know *what* truth is and then the ethical question is whether or not to tell it, or how much of it to tell. Behind that is the assumption that truth is a simple matter of speaking with our lips the facts as we understand them. On reflection, however, alcoholics should know the insufficiency of this approach. After all, during our heaviest drinking we were quite accomplished at using factual words to deceive. (Example: Spoken words to spouse: "I'm not drinking any more than I used to." Unspoken: "For a long time I've been drinking a lot more than you know.") Truth is not an objective "what." It is a life-giving quality embodied in a *relationship*.

In his essay "What Does It Mean to Tell the Truth?" Dietrich Bonhoeffer provided a clear example.[6] It was the child being confronted in front of the class by the teacher's question, "Is it true that your father often comes home drunk?" The child denied it, when in fact he sadly knew that those *were* the facts of the situation. Bonhoeffer's point, however, is that truth is always deeper and more complex than factual words. While truth involves words, it is basically a matter of making those communications congruent with life-giving relationships of integrity. The teacher had no right to invade the family relationship in that confrontive, public way. The youngster was right in defending that relationship in the only way he knew how, trying as best he could to salvage anything of family self-respect in that stressful moment.

A recovering alcoholic may choose to reveal the fact of her alcoholism to X, but not to Y. She makes the judgment that X deserves this knowledge, which will enrich their relationship in mutually life-giving ways, but that (for whatever reasons) the same is not the case with Y. In the latter instance, she chooses her words with care, trying never to convey false facts, but also believing that withholding this information from Y has more fidelity to this relationship than her self-disclosure would have. It is *not* the case that this recovering alcoholic was truthful to X but not to Y. She was attempting to be truthful to both, not truthful in the abstract but in two quite different, concrete relationships.

Careful listening is critical for knowing the truth. Alcoholism is different from most diseases to which we are subject. We are accustomed to experiencing symptoms and then going to the doctor for professional diagnosis. But alcoholism must be diagnosed by the *patient*, and so to know this truth about ourselves we have to listen carefully to our own lives telling us who we are and what we have become.

In spite of being well into mid-life when I became actively alcoholic, and in spite of years of dealing professionally with issues of the deeper self, I was still listening too intently to others' voices telling me who I was. From our early grade-school days we are taught to listen to everyone but ourselves, and when those outside clues get built into our egos it is difficult to hear the deeper and truer voice within. This is *heteronomy*, listening to "the strange god."

If recovery is to begin, there must be "truth in the inward being." I had to listen for truth about myself, including what I did not want to hear. It takes patience. Parker Palmer reminds us that the soul is often "like a wild animal—tough, resilient, savvy, self-sufficient, and yet exceedingly shy. If we want to see a wild animal, the last thing we should do is to go crashing through the woods, shouting for the creature to come out." But if we remain still in the woods for a long time, the creature may emerge and we will glimpse its precious wildness.[7]

In that listening I learned to name the thirst I really felt within, and it was a thirst beyond that for alcohol. The truth leading to recovery had to come *theonomously*—by hearing and recognizing the voice of God within myself. In his play about Joan of Arc, George Bernard Shaw depicts the young martyr being interrogated about her conversations with God. "How do you mean, voices?" her examiner says. She responds, "I hear voices telling me what to do. They come from God." Her questioner persists, "The voices come from your imagination." But to this, Saint Joan replies, "Of course, that is how the message of God comes to me."[8]

Truth is relational, and it comes by careful listening. It is also an *event*. The Greek word for truth typically used by New Testament authors was *aletheia*, bearing several meanings. Though it sometimes meant "the facts," sometimes "trustworthiness," beyond these it meant the disclosure of a reality previously hidden. Early Christian usage added something more: truth was a revelatory event.

Thus, in encountering truth, we point to something that has happened to us, perhaps exceeding our expectations, possibly going beyond our comprehension, but somehow revealing the divine Presence in our midst. That is why Jesus' followers interpreted him as "the truth." In him they experienced someone who was fully open to God, to his neighbors, and to himself. So also, that is why the Fourth Gospel uses such phrases as "doing the truth," "being the truth," and "I am the truth"—word combinations that, as Tillich says, "indicate that truth in Christianity is something which *happens*, something which is bound to a special place, to a special time . . . an event which has taken place and which takes place again and again."[10]

Some of us have met truth in a decisive and compelling way in Jesus the Christ. Some of us also affirm that God is active and has been active in all times and places, not only in that one event. These two claims seem incompatible to some believers, but they need not be. Norman Pittenger recognizes their harmony, saying that in the Christ event something happens "so that what is always true is now *known to be true*. A vivid self-revelation in that one place has provided the clue to all the rest of God's operation in the world."[11] Through such a vivid, decisive act we now see things differently than we did before.

Recovery experience helps us grasp this new vision. It is not that God's favor suddenly turned toward us when we stopped drinking. Rather, hitting bottom and beginning recovery was a decisive act allowing us to see what was always true. Since this event we have seen the world through different lenses. Truth *happens*.

Every recovering alcoholic I know has a unique story of how the movement from deception to more truthful living happened. Many things contributed to my own "moment of truth": increased "maintenance drinking," periodic blackouts, morning drinking, increasing social withdrawal, a seriously strained marriage. All of those things happened over time. But there was also a decisive moment, the moment when an almost unrecognizable face stared back from the mirror on the sixth morning of a crazy binge. It was the event when God's truth broke through. Most of us can recite the exact time and circumstances when truthfulness broke in. For this reason, along with many recovering companions, my biological birthday has been eclipsed in personal significance by my sobriety birthday ("my *real* birthday").

If truth is event, it comes not only by listening but also by *doing*. Difficult enough for stubborn rationalists, this reality is even tougher for active
alcoholics. When self-doubts came during my time of heavy drinking, I
found myself clinging to the fiction that I had to understand fully what was
happening to me before I could do anything about it. Like the proverbial
Titanic passenger refusing the lifeboat, I said, "I'm not getting off this ship
until I understand exactly why it's going down!"

But often we need to act ourselves into understanding. Such is the
homely wisdom in A.A.'s advice: "Get your body to the meeting, and your
mind will follow." That wisdom is not far from the Fourth Gospel's reference to "those who do what is true" (John 3:21).

Part of recovery wisdom says that we must "live life on life's terms."
Thus, *accepting reality* can be a way of doing the truth. Neither passivity
nor fatalism, it is a recognition that much of life's pain comes not because
of life itself but because of our resistance to life.

The homeopathic approach to disease healing illustrates an alternative
way. Two hundred years ago it was developed by Dr. Samuel Hahne-
mann, who discovered that patients would heal given a very small dose of
natural drugs that, in larger doses, would produce symptoms of the disease itself. It was based on the assumption that *like* can be cured by *like*.

Mark well, I do not assume that small doses of alcohol would benefit
my alcoholism. Alcoholics trying that route have courted utter failure.
But I do find the notion of "the homeopathic move" very suggestive: you
don't run *from* the disease, you run *into* it. My efforts to compensate for
my unattractive character traits and emotional deficiencies by striving to
produce the opposite have not been resoundingly successful. Alterna-
tively, the homeopathic move honors the symptoms by listening to and
learning from them (back to the wild animal in the woods). It is a matter
of becoming willing to stop running from the emotional pain and instead
befriend its reality, listen to it carefully, and hear its truth. It may be a
voice of the soul. So it means wrestling with the assailant like Jacob at Pe-
niel, saying, "I will not let you go, unless you bless me" (Gen. 32:26).[12]

The truth of living into reality also means *willingness to live with ambiguity*. Long ago I accepted ambiguity as part of my theological understanding
of life, but the capacity to live with it has grown during sobriety. After all,
ambiguity is intrinsic to a disease for which there is no cure, only remission.
Even though, as of this writing, my abstinence has been unbroken for the
past decade, I cannot guarantee anything about the future. Furthermore I
know that my emotional recovery (the transformation of my attitudes,
emotions, and thinking) has been only gradual and incremental, and not
without setbacks—in other words, ambiguous. But I take comfort from

baseball. Commissioner Fay Vincent once commented on how that sport teaches us to live with failure. He said he found it "fascinating that baseball alone in sport considers errors to be part of the game, part of its rigorous truth."[13] Indeed, the best hitter of all time struck out six times out of ten. So also, part of the rigorous truth of sobriety is, as one addiction therapist put it, "the clarity of mind to know that, in many instances, there will be no particular clarity of mind."[14]

Biblical faith typically connects truth with *freedom*: "If you continue in my word, you are truly my disciples; and you will know the truth, and the truth will make you free" (John 8:31–32). According to the Fourth Gospel, this oft-quoted statement came in the midst of a religious dispute. Jesus' detractors immediately countered, "We . . . have never been slaves to anyone. What do you mean by saying, 'You will be made free?'" (John 8:33). I find this dialogue unsettlingly familiar. I thought my freedom to drink was genuine freedom, and only gradually did the reality of my slavery become clear to me. And only when conscious of my slavery did I thirst for the truth that would make me free.

Common testimony at recovery meetings is that commitment to truthful living produces an amazing sense of freedom and makes one feel a thousand pounds lighter. No more need I tax my memory trying to remember what I said last night. No more need I try to remember the excuses I made yesterday so that I can appear consistent today. No more need I fear someone getting too close and discovering the secret of my addiction. Now I have more energy for life since I am not devoting it to protecting myself from being found out.

Mark Twain's advice was "Tell the truth. It will confound your enemies and astound your friends." More than that, it can keep us sober, for our secrets will kill us. In one of his parables about the realm of God, Jesus said, "'Is a lamp brought in to be put under the bushel basket, or under the bed, and not on the lampstand? For there is nothing hidden, except to be disclosed; nor is anything secret, except to come to light'" (Mark 4:21–22). Recovering people know something about that. They also know the truth of Kahlil Gibran's observation that to reveal yourself you must either dance naked in the sun or carry your cross. Recovery seems to involve some of both.

A Journey into Time

Throughout the ages philosophers and theologians have struggled with the meanings of time. So have alcoholics. It has been—and still is—quite literally a matter of life and death. In fact, the first name for the young Alcoholics Anonymous group was "The Day at a Time Program."[15]

That title was based on two clear perceptions. The first conviction was that drinking alcoholics were locked into a skewed understanding of time. They wanted only a truncated present moment (a drink *now*) and were incapable of either learning from the past or caring about the future. The second realization was that drunks were unable to make a sobriety promise extending endlessly into the future, but they did have a chance of choosing not to drink *today* (or if today was too long, for an hour).

As a practicing alcoholic my sense of time was distorted in several ways. For one, there was never enough of it. My approach was epitomized in a solo I had in a high school choral concert (I remember it clearly): "I love life and I want to live, to drink of life's fullness, take all it can give; I love life, every moment must count. . . ." *Every moment must count.* I must squeeze everything possible out of the time available. Decades later during active alcoholism, time seemed to turn against me. I didn't want to look at my wristwatch, and I hated the sight of wall clocks, for the future was coming far too quickly. Since grace was too unreal to me, there was never enough time to prove my worth.

The distortion of the present in Kierkegaard's description of "the aesthete" was also uncomfortably true of me. Since time has become a series of "now-moments" to be filled with pleasurable distractions, the aesthete races through life fearing that he is missing out on gratifications. But he has lost his freedom in this constant flight from his own mortality.[16]

As an active alcoholic when I wasn't anxiously seizing the present moment, I was twisting the past out of shape. Alcohol invited rumination and brooding over yesterday—part of my delusion of control, the absurd belief that I had the power to change what was past. But trying to control what was impossible to control was an exercise in frustration and thus another invitation to drink.

Since the past is always where injury and trauma to the spirit reside, it is where resentments live. The addicted one perceives that the present is really no different from the past. Indeed, the word "resentment" literally means "to feel again," thus to scrape the scab off the sore; to feel the old injury, fear, and anger as if they existed freshly in the present. This way, clinging to the past furnished more justifications for numbing myself with alcohol. The disease created in me a world where the past was indistinguishable from the present, thus spawning ever more occasions for self-medication.[17]

The future was similar. In my youth I had been significantly shaped by the Boy Scouts and had thoroughly internalized their motto, "Be Prepared." My alcoholic drinking, however, turned realistic preparation for the future into chronic worry. After all, if I didn't worry about something, it would certainly happen! Living so much in the future predictably nurtured my sense of inadequacy and sapped the present of its strength. But I now had still another reason to drink: to numb my anxiety about what surely lay ahead.

Condemned to live in a remorseful past, in a fearful future, or in an escapist present, the drinking alcoholic has no real *now*. On the other hand, recovery brings fresh ways to experience time. An unnamed writer who lived two hundred years before Jesus' birth provided a foundational insight for this. He was a man schooled in Greek wisdom and shaped by Jewish piety, and his familiar words are found in the Hebrew Scripture's book of Ecclesiastes:

> For everything there is a season, and a time for every matter under heaven:
> a time to be born, and a time to die;
> a time to plant, and a time to pluck up what is planted;
> a time to kill, and a time to heal;
> a time to break down, and a time to build up;
> a time to weep, and a time to laugh;
> a time to mourn, and a time to dance.
>
> (Eccl. 3:1–4)[18]

Though the words sound lyrical, they produce a picture of pessimism and despair. It reminds me of my own alcoholic thinking. Though everything has its proper time and season, life is cyclical and nothing new ever emerges. All is vanity; everything is in vain.

Nevertheless, there is a deep wisdom here. It begins in recognizing that we do have our limits. Our years are limited, our knowledge is limited, and our own sense of timing is a secondary matter. The writer knows that *the right time* depends on a Wisdom infinitely greater than ours.

That notion is often called *kairos*. It is one of two Greek words for time, the other being *chronos*—chronological time, quantitative time, time as measured by the hands of a clock. But *kairos* refers to something qualitatively different. It is a unique moment in the temporal process. The closest we can get to it in English is probably "timing" or "at the right moment." It is this latter meaning of which the writer of Ecclesiastes speaks: there is a right time to mourn and a right time to dance.

During my alcoholic drinking I seemed to experience no *kairos* moments. Nothing seemed to happen just at the right time. Present moments were too often poisoned by the remorseful past and the fearful future, thus becoming the time for numbing escape. *Chronos* had become threatening, finally, because the clocks were telling me that *I was timed.* Clocks reminded me not only of appointments and deadlines, but also of the finality of it all. In the race with time, I was losing out and none of my achievements would finally count.

If the book of Ecclesiastes declares that there *is* a right time known by Wisdom, the Gospels give clues about its meaning. According to Mark, Jesus' first public teaching was this: "'The time is fulfilled, and the kingdom of God has come near; repent, and believe in the good news'" (Mark 1:15). *The time is fulfilled.* Eternity is infusing the present with victory over a chronological time that had become chaotic and meaningless.

While Jesus' announcement of the realm of God is one expression of this inbreaking of eternity, perhaps the most dramatic symbol of such *kairos* is his resurrection. When I affirm Christ's resurrection I am not concerned about a physical resuscitation, an angel rolling a stone from the door of a tomb, or a body miraculously appearing from nowhere and then disappearing into the air. Easter faith, as I understand it, does not depend on such proofs, nor must twenty-first-century believers use all of the thought forms of an earlier era. I accept these accounts as powerful testimonies in first-century language about a person who was so utterly filled with God that death could not define him, contain him, or conquer him. I want to celebrate that same life-giving God.[19]

During his ministry Jesus showed no desire to monopolize the divine incarnation. To the contrary, he tried to spread God's embodied presence far and wide. So, also, in death Jesus had no intent to monopolize resurrection. Quite the opposite. In accepting his cross he proclaimed to the ages that being is stronger than nonbeing and that love is stronger than death. The apostle Paul's outburst of resurrection faith says what finally needs to be said: "For I am convinced that neither death, nor life, nor angels, nor rulers, nor things present, nor things to come, nor powers, nor height, nor depth, nor anything else in all creation, will be able to separate us from the love of God in Christ Jesus our Lord" (Rom. 8:38–39).

What difference can this make for an alcoholic's recovery? Christ's resurrection, as I understand it, is not about conquering *death*—as if to say that it erases death's reality. But it is very much about conquering *the fear of death* and, perhaps even more, *the anxiety about having to die.* Our mortality can frighten us into a host of distorted, destructive meanings, and drinking alcoholics are particularly vulnerable. So, the clocks on the walls haunted me. Tillich observes, "Time is the central category of finitude," and it is not primarily the fear of death as such that haunts us; it is our finitude, our anxiety about *having* to die.[20] It is our melancholy awareness that we are on a journey from being alive to not being here at all.

The Big Book says that without sobriety the alcoholic is likely to end up in prison, in a mental hospital, or dead, and I suspect that most of us would be prematurely dead. Over and over at recovery meetings I hear, "Without this program I wouldn't be alive today," and the speakers appear to mean that quite literally. While a daily awareness of death might be depressing to many people, it seems just the opposite for recovering people: it is a daily awareness of resurrection.

Still, some might say that it is primarily fear—especially fear of death—that keeps us sober. It is the fear that next time there might be no recovery and the consequences might be fatal. I do not doubt the reality of these fears, but I strongly doubt that they are the central energies behind recovery for most people. Rather, it is an overwhelming sense of gratitude—gratitude for new life, for resurrection, for the Now.

The postresurrection accounts in the Gospels are not shrouded in ghostly otherworldiness. They are astoundingly daily, bodily, and material. Thus the Fourth Gospel reports the risen Christ standing on the beach encountering the disciples who are discouraged about their fishing. They have not recognized him. "'Children, you have no fish, have you?' They answered him, 'No.' He said to them, 'Cast the net to the right side of the boat, and you will find some.' So they cast it, and now they were not able to haul it in because there were so many fish" (John 21:5–6).

The account is typical of the postresurrection reports. They are stories of fishing, of eating breakfast on the beach, of walking on a road and talking with a stranger, of having supper. How is it going? What's happening in your life today? Are you getting any fish? These are the earthy, practical questions. Not, are you spiritual? Or, have you started building that temple? Rather, have you caught anything yet? Try the other side of the boat, for the other side is here and now, not in the sky by and by. As Peter Gomes says, these postresurrection accounts of Jesus are told in the most material and fleshly ways possible "to remind us that this other side is tangible and real, not a ghostly metaphor but something that lives in living people here and now, and that you do not have to die to know the resurrected life."[21]

So it was with the early "Easter people" of the New Testament. Their focus was not on *how long* they would live now that Christ's resurrection had occurred, but on *how* they could live now. *How long* is *chronos*. *How* is the qualitative question. It is *kairos*, the right time, the eternal Now.

Regardless of our varied religious orientations or lack thereof, recovering people tend to speak in resurrection-like language, for we have received new life. True, it is a gradual thing for most of us, but we can date its beginning and we have absolutely no doubt that it is qualitatively different. Since the event of our resurrections, our lives no longer look only like an unexpended stretch of time. They no longer feel like the balance remaining in the checking account, but instead like someone has burned the mortgage. The house where we once lived, a habitation not really our own, is now truly ours free and clear.

Life feels different because we *perceive* it differently. Just as addiction is a disease of perception, so also recovery is the gift of a new way of seeing. In the Christian tradition, it is a familiar way of understanding redeemed life. In his *Treatise Concerning Religious Affections* Jonathan Edwards described how "the saints" have "a new inward perception or sensation of their minds, entirely different in its nature and kind from anything that ever their minds were the subjects of before they were sanctified."[22]

Though more comfortable calling themselves "just a bunch of drunks" than "saints," recovering alcoholics are familiar with this phenomenon and use language not too different from that of Edwards. Certainly these alcoholics know healing, but their language moves even beyond the healing imagery. They are not just talking about being restored to a previous condition—the way they were before the addiction set in. They are talking about something *new*, a way of seeing things that is truly different from the way they perceived things before. It is resurrection language.

For one thing, the past looks and feels different. The Big Book promises, "We will not regret the past nor wish to shut the door on it."[23] True, I do have many regrets about my drinking past; I deeply wish it had been different. But I can live without wallowing in the past. Regret need not become remorse. Forgiven and accepted by the Gracious One, I need not slam the door on the past in self-defense. Rather, I can remember it—literally *re-member* it—put the past back together in a new and different way. Then I perceive my alcoholic history as a source of wisdom for life, not a paralyzing burden of guilt and shame.

What about the future? When I was drinking, the future seemed full of contradiction. I lived for it and thus missed much that was happening in the present. But even more, I was anxious about the future for it meant limited time, mortality, and death. Yes, the future could drive a man to drink.

Now I know that this death anxiety is a place of failure to which Jesus crossed over. In my experience of resurrection, I have new confidence in Jesus' resurrection, and his tells me that in life and in death there is no separation from the God who loves us absolutely. There is no need for alcoholic medication. If the future is given to us, we can live now. To know that we are the desire of God's heart, as Martin Smith so well says, "is not like being born again. It *is* being born again. It is to rise from the dead *now*. It is time for us to cross over with Jesus into the place of death and discover it is the only place where we can truly come alive."[24]

Thus, living in the present is possible in a new way. Early in recovery I found the counsel "one day at a time" (or one hour or ten minutes at a time if necessary) essential for abstinence. Now, years later, the temptation to drink surfaces only occasionally, and the obsession with drinking has long ago disappeared. Yet I have no doubt that the obsession would return in full fury were I to try drinking once more. The evidence for this pattern is simply too compelling for me to think otherwise.

Today, however, my daily vow is focused on emotional and spiritual recovery as much as on abstinence from alcohol. In speaking of the realm of God and the resurrection, New Testament writers are genuinely urgent about the present tense. They see it as a matter of life and death. Without God in the present, we are condemned to slow spiritual starvation or quicker forms of self-destruction.

That is true of my recovery. If I could not live in the present, I would live in a past filled with remorse and a future filled with fear. Then I would be living as "a dry drunk"—abstinent, but filled with typical alcoholic emotions and perceptions of life. Take that one step further. If for a considerable time I were not in emotional recovery, it would be next to impossible to retain equilibrium. In such cases, emotional relapse is highly predictable and, sooner or later, drinking begins once again.

During their long journey in the desert the Israelites learned the hard way that they could not store up today's manna for tomorrow—it rotted. They had to trust Yahweh's gifts today. Tomorrow they would have to rely once again on that same divine favor, but by then tomorrow would be today. That is also the word of the New Testament. The time is fulfilled. The tomb is empty. It is time to believe and to declare that "the sins of the world do not take away the Lamb of God—it's the other way around."[25]

A Journey into Community

When still drinking I looked on recovery groups with suspicion if not disdain. I was mighty glad that *I* didn't need them. A couple of my uncles did, but then they were nervous people, always sneaking away from family gatherings without telling us where they were going, gloomily heading toward some church basement where other people in windbreakers and faded jeans would drag plastic chairs into a circle, and then all sit around repeating bumper sticker clichés or telling their stories about booze until a normal person would die of thirst or boredom.[26] I have changed my mind completely. My recovering companions are indispensable strength, wisdom, and good humor for the journey.

We are such thoroughly social selves that our language, our feelings, our sense of who we are all depend on the relationships in which we are immersed. Anthropologists tell us that—lacking human speech, thought patterns, and emotional expressions—children reared by wolves are not recognizably human in any way except physical appearance. Throughout our lives we understand ourselves by interpreting ourselves to others. To remember how my addiction has affected my identity and to celebrate my recovery with them, I regularly say to my recovery group, "My name is Jim, and I'm an alcoholic." Our Creator has so designed human life that we are destined to think, speak, dream, and know ourselves by virtue of community. T. S. Eliot recognized that clearly in his "Choruses from 'The Rock'":

> What life have you if you have not life together?
> There is no life that is not in community.[27]

Religious faith is also thoroughly social. At times some have thought otherwise, as did the person (once described by Archbishop William Temple) who said, "I believe in one holy infallible Church, of which I regret to say that at the present time I am the only member." Nevertheless, the "private Christian" is an oxymoron, and so is "personal faith," if that means a faith belonging to me alone. Biblical faith, both Hebrew and Christian, is thoroughly social—not a saga of individuals heroically struggling by themselves to live faithfully, but rather the story of divine revelation received and faith lived out in community. Thus, continuing his poem, Eliot affirms that all genuine community is lived in praise of God. Furthermore, he reminds us, even the anchorite—the cloistered monastic dedicated to a life of solitary prayer—continually prays for the church, the communal Body of Christ.

In my experience, recovery is just as thoroughly social as religion. Medieval theologians developed a doctrine about the indispensability of the church. They called it *Extra ecclesium nulla salus* ("Outside of the church there is no salvation"). While I want no part of Christian imperialism or exclusivism, I do find considerable truth in one aspect of that doctrine: saving requires a saving community, and healing requires a healing community. Correspondingly, I have no doubt that my recovery requires a recovering community.

Surprisingly, Alcoholics Anonymous was not originally envisioned by its shapers as a group experience. Rather than meetings, the Big Book, its Twelve Steps, and individual contacts were to be the core of the program. Even so, the Big Book itself conveys a sense of the communal enterprise through its constant emphasis on shared experience, and within a few years of A.A.'s founding, regular group meetings became standard for the movement. The twelve "Traditions" were soon formulated to guide the life of the now avowedly communal movement.

Certainly there are other approaches, and some folk find their way to sobriety without much communal support. For example, the "Rational Recovery" movement appeals to a sense of radical independence: sobriety without reliance on other people or on Higher Powers. But for most of us, sobriety is no do-it-yourself project, thus the A.A. motto "You alone can do it, but you can't do it alone."

My treatment counselor said to me more than once, "Jim, your mind is like a bad neighborhood. Never go there by yourself." Alcoholism is a disease of isolation, and precisely because of that, together with my alcoholic capacity for denial and self-deception, I have needed help from others every step of the way.

What kind of help? I need reminders from others when I take inventory of my life. I need to unburden myself to others, tell my story, and listen carefully to others' stories. I need the relief that someone else knows what it's like. I need to extend my help to others, not only for their sakes, but also to reinforce my own sobriety. In short, I need a community with whom I can share experience, strength, and hope.[28]

My recovery community, with good reason, dissociates itself from any religious identifications or pretensions. I understand that and affirm it. At the same time, I am an alcoholic whose faith has been shaped by *Christian* community, and I cannot live in two disparate worlds. In fact, whenever I try to name those aspects of the recovery community particularly important to me, I find them to be aspects I also cherish in the best of my church experience: the *storytelling*, the *vulnerability*, the *grace*, the *accountability*, the *mission*. Both communities feed me in these ways, and each enriches my understanding and appreciation of the other.

Both recovery community and church are obviously *storytelling* groups, each illustrating the biblical axiom that community and story depend on each other. Sadly, one can see the negative illustration of this in a certain group of alcoholics. Jefferson Singer's depth study of hard-core addicted men of the streets depicts men who lack both a community and a story. Theirs is neither the alternative lifestyle story of the homeless adventurer's freedom, nor the story of the principled dropout from a corrupt society. Rather, chemical use has freed them from the burden of having to shape a story at all. Concludes Singer, "Their lack of narrative keeps them from participating in any form of living community; without a story there exists no means to locate their identity in a shared narrative of common experience."[29]

But in the recovery group there is a pervasive sense of shared stories. The storyteller's autobiographical account provides others with practical advice and encouragement. Perhaps above all it gives a sense of mutual identification and belonging. When in a meeting my story mentions hidden vodka bottles in my office filing cabinets, heads nod, acknowledging our common insanity. When I tell of my immense gratitude now for a life without hiding, there are smiles of shared thanksgiving. In such ways the little stories of individuals are placed in the framework of the larger story. It is the recovery community's story of what alcoholism looks like and of what makes sobriety possible—how we got that way and what it's like now.

For me, however, the larger story is still more encompassing. It involves the stories of Abraham and Sarah, Isaac and Rebekah, James and John, Mary and Martha, and an itinerant rabbi from Nazareth whom his followers called the Christ. It is the story this faith community tells about God. Drunkenness and recovery may be a strange story, but the gospel is at least as strange. It is the story of holy vulnerability, of God's caring more about us than we care about ourselves, the story of divine life-giving even in the midst of death.

Those of us who identify with Christian community know the meaning of the gospel hymn "Tell Me the Old, Old Story," for the church is constituted by its own story told repeatedly in a thousand different ways. One line in that hymn says, "Tell me the old, old story, for I forget so soon. . . ." If I cannot remember and meaningfully claim the Christic story as my own, my faith and identity will be something other than Christian. Nor can I as a recovering person afford to forget the alcoholic part of my story. If I cannot remember my last drunk, it will not likely be my last drunk.

Vulnerability is another dimension of the saving community for me, and when true to their origins, both church and recovery groups know well how we are bound together more by our shared weaknesses than by our shared strengths. The church, as the Reformers insisted, is more a hospital for the sick than a society of saints. Or, as a medieval manuscript reportedly put it, "The church is something like Noah's ark: if it weren't for the storm outside, one could hardly stand the smell inside."

Twelve Step groups share this characteristic as communities of imperfection and often seem more conscious of it than are churches. Bill Wilson and his confidant Fr. Ed Dowling spoke of A.A. as "a democracy of people helping through mutual vulnerability."[30] Wilson once wrote to a member who was troubled by certain "goings-on" in the movement, "Alcoholics Anonymous is a terribly imperfect society because it is made up of very imperfect people. . . . [B]ecause we are very human and very sick, we often fall short. I know because I constantly fall short myself."[31]

When you fail again and again in your resolutions, and when you are driven to your knees by a life out of control, the recognition of imperfection comes readily. Yet this sense of shared weakness in the recovery group does not erase the appreciation of each other's strengths. When I recognize that vulnerability is our common bond, I also can see the strengths of others in my group not as threats but as hope and assurance: they will be there for me when I need them.

Such is *a community of grace*, which is another shared feature of church and recovery group. A decade ago, both Wilys Claire and I wanted our congregation in Minneapolis—First Congregational Church—to be aware of my being in treatment, because each of us needed their support. Both congregation and pastoral staff were unfailing in giving it to us—sensitively, warmly, nonjudgmentally. The same was true of United Seminary. These gracious communities were enormously sustaining.

Likewise, I experience that grace in every recovery meeting I attend. The warmth in those rooms signifies more than cheery good fellowship, for each person knows that we are arm-in-arm on a shared journey from death back to life. Any one of these folk would respond without hesitation to a 3:00 a.m. phone call from me, as I would from them. The acceptance goes beyond words.

Communities of grace are marked by "a non-competitive understanding of things," in Kathryn Tanner's apt phrase.[32] Divine grace is an economy of abundance, not of scarcity. There is enough for everyone, and then some. Indeed, as the familiar A.A. saying has it, "If we want to keep it, we have to give it away."

These communities are also places of *accountability*. Sobriety requires regular disciplines and those in turn need regular reinforcement. It is clear to me that my group expects my regular participation, seriousness about the steps of the program, honesty about myself, and my support for other alcoholics. These expectations are very real, but they are not a burden imposed on me from an external authority. Not "law," they are truly "gospel"—good news for my sobriety. Furthermore, I hold that sobriety as a trust from this community. If I am seriously tempted to drink again, I profoundly hope that the faces of these companions will flash through my mind before I ever take the glass in hand.

My present church congregation in Tucson is also a community of accountability for me. Accountability is a two-way street, and a tangible expression of theirs to me comes in the bulletin each Sunday that we celebrate communion. The announcement reads, "[O]ur custom at Southside is to celebrate Holy Communion with grape juice rather than wine. This is to include all God's people in the sacrament—children, folks with addictions, and expectant mothers." It is a mark of caring and inclusiveness, as are the congregation's ministries of justice and aid for street people, many of whom are addicted to alcohol and other drugs. In our corporate prayer time on the Sunday nearest my sobriety anniversary I publicly ask prayers for all people affected by addiction and give thanks for my own recovery—a custom of some others in the congregation as well.

On the matter of *mission* to others affected by addiction my two communities differ. While Alcoholics Anonymous is impressively faithful in its central mission to suffering individuals, it avoids public issues and matters of social change with all the rigor that recovering alcoholics avoid alcohol. A.A.'s Tradition 6 warns against identifying the group with any "outside enterprise," and Tradition 10 declares, "Alcoholics Anonymous has no opinion on outside issues; hence the A.A. name ought never be drawn into public controversy." It is a program that exists solely for personal change with, according to Tradition 5, "but one primary purpose—to carry its message to the alcoholic who still suffers."[33]

The churches of which Wilys Claire and I have been part over the years are far different, readily embracing mission not only to individuals but also to the structures of society. I fully affirm this approach: not only social welfare but also social justice. Indeed, we need to build the hospital at the bottom of the cliff to heal the wounded who have fallen over, but we also need to confront the principalities and powers who control the top of the cliff so that we can build a protective fence there.

Soon after its founding and after toying with the temptations to own hospitals and treatment centers and to involve itself in the public arena, Alcoholics Anonymous drew a clear line opposing all such action. This clarity has been part of its genius as a movement. It has avoided public controversy, power struggles, battles over money, and schisms. Its single-minded focus on the ongoing recovery of its members and on its person-to-person outreach to the still-suffering alcoholic has allowed A.A. to survive and thrive. I would not have it otherwise.

Nevertheless, my sobriety has been shaped by the church's story as well. I need to help build the fence as well as the hospital, and sheer gratitude for emergence from "the kingdom of night" will not let me rest easily with silence on the public issues. "The personal is political." This rallying cry of liberation theologies makes eminently good sense in matters of addiction and recovery, for personal suffering from alcohol and other drug addiction is greatly magnified and unnecessarily prolonged by skewed public policies. A three-year, state-by-state study by the National Center on Addiction and Substance Abuse at Columbia University estimated that in recent years states have spent an average of 13 percent of their budgets on matters of substance abuse. However, only 4 percent of that sum was spent on prevention, while 96 percent was spent, as the report put it, "shoveling up the wreckage." "This is truly insane public policy," said Joseph A. Califano, Jr., president of the National Center at Columbia.[34]

Social costs as well as personal costs of alcoholism and other drug dependence are enormous. By any count, it is the nation's number one health problem, destroying lives, damaging families, straining the health care system, bleeding the economy, and threatening public safety. On average, untreated alcoholics have health care costs at least 100 percent higher than nonalcoholics; fetal alcohol syndrome is the leading known environmental cause of mental retardation; and substance abuse is now the principal overall cause of death and disability in the United States. At the time of this writing, the estimated cost of untreated addiction to the economy is $276 billion a year—more than cancer, heart disease, and diabetes combined.

For every dollar spent on addiction treatment, approximately seven dollars are saved in reduced health and social costs. Yet overall funding, access to treatment, and chemical addiction research all continue to diminish. Specifically regarding drug addiction, the federal government currently allocates two-thirds of its budget to attempts to interdict the supply rather than treating the demand. Added to all this, the costs of our failing "war on drugs" include significant American contributions to militarization and oppression in drug-supplying countries elsewhere and a shocking expansion of the prison population and the prison culture at home.[35]

In spite of overwhelming evidence of the critical need for expanded prevention and treatment resources, alcohol and other drug addiction is the only major disease without a large vocal and visible constituency. Cancer, tuberculosis, multiple sclerosis, and all the rest—even HIV/

AIDS—have their telethons, marathons, walk-a-thons, and fund drives, but not chemical addiction. The reason should be obvious: *chemical addiction is still too often seen as a moral or criminal issue, and those affected remain largely invisible, hiding behind a curtain of stigma and shame.*

Given the current politics of addiction, the insurance industry and the U.S. Chamber of Commerce have little trouble engineering the defeat of expanded treatment coverage. Even working people who do have insurance coverage and need treatment oftentimes do not avail themselves of it. An Arizona state study recently reported that many insurance-covered substance abusers and addicted persons either do not claim treatment or pay out of their own pockets for one simple reason: "Many working people still fear reprisals."[36]

But some of us are freer to speak without significant reprisal. We might take a page from the record of the desert monks in the early years of the Christian empire. The situation of those monks (who, remember, relied on their communities of mutual support) was not lost on the empire's authorities. The monks were free to take risks in their loving. Living in the desert in voluntary poverty, they wanted nothing, hence they could not be coopted or frightened into submission. Belden Lane observes, "It was no wonder that prelates and emperors continually sought to curry the favor of these desert athletes, recognizing the intense political danger of a people who had nothing whatever to lose.[37] Those monks are part of "the great cloud of witnesses" who surround us. For those of us who are recovering they can be both inspiration and prod, because we, like they, have gained so much that we have little to lose.

Before my addiction I had known the genuine power of community. I knew it in the bonds of family and friends, in the church, in the seminary where I taught. But I did not fully appreciate it until I experienced its loss during the worst days of active alcoholism. My communities did not in any way abandon me. Rather, in my disease I withdrew from them. In spite of that, they stood by me with amazing staying power and grace. Great was their faithfulness.

Now in better days and in myriad ways people continue to support my recovery. Most of these folk are, in one way or another, part of that cloud of witnesses in the church, which in worship opens its life to the Source of all true community. It is this church that calls me to public mission in certain ways that my recovery community does not. It will not let me forget the story of Jesus and of Isaiah before him who identified God's cause as bringing good news to the poor, proclaiming release to the captives, recovery of sight to the blind, and freedom for the oppressed (Luke 4:18).

In my two communities there is an overlap of membership, to be sure. Some members of my recovery groups are active church members; many are not. But my recovery community shows me regularly and with moving power what the radical fellowship of love is meant to be. Though it rightly shuns all formal religious ties, its capacity for honesty, for authentic acceptance, and for iconoclastic humor often makes me wonder if I am among some first-century Christians freshly excited by the experience of the resurrection.

The Journey Is Our Home

Stories of the desert journey of our ancestors-in-faith are followed by accounts of their struggle to possess the promised land. Victories are punctuated by defeats. After one setback Joshua and the elders of Israel despaired, tearing their clothes, putting dust on their heads, and falling to the ground. Joshua then prayed loudly, informing the Holy One of their complaint (as if God didn't know): "Ah Lord GOD! Why have you brought this people across the Jordan at all, to hand us over to [the enemy] . . . so as to destroy us?" (Josh. 7:7). God's reply sounds like words to a struggling alcoholic: "Stand up! Why have you fallen upon your face?" (Josh. 7:10). Then comes a warning for anyone who has ever let other things take priority over recovery: "There are devoted things [objects believed to have special holiness] among you, O Israel; you will be unable to stand before your enemies until you take away the devoted things from among you" (Josh. 7:13).

I know that I must befriend my addiction as well as fight it, and in recent pages have emphasized befriending it. Now the Hebrew saga of conquest of the land reminds me of the other side of that paradox. And a valid side it is, for if I lose proper respect for the power of my adversary the disease will return in full force. Even in remission I must stand my ground against it, claiming what I need in order to resist whatever would invite relapse.

Returning to the desert journey part of the story, forty years in the wilderness was a long, long time. I do not expect ever to be cured of my alcoholism, but I do hope for progress in my emotional-spiritual recovery. A decade ago I began recovery still acting like an addict: I wanted recovery *now*, and I wanted to do it *right*. Now I have a little more humility.

I also have a little more patience. It took a long time of soul neglect to develop my disease, and it will take a long time of soul care to make a significant difference. It takes time to honor the soul's expressions, time to let the interior life reveal itself, time to live in a way that nurtures depth, time to absorb the wisdom of that cloud of witnesses. Gracie Allen was right in what she reportedly wrote to George Burns: "Never put a period where God has placed a comma."

Writing this book has been extraordinarily helpful. Like recovery itself, it has had its ups and downs. In part it has been a welcome challenge to put some puzzle pieces of an alcoholic's experience together. In part, it has been plain hard work in knowing what to say and how best to say it. I have wanted to speak for myself, studiously respecting confidentiality, and yet tearing another little opening in the curtain of silence that still surrounds this addiction. I have wanted to deal seriously with theology, yet in ways accessible to those who would never darken a seminary door.

But in a particular way the writing process has been a parable of the wilderness journey. When I have not been sure where I was going, I have tried to remember that wisdom from E. L. Doctorow. When asked how he wrote a novel, whether he had the entire plot clearly in mind from the beginning, Doctorow said that "writing a novel is like driving a car at night. You can see only as far as your headlights, but you can make the whole trip that way."[38] So also, if you can see a few feet ahead in this life of recovery (or in writing about it) maybe that is enough—if your journey is made in faith.

Back to the desert story. Now I want to return to Moses, for he (more than his successor Joshua) truly symbolizes this process. Moses never actually set foot in the promised land. But he dreamt of it. His life was shaped by it. He actually saw it from Mount Pisgah. But he died with the journey still underway and with God still going ahead of him. And that was enough for him.

A short time before his assassination, Martin Luther King Jr. preached a sermon recapitulating this story. He had a premonition of his own death and like Moses was content with a vision of the land for which he had worked so tirelessly. It may seem unfair that Moses and King never saw the trip completed. Likewise, it may seem unfair that everyone else who has ever given themselves wholeheartedly to whatever significant life journey they are called to make will never see that trip completed either. But God has not promised that we will be allowed to *complete* what *we* have begun. The gracious promise is that we are allowed to *participate* in what *God* has begun.[39]

So it is with recovery. The journey God has begun with us gives us realistic hope. It is not a hope that says everything will turn out well, but a hope convinced that things will make sense regardless of how they turn out.[40] After all, in the gift of recovery God has been helping us make sense of our addiction, and that is no small miracle.

So we keep on keeping on, with gratitude for each new day, one day at a time. And each one is not only marked by ongoing struggle but is also a day of our resurrection. The glimpse of all things made new in God, this vision that informs our endless journey, does not whisk us out of the present into some distant future. It is not *chronos*, but *kairos*—God bathing this ordinary today in the Eternal Now.

As I was writing this last chapter and reflecting about recovery's endless journey, I went to the final book of the Bible to read once more those words about God's "new heaven and new earth." The book of Revelation contains a stunning vision of God, the Holy One now completely present and at home among us, wiping the tears from our eyes because death and mourning, crying and pain have all passed away. After pondering that familiar, still gripping passage, I read on. Soon I came to some other words I had forgotten. They leapt from the page and wrapped themselves around the mind and heart of this recovering drunk: "And let everyone who is thirsty come" (Rev. 22:17).

Notes

Preface

1. Alcoholics Anonymous World Services, Inc., *Alcoholics Anonymous* ("The Big Book"), 4th ed. (New York: Alcoholics Anonymous World Services, Inc., 2001), 153.

Chapter 1: Silence and Speech

1. I discovered Maurois's insight in Rollo May, *Love and Will* (New York: W. W. Norton, 1969), 170, and drew on it in the opening pages of my book *Embodiment: An Approach to Sexuality and Christian Theology* (Minneapolis: Augsburg, 1978), 9.
2. Anne Lamott, *Bird by Bird: Some Instructions on Writing and Life* (New York: Doubleday, 1995), 3.
3. May Sarton, *At Seventy* (New York: W. W. Norton, 1987), 105.
4. The phrase is Martin L. Smith's, *Nativities and Passions* (Cambridge, Mass.: Cowley Publications, 1995), 26.
5. Quoted in Smith, *Nativities and Passions*, 66.
6. I am indebted to my good friend and mentor, Douglas Federhart, for a clarifying discussion about the aims of this project.
7. Smith, *Nativities and Passions*, 35.
8. Quoted in Robert Fitzgerald S. J., *The Soul of Sponsorship: The Friendship of Fr. Ed Dowling, S. J. and Bill Wilson in Letters* (Center City, Minn.: Hazelden, 1995), 39.
9. Alcoholics Anonymous World Services, Inc., *Twelve Steps and Twelve Traditions* (New York: Alcoholics Anonymous World Services, Inc., 1952, 1953, 1981), 184.
10. *Twelve Steps and Twelve Traditions*, 187.
11. See William L. White, *Slaying the Dragon: The History of Addiction Treatment and Recovery in America* (Bloomington, Ill.: Chesnut Health Systems, 1998), chap. 2.
12. *Twelve Steps and Twelve Traditions*, 132.
13. *Alcoholics Anonymous*, 59, italics mine.
14. See, for example, Otto Maduro, "Liberation Theology," in Donald W. Musser and Joseph L. Price, eds., *A New Handbook of Christian Theology* (Nashville: Abingdon Press, 1992).

15. Dietrich Bonhoeffer, *Life Together*, trans. John W. Doberstein (New York: Harper & Brothers, 1954), 97f.
16. Toni Morrison is quoted in Lamott, *Bird by Bird*, 193.
17. *Alcoholics Anonymous*, 58, 132.
18. Arthur Kleinman, *The Illness Narratives: Suffering, Healing, and the Human Condition* (New York: Basic Books, 1988), 3.
19. John D. Barbour, "The *Bios* of Bioethics and the *Bios* of Autobiography," an unpublished paper written for the "Religion, Ethnography, and Public Life" project of the Poynter Center, Indiana University, 1998.
20. George W. Stroup, "Narrative Theology," in Musser and Price, *A New Handbook*, 325.
21. H. Richard Niebuhr, *The Meaning of Revelation* (New York: Macmillan Co., 1941), 93.
22. Roxana Robinson, "The Big Chill," *The New York Times Book Review*, 7 January 2001, p. 31.
23. I am indebted to Peter J. Gomes, *Sermons: Biblical Wisdom for Daily Living* (New York: Wm. Morrow & Co., 1998), esp. 222.
24. See 1 Corinthians 1:20–25.

Chapter 2: God Thirst and Alcoholic Thirst

1. Ernest Kurtz and Katherine Ketcham, *The Spirituality of Imperfection* (New York: Bantam, 1992), 5.
2. Surely, the indictment of religion is not universal among A.A. members by any means. In fact, many groups continue to use the Lord's Prayer as part of a beginning or closing ritual. However, though that prayer is clearly part of the Christian tradition, its use is understood by many members as "spiritual" and "not religious."
3. Karen Armstrong, "Preface," in *Islam: A Short History* (New York: Modern Library, 2000), as quoted in *The New York Times Book Review*, 3 September 2000, p. 8.
4. Quoted by Ronald Rolheiser, *The Holy Longing: The Search for Christian Spirituality* (New York: Doubleday, 1999), 3.
5. Ibid.
6. Ibid., 4.
7. Augustine, *The Confessions of St. Augustine*, trans. R. S. Pine-Coffin (Harmondsworth, England: Penguin Books, 1961), 24.
8. Fran Ferder and John Heagle helpfully describe this spiritual dynamic, especially as it affects our sexuality. See *Tender Fires: The Spiritual Promise of Sexuality* (New York: Crossroad, 2002).
9. See Kerry Walters, *Godlust: Facing the Demonic, Embracing the Divine* (Mahwah, N.J.: Paulist Press, 1999), 9.
10. Walters, *Godlust*, 10. Augustine's words in *Confessions* (see note 6, above) might be translated, "Thou madest us toward [*ad te*, frequently mistranslated as 'for'] Thyself, O God, and our hearts are restless until they repose in Thee." See the translation by Henry Chadwick (New York: Oxford University Press, 1992), 4.
11. For this interpretation of Buddhism, including the Shaw illustration, I am indebted to Huston Smith, *The World Religions* (San Francisco: HarperSanFrancisco, 1991), 102.
12. Ibid., italics added.
13. Rolheiser, *The Holy Longing*, 11.
14. Paul Tillich, *Dynamics of Faith* (New York: Harper & Brothers, 1957), 4.

15. Donald W. Goodwin, *Alcoholism: The Facts*, 3d ed. (Oxford: Oxford University Press, 2000), 90.
16. Bruce Wilshire, *Wild Hunger: The Primal Roots of Modern Addiction* (Lanham, Md.: Rowman & Littlefield, 1998), xii–xiii.
17. Thomas Wolfe, *Look Homeward Angel: A Story of Buried Life* (New York: Charles Scribner's Sons, 1947), 525. Cf. Howard Clinebell, *Understanding and Counseling Persons with Alcohol, Drug, and Behavioral Addictions*, revised and enlarged (Nashville: Abingdon Press, 1998).
18. Quoted in Clinebell, *Understanding and Counseling*, 272.
19. Gerald G. May, *Addiction and Grace* (New York: HarperCollins, 1988), 1.
20. The correspondence was reprinted several times in *The A.A. Grapevine*, e.g., January 1963 and January 1968. For the full text see Gerhard Adler, et al, ed., *C.G. Jung: Letters, 1951–1961*, Bollingen series, xcv, no. 2 (Princeton: Princeton University Press, 1992), letter of 30 January, 1961.
21. Saul Bellow, *Henderson the Rain King* (New York: Penguin, 1976), 24. Cf. Smith, *Nativities and Passions*, 36f.
22. Arnold M. Ludwig, M.D., *Understanding the Alcoholic's Mind* (Oxford: Oxford University Press, 1988) is particularly helpful on the matter of craving.
23. Ibid., 92.
24. Walters, *Godlust*, 6f.
25. Daniel Day Williams, *The Demonic and the Divine*, ed. Stacy A. Evans (Minneapolis: Fortress Press, 1990), 6–14. Cf. Walters, *Godlust*, 27.
26. Antoine de Saint-Exupery, *The Little Prince* (New York: Harcourt Brace Jovanovich, 1971), 50–52. I am indebted to Francis F. Seeburger, *Addiction and Responsibility: An Inquiry into the Addictive Mind* (New York: Crossroad, 1993), 20, for reminding me of this story.
27. I am grateful to Ferder and Heagle, *Tender Fires*, for reminding me of John Bradshaw's phrase.
28. Kurtz and Ketcham, *Spirituality of Imperfection*, 20.
29. See Smith, *The World Religions*, p. 39f.
30. See Thomas Moore, *Care of the Soul* (New York: HarperCollins Publishers, 1992), 166.
31. See note 6, above.

Chapter 3: Disease and Sin

1. Frank McCourt, *Angela's Ashes* (New York: Simon & Schuster, 1999), 23ff.
2. For various definitions of alcoholism, see David E. Smith and Richard B. Seymour, *Clinician's Guide to Substance Abuse* (New York: McGraw-Hill, 2001), 18ff.; Clinebell, *Understanding and Counseling*, 24; May, *Addiction and Grace*, 26ff; and "Helping Patients with Substance Abuse Problems," a guide to accompany "Moyers on Addiction: Close to Home," Public Broadcasting System, 1998, i–ii.
3. Goodwin, *Alcoholism*, 32, 83.
4. Howard Clinebell, "Alcohol Abuse, Addiction, and Therapy," in *Dictionary of Pastoral Care and Counseling*, Rodney J. Hunter, gen. ed. (Nashville: Abingdon Press, 1990), 18.
5. The term "oops phenomenon" is from Alan Leshner, Director of the National Institute on Drug Abuse, quoted in "Addiction: A Brain Disease with Biological Underpinnings," *Hazelden Voice* 6, no. 1 (Winter 2001): 1.

6. From Lord Byron, "The Prisoner of Chillon," *Selected Poems* (London: Penguin, 1996), 41.

7. See Goodwin, *Alcoholism*, chap. 6.

8. Barbara S. Cole, *Gifts of Sobriety: When the Promises of Recovery Come True* (Center City, Minn.: Hazelden, 2000), 72f.

9. William Shakespeare, "Macbeth," Act II, scene iii, *The Arden Shakespeare Complete Works*, ed. Richard Proudfoot, et al. (Walton-on-Thames, Surrey: Thomas Nelson & Sons, 1998), 781.

10. The empirical data are helpfully summarized in Clinebell, *Understanding and Counseling*, chap. 2; Goodwin, *Alcoholism*, chaps. 2, 7, 9, 11; and Smith and Seymour, *Clinician's Guide*, chaps. 3 and 4.

11. Clinebell, *Understanding and Counseling*, 60.

12. Clinebell, "Alcohol, Abuse, Addiction, and Therapy," 19.

13. Goodwin, *Alcoholism*, 107.

14. While I have developed my own version of this continuum, I am particularly indebted to Clinebell, *Understanding and Counseling*, 287ff., and Francis F. Seeburger, *Addiction and Responsibility* (New York: Crossroad, 1993), chap. 5.

15. White, *Slaying the Dragon*, 1ff.

16. Proceedings of the A.A.C.I., 1870, 8, quoted in White, *Slaying the Dragon*, 26.

17. Ibid., 197.

18. Ibid., 187.

19. Dr. Paul O., *There's More to Quitting Drinking than Quitting Drinking* (Laguna Niguel, Calif.: Sabrina Publishing, 1995), 14f.

20. This definition is that of D. C. Lewis. See "Addiction: A Disease Defined," *Research Update* (The Hazelden Institute, August 1998), 1.

21. Smith and Seymour, *Clinician's Guide*, 18.

22. *Alcoholics Anonymous*, 62.

23. Paul O., *There's More to Quitting*, 20.

24. *Twelve Steps and Twelve Traditions*, 24.

25. Herbert Fingarette, "Rejecting the Disease Concept," *Harvard Mental Health Letter* (February 1990): 1.

26. For a fuller discussion, see James B. Nelson, *Body Theology* (Louisville, Ky.: Westminster/John Knox Press, 1992), 46ff., 166ff.

27. Susan Sontag, *Illness as Metaphor* (New York: Farrar, Straus & Giroux, 1978); and *AIDS and Its Metaphors* (New York: Farrar, Straus & Giroux, 1989).

28. See Goodwin, *Alcoholism*, 33.

29. Deepak Chopra, *Overcoming Addictions: The Spiritual Solution* (New York: Three Rivers Press, 1997), 92.

30. I am indebted to the Rev. Eric Nelson's sermon at First Congregational Church of Minnesota, Minneapolis, March 11, 2001, for reminding me of Officer Krupke.

31. Fingarette, "Rejecting the Disease Concept," 2.

32. Ibid.

33. Clinebell, *Understanding and Counseling*, 293.

34. See Robert Lowry Calhoun, *Lectures on the History of Christian Doctrine*, vol. 2 [private circulation] (New Haven, Conn.: Yale Divinity School, 1948), 220ff.

35. Emily Dickinson, *The Poems of Emily Dickinson*, ed. Thomas H. Johnson (Cambridge, Mass.: The Belknap Press of Harvard University Press, 1951, 1955, 1979), 439.

Chapter 4: Sin and Disease

1. Annie Dillard, *Pilgrim at Tinker Creek* (New York: HarperCollins, 1974), 123.
2. Cole, *Gifts of Sobriety*, 107.
3. Linda A. Mercadante, *Victims and Sinners: Spiritual Roots of Addiction and Recovery* (Louisville, Ky.: Westminster John Knox Press, 1996), ix.
4. Phillip Rieff, *The Triumph of the Therapeutic: Uses of Faith After Freud* (New York: Harper & Row, 1966).
5. Oliver J. Morgan provides a useful summary of the biblical consensus on alcohol itself as well as summarizing wider biblical themes. See "Practical Theology, Alcohol Abuse and Alcoholism: Methodological and Biblical Considerations," *Journal of Ministry in Addiction and Recovery* 5, no. 2 (1998): 39ff. See also John Patton, *Pastoral Care in Context: An Introduction to Pastoral Care* (Louisville, Ky.: Westminster/John Knox Press, 1993), 169–83.
6. Walter Brueggemann and Paul S. Minear, *The Bible and Alcohol and Drugs: A Study Guide* (New York: United Church of Christ, n.d.), 6.
7. Jesus' positive acceptance of wine is most vividly reflected in John's account of the wedding miracle in Cana (John 2:1–11). But in his teachings he also condemned the unfaithful steward who, sensing a delay in the master's return, got drunk and beat those in his charge (Matt. 24:45–51; Luke 12:42–46). In addition to its ordinary use, Paul recommended wine medicinally and at the same time believed that drunkenness could exclude a person from the realm of God (1 Tim. 5:23; 1 Cor. 6:10). A Presbyterian policy statement is a good summary of the biblical teaching: "The consumption of alcohol is not itself a sinful act. Drinking of wine is described without condemnation throughout the Bible. Alcohol abuse, however—the use of alcohol in a manner that invokes harm or the risk of harm to oneself or others—is sinful in its violation of Shalom. Intoxication is uniformly condemned in the Scriptures as a misuse of alcohol that damages one's relationship to God, to others, and to society." Presbyterian Church, (U.S.A.), *Alcohol Use & Abuse: The Social and Health Effects* (Reports and Recommendations by the Presbyterian Church (U.S.A.), 198th General Assembly, 1986), 34.
8. Anon., *Twenty-Four Hours a Day* (Center City, Minn.: Hazelden 1954, 1975), reading for Nov. 26.
9. See Brian L., *Perfectionism* (Center City, Minn.: Hazelden, 1985).
10. See Smith's discussion of this point in *Nativities and Passions*, 116.
11. Quoted in Ernest Kurtz, *Not-God: A History of Alcoholics Anonymous* (Center City, Minn.: Hazelden, 1979), 120.
12. *Alcoholics Anonymous*, 62.
13. Quoted in Kurtz, *Not-God*, 243f.
14. Christina Grof, *The Thirst for Wholeness: Attachment, Addiction, and the Spiritual Path* (New York: HarperCollins Publishers, 1993), 139f.
15. Ibid., 142.
16. May, *Addiction and Grace*, 14ff.
17. *Confessions*, xxxiii, 48, as quoted in H. Richard Niebuhr, *Christ and Culture* (New York: Harper & Brothers, 1951), 210.

18. John C. Ford. *What About Your Drinking?* (Glen Rock, N.J.: Deus Books, 1961), 51.
19. *City of God*, XIX, 13; cf. Niebuhr, *Christ and Culture*, 211.
20. This wording is Reinhold Niebuhr's, who recaptured much of Augustine's theology for a modern age. See *The Nature and Destiny of Man* (New York: Charles Scribner's Sons, 1941, 1943, 1949).
21. Walter Rauschenbusch, *A Theology for the Social Gospel* (New York: Macmillan Co., 1917), 67.
22. May, *Addiction and Grace*, 11.
23. Mercadante, *Victims and Sinners*, 80.
24. Grof, *Thirst for Wholeness*, 110.
25. See Seeburger, *Addiction and Responsibility*, 39ff. In using the slavery metaphor for alcoholism, I intend no disrespect for the African American experience, wherein slavery was institutionalized by a system far more insidious than usually recognized—in the North as well as the South (see Brent Staples, "Slaves in the Family: One Generation's Shame Is Another's Revelation," *New York Times*, 15 June 2003, Sec. 4, 12). Indeed, the image of slavery should be used with care. However, I do find it utterly appropriate to the late stages of active alcoholism because of the word's denotations of total domination and ownership with consequences for absolutely every aspect of life.
26. *Twelve Steps and Twelve Traditions*, 24.
27. White, *Slaying the Dragon*, 330.

Chapter 5: Body and Spirit

1. Parts of this chapter are adapted from my "Masculine Spirituality and Addiction: A Personal Journey," in Ursula King, ed., with Tina Beattie, *Spirituality and Society in the New Millennium* (Brighton, U.K. and Portland Oreg.: Sussex Academic Press, 2001); also my Carpenter Lecture at the Seventh Annual Conference of the American Men's Studies Association, Vanderbilt University, March 13, 1999, and one of my Spring Convocation Lectures at United Theological Seminary of the Twin Cities, May 4, 2000, all used here by permission.
2. Walter A. Hunt and Sam Zakhari, eds., *Stress, Gender, and Alcohol-Seeking Behavior*, Research Monograph No. 29 (Bethesda, Md.: National Institutes of Health, 1995), 7; Christopher T. Kilmartin, *The Masculine Self* (New York: Macmillan Publishing Co., 1994), 160.
3. See "Fact Sheet," June 1999, National Council on Alcoholism and Drug Dependency, Inc. (national@ncadd.org); also Joseph Nowinski, *Hungry Hearts: On Men, Intimacy, Self-esteem, and Addiction* (New York: Lexington/Macmillan, 1993), viii.
4. Hunt and Zakhari, *Stress, Gender, and Alcohol-Seeking*, 23.
5. Christie Cozad Neuger, "Gender and Addiction," public lecture at United Theological Seminary of the Twin Cities, New Brighton, Minn., 14 November 1998 (unpub.), 3; Sheila Blume, "Alcohol and Other Drug Problems in Women," in Joyce Lowinson, et al., *Substance Abuse: A Comprehensive Textbook*, 2d ed. (Baltimore: Williams & Wilkins, 1996), 798. Cf. Stephanie S. Covington, *A Woman's Way through the Twelve Steps* (Center City, Minn.: Hazelden, 1994).
6. See Neuger, "Gender and Addiction," 15; also statistics from the National Council on Alcoholism and Drug Dependence, national@ncadd.org, updated regularly.

7. For overviews on gay men and alcoholism, see Thomas S. Weinberg and Jacqueline P. Wiseman, *Gay Men, Drinking, and Alcoholism* (Carbondale, Ill.: Southern Illinois University Press, 1994); and Robert J. Kus, ed., *Addiction and Recovery in Gay and Lesbian Persons* (New York: Haworth Press, 1994).

8. Owen Wilson (pseud.), *The Inside Man: The Social Construction of Masculinity in the Culture of Alcoholics Anonymous*, M.A. thesis, unpub. (University of Kansas, 1998), 40.

9. Quoted in John W. Crowley, *The White Logic: Alcoholism and Gender in American Modernist Fiction* (Amherst, Mass.: University of Massachusetts Press, 1994), 44.

10. See Wilfrid Sheed, *In Love with Daylight: A Memoir of Recovery* (New York: Simon & Schuster, 1995), 91.

11. See ibid., 199.

12. David C. McClelland, et al., *The Drinking Man* (New York: Free Press, 1972), 300.

13. David Gilmore, *Manhood in the Making: Cultural Concepts of Masculinity* (New Haven, Conn.: Yale University Press, 1990), 77.

14. McClelland, *The Drinking Man*, 336.

15. See Nowinski, *Hungry Hearts*.

16. Jefferson A. Singer, *Message in a Bottle: Stories of Men and Addiction* (New York: Free Press, 1997), 21, italics mine.

17. William Meehan et al., "Guilt, Shame, and Depression in Clients in Recovery from Addiction," *Journal of Psychoactive Drugs* 28, no. 2 (April–June 1996): 132; also Ernest Kurtz, *Shame and Guilt: Characteristics of the Dependency Cycle* (Center City, Minn.: Hazelden Foundation, 1981), 8.

18. Cf. Robert H. Albers, *Shame: A Faith Perspective* (London: Haworth, 1995), 41.

19. See Lee Jampolsky, "Healing the Addictive Mind," for a further discussion of beliefs of the addictive thought system, in Oliver J. Morgan and Merle Jordan, eds., *Addiction and Spirituality: A Multidisciplinary Approach* (St. Louis: Chalice Press, 1999), 72.

20. Ibid., 56. I am persuaded that "spiritualistic dualism," the assumption of a disembodied spirit, greatly augments the problems of addiction, and I have emphasized that in this chapter. It is also the case, however, that certain forms of the disease theory err by putting the focus solely on *body* devoid of spirit. Science has taken a disease model developed for other sicknesses and applied it to chemical dependency, attempting to correlate processes and establish causal linkages. In the course of things it has also objectified and quantified the body. To the extent that that happens, however, critical features of the body *as a self* are masked. Consider, for example, a strictly physiological definition of alcoholism: "the adaptation of cell metabolism to alcohol and the experience of withdrawal symptoms when the body is deprived of alcohol." While this is true as far as it goes, the description is incomplete. Questions about meaning elude the medical laboratory. Another example is brain research on dopamine and seratonin, a highly valuable but still partial approach to chemical addiction. Imbalances in these neurotransmitters are now demonstrably associated with addictive cravings. But what lies behind the imbalances in the first place? To answer this question we cannot look only at the brain. We must see the brain as part of a particular human being with a particular history, immersed in certain social contexts within a natural environment—a human being who in the midst of it all is seeking meaning.

21. May, *Addiction and Grace*, 90.

22. Wilshire, *Wild Hunger*, xv.

23. Ibid., xi.
24. See ibid., xii.
25. Cornel West, *Race Matters* (New York: Vintage Books, 1994), 122.
26. See ibid., 128f.
27. See Rhonda Jones-Webb, Dr. P. H., "Drinking Patterns and Problems among African-Americans: Recent Findings," *Alcohol Health and Research World* 22, no. 4 (1998). Cf. Henry L. Francis, M.D., "The Medical Consequences of Drug Use in Minority Populations," paper given at the conference "Bridging Science and Culture to Improve Drug Abuse Research in Minority Communities," Philadelphia, Sept. 24–26, 2001 (see abstract, National Institute on Drug Abuse, www.nida.nih.gov).
28. West, *Race Matters*, 129.
29. Quoted in Sheed, *In Love with Daylight*, 79.
30. Quoted in Kurtz, *Shame and Guilt*, 41.
31. Cf. Kurtz & Ketcham, *Spirituality of Imperfection*, 126.
32. See esp. Seymour Fisher, *Body Consciousness* (Glasgow: William Collins, 1976), and Seymour Fisher and S. E. Cleveland, *Body Image and Personality* (New York: Dover, 1968).
33. See James B. Nelson, *The Intimate Connection: Male Sexuality and Masculine Spirituality* (Philadelphia: Westminster Press, 1988), chap. 5; Stephen B. Boyd, *The Men We Long to Be* (San Francisco: HarperSanFrancisco, 1995).
34. John Dewey, *Art as Experience* (New York: G. P. Putnam's Sons, 1980 [1934]), 22.
35. See, for example, Romans 8:1–17.
36. John A.T. Robinson describes the pervasive body imagery in Paul's understanding of the gospel: "It is from the body of sin and death that we are delivered; it is through the body of Christ on the Cross that we are saved; it is into His body the Church that we are incorporated; it is by His body in the Eucharist that this Community is sustained; it is in our body that its new life has to be manifested; it is to a resurrection of this body to the likeness of His glorious body that we are destined." *The Body: A Study in Pauline Theology* (London: SCM, 1952), 9.
37. Quoted in Moore, *Care of the Soul*, 163.
38. Ibid ., 164f.; cf. 171f.
39. Chopra, *Overcoming Addictions*, 4f.
40. The references are to e. e. cummings's poem, "I thank You God for most this amazing," *E.E. Cummings Selected Poems*, ed. Richard S. Kennedy (New York: W. W. Norton & Co., 1994), 167.
41. Belden Lane, *The Solace of Fierce Landscapes: Exploring Desert and Mountain Spirituality* (New York; Oxford: Oxford University Press, 1998), 41f.
42. Boyd, *The Men We Long to Be*.
43. Quoted in Merle Fossum, *Catching Fire: Men's Renewal and Recovery through Crisis* (Center City, Minn.: Hazelden, 1989), 61.

Chapter 6: Power and Powerlessness

1. Because during his early recovery Bill Wilson had been so affected by William James's *The Varieties of Religious Experience*, he spoke of him as "one of the founders" of Alcoholics Anonymous. James is quoted in Andrew Delbanco and Thomas Delbanco, "Annals of Addiction: A.A. at the Crossroads," *New Yorker* (20 March 1995): 59.
2. The hymn text is by George Matheson.

3. Covington, *Woman's Way*, 12.
4. Ibid., 23.
5. Ibid., 24.
6. Douglas J. Federhart, "Issues of Addiction, Recovery and Spirituality for Gay, Lesbian, Bisexual and Transgendered People," (unpublished lecture presented at United Theological Seminary of the Twin Cities, 12 June 2000), 9.
7. Ibid.
8. Ibid.
9. Charlotte Davis Kasl, *Women, Sex, and Addiction: A Search for Love and Power* (New York: Harper & Row, 1989); *Many Roads, One Journey: Moving Beyond the Twelve Steps* (New York: Harper Collins, 1992). Cf. Clinebell, *Understanding and Counseling*, 163, 247ff.
10. Kasl, *Many Roads*, 338.
11. Mercadante, *Victims and Sinners*, 37.
12. *Alcoholics Anonymous*, 31.
13. Abraham J. Twerski, M.D., *The Spiritual Self: Reflections on Recovery and God* (Center City, Minn.: Hazelden, 2000), 8f.
14. See Cole, *Gifts of Sobriety*, 15, for an excellent discussion of this.
15. Twerski, *Spiritual Self*, 75.
16. Many others have experienced a similar path. Cf. John A. Martin, *Blessed Are the Addicts: The Spiritual Side of Alcoholism, Addiction, and Recovery* (San Francisco: HarperSanFrancisco, 1990), esp. 39ff.
17. Seeburger, *Addiction and Responsibility*, 93. See his entire analysis of this phenomenon, 89–93.
18. At points the Big Book clearly embraces the disease model ("an allergy of the body and an obsession of the mind") and removes the responsibility for being alcoholic from the individual. Elsewhere, there is different language that strongly suggests personal culpability: "So our troubles, we think, are basically of our own making . . . and the alcoholic is an extreme example of self-will run riot." *Alcoholics Anonymous*, 62.
19. *Alcoholics Anonymous*, 58. Cf. Mercadante, *Victims and Sinners*, 88f.
20. See Mercadante, *Victims and Sinners*, 87f.
21. Kant's argument comes in his *Critique of Practical Reason* (1788). See John Macquarrie, "Free Will and Determinism," in James F. Childress and John Macquarrie, eds., *The Westminster Dictionary of Christian Ethics* (Philadelphia: Westminster Press, 1986), 237f. for a summary of the philosophical issues.
22. Quoted in Delbanco and Delbanco, "Annals of Addiction," 62.
23. Ibid.
24. Ibid.
25. See *The Westminster Dictionary of Christian Ethics*, 238.
26. I am grateful to Prof. Sterling Vinson for directing me to the passage in *The Confessions* where Augustine describes his own mother's alcohol problem in adolescence. Monica's parents, believing her trustworthy, would send her to the cellar to draw wine from the cask. She began sipping a few drops, initially disliking the taste. But each day she added a bit more. (At this point in Augustine's description, he quotes Ecclesiasticus (Sirach) 19:1, "But little things despise, and little by little you shall come to ruin.") Soon she was drinking "almost by the cupful." Asking how God cured her "disease," Augustine reports that God used a servant girl who would accompany his mother to the cellar. One

day in a quarrel with her mistress, the servant called her "a drunkard," whereupon Monica came to her senses and renounced her drinking. Augustine concludes his account, "You, O Lord, Ruler of all things in heaven and on earth, who make the deep rivers serve your purposes and govern the raging tide of time as it sweeps on, you even used the anger of one soul to cure the folly of another." *The Confessions*, Book 9, 194.

27. Cole, *Gifts of Sobriety*, 52.
28. See ibid., 95f.
29. Fossum, *Catching Fire*, 32.
30. Nowinski, *Hungry Hearts*, viii.
31. Cf. Gregory Bateson, *The Cybernetics of "Self": A Theory of Alcoholism* (Center City, Minn.: Hazelden, 1991).
32. Kurtz and Ketcham, *Spirituality of Imperfection*, 126.
33. Twerski, *Spiritual Self*, italics mine, 62.
34. The image is Coles's; see *Gifts of Sobriety*, 16f.
35. Cf. Kurtz, *Shame and Guilt*, 10
36. Cf. Martin, *Blessed Are the Addicts*, 85ff.
37. The account of the young ruler is found in Matthew 19:16–22, Luke 18:18–23, and Mark 10:17–22.
38. Cole describes this particularly well. See *Gifts of Sobriety*, 140f. I believe that she errs, however, in finally describing losing as "the perfect strategy" to win the war against addiction. To see the loss or surrender as a strategy is to miss its radical nature.
39. Ibid., 140.
40. Quoted in Kurtz and Ketcham, *Spirituality of Imperfection*, 127.
41. Step 2 ("Came to believe that a Power greater than ourselves could restore us to sanity") thus prepares for Step 3 ("Made a decision to turn our will and our lives over to the care of God *as we understood Him*"). Succeeding steps are also paired: Step 4 prepares us with willingness for Step 5; Step 6, for Step 7; Step 8, for Steps 9 and 10; and Step 11, for Step 12. There is the repeated recognition that *willingness* must precede our actual decision (willing) to take the steps that will open us to the gift of sobriety. Kurtz and Ketcham give a helpful commentary on this in ibid. 127f.
42. See ibid., 170.
43. Kathleen Norris, *Amazing Grace* (New York: Penguin Putnam, 1998), 32.
44. Quoted in Fitzgerald, *Soul of Sponsorship*, 40.
45. Quoted in ibid., 61.
46. Thomas Merton, *Conjectures of a Guilty Bystander* (Garden City, N.Y.: Doubleday & Co., 1976), 73.
47. The delightful Cinderella image is from Smith, *Nativities and Passions*, 42f.
48. Wilshire, *Wild Hunger*, 14.
49. Quoted in Delbanco and Delbanco, "Annals of Addiction," 59.
50. Ibid.
51. James, *Varieties of Religious Experience*, 99. Cf. Kurtz and Ketcham, *Spirituality of Imperfection*, 169.
52. *Alcoholics Anonymous*, 83. The first 164 pages of the Big Book are considered sacred scripture by many A.A. members. In the fourth edition (2001) these pages were left entirely unchanged, while the remaining two-thirds of the book ("Personal Stories") underwent revision. As sacred scriptures are used over time in any religious or

quasi-religious movement, "canons within the canon" typically emerge—authoritative and oft-quoted passages that interpret the larger text. "The Promises" are such a canonical passage, often quoted, often used liturgically in A.A. meetings.

53. Cole, *Gifts of Sobriety*, 13.
54. Paul O., *There's More to Quitting*, 71f.
55. Lamott, *Bird by Bird*, 46.
56. Gomes, *Sermons*, 76.
57. Ibid., 77.
58. See the language of the first chapter of Mark concerning the calling of the disciples and Jesus' early healings. The word "immediately" recurs again and again.
59. *Alcoholics Anonymous*, 62.
60. Kurtz and Ketcham, *Spirituality of Imperfection*, 21.
61. See Smith, *Nativities and Passions*, 139ff., for a suggestive interpretation of Jesus' "crossing over" on which I am drawing here.
62. Ibid., 140.

Chapter 7: Grace and Brokenness

1. *Alcoholics Anonymous*, 84.
2. See Kathryn Tanner, *Jesus, Humanity and the Trinity* (Minneapolis: Fortress Press, 2001), chap. 3; Martin E. Marty, "Grace" in Musser and Price, *A New Handbook*, 209ff.; P. S. Watson, "Grace" in Alan Richardson, ed., *A Dictionary of Christian Theology* (Philadelphia: Westminster Press, 1976), 147ff. Cf. May, *Addiction and Grace*, 16f.; and Mercadante, *Victims and Sinners*, 171ff.
3. Inclusive Language Lectionary translation.
4. From a letter of Bill Wilson to Fr. Marcus O'Brien, 21 January 1943, quoted in Fitzgerald, *Soul of Sponsorship*, 32.
5. Gregory Baum, *Faith and Doctrine* (New York: Paulist Press, 1969), 15f.
6. In this paragraph I have depended on Stephen Mitchell's helpful way of expressing grace. See *The Gospel According to Jesus* (New York: HarperCollins, 1993), 10.
7. Belden Lane describes O'Connor well, and I am indebted to him for some of the thoughts in this section on the grotesque. *Solace of Fierce Landscapes*, 29ff.
8. James Luther Adams and Wilson Yates, eds., *The Grotesque in Art and Literature: Theological Reflections* (Grand Rapids: Wm. B. Eerdmans Publ. Co., 1997), xiv.
9. See Robert Doty's definition, ibid., xv.
10. See Lane, *Solace of Fierce Landscapes* for an extended discussion of this topic, 32ff.
11. Though the substance of this story is true, I have changed details to ensure anonymity.
12. Adams and Yates, *The Grotesque*, 190.
13. Christine M. Smith, *Risking the Terror: Resurrection in this Life* (Cleveland: Pilgrim Press, 2001), 47.
14. Ibid.
15. I have alluded here to Auden's words in "For the Time Being: A Christmas Oratorio," *Collected Poems*, ed. Edward Mendelson (New York: Random House, 1976), 303. One reason for my guilt, I am convinced, was bound up in my inability to depend on grace to satisfy my thirst for wholeness. I thirsted for God, but depended on my own efforts. Then in a variety of ways I experienced my inability to realize my deepest needs and capacities for ecstatic wholeness, and I experienced that as a

failure of responsibility to myself. But that failure also engendered guilt—particularly free-floating guilt. Increasingly I dealt with the guilt not through confession, forgiveness, and amendment of life, but rather by diluting the guilt with alcohol. For a different and insightful description of this dynamic see Wilshire, *Wild Hunger*, 62ff.

16. Twerski, *Spiritual Self*, makes this distinction helpful. See 113.

17. This phenomenon is "writ large" in the history of oppressed peoples. The genocidal oppression of Native American people has taken its toll in myriad ways, not the least of which is the self-hatred experienced by both individuals and whole Indian communities. When that self-hatred is internalized, it results in high rates of suicide and alcoholism. When it is externalized, anger is often vented in domestic violence. When that happens, it serves a dual purpose: "The perpetrator of violence can achieve momentary catharsis and relief while at the same time destroying the part of him/herself that reminds him/her of that helplessness and lack of hope." Eduardo Duran and Bonnie Duran, *Native American Postcolonial Psychology* (Albany: State University of New York Press, 1995), 30.

18. Kurtz and Ketcham, *Spirituality of Imperfection*, 218.

19. Garret Keizer, "The Other Side of Rage," *The Christian Century* 119, no. 16 (31 July–13 August 2002): 23. I am indebted to Keizer also for his insights into the limits of rationalism in forgiveness, and the connection between forgiveness and resurrection.

20. Ibid., 27.

21. Ibid.

22. See Kurtz, *Shame and Guilt*, 7.

23. See Fossum, *Catching Fire*, chap. 4; cf. Merle A. Fossum and Marilyn J. Mason, *Facing Shame: Families in Recovery* (New York: W. W. Norton & Co., 1986); Gershen Kaufman, *Shame: The Power of Caring* (Cambridge, Mass.: Shenkman Press, 1980); and Roy U. Schenk and John Everingham, eds., *Men Healing Shame: An Anthology* (New York: Springer Publishing Co, 1995). To be sure, shame has different manifestations in different cultures, and I am speaking out of my experience in a white middle-class American culture. For a powerful example of the development and functioning of shame in another culture, see Duran and Duran, *Native American Postcolonial Psychology*. The high rate of alcoholism among male Native Americans cannot be understood, the Durans argue, without understanding the power of shame in a culture under constant attack. "Shame is of critical concern within a warrior tradition. Shame is akin to existential death, and the split-off segment of the warrior must react to the shame incurred" (p. 39). The destructive use of alcohol, the authors argue, thus helps in the formation of an "oppositional identity" that is a protest against assimilation of the native culture. "The drunken Indian" stereotype, imposed and caused by white colonialism, is turned around and used as a weapon against the colonizer.

24. C. D. Schneider, "Shame," in Rodney J. Hunter, ed., *Dictionary of Pastoral Care and Counseling* (Nashville: Abingdon Press, 1990), 1162. Cf. Kurtz, *Shame and Guilt*, 9.

25. See Gershen Kaufman, "Men's Shame," in Shenk and Everingham, *Men Healing Shame*, 31ff; and Francis Baumli, "On Men, Guilt, and Shame," in Shenk and Everingham, *Men Healing Shame*, 161ff. Theological treatments of addiction written by nonaddicted people seldom grapple with this issue sufficiently, doubtless because it is difficult for the nonaddicted to understand the depths of shame that most addicts seem to feel.

For example, Linda Mercadante briefly mentions shame, but then dismisses it as obscuring the theological roots of the addiction issue; see *Victims and Sinners*, 22. Gerald May, in *Addiction and Grace*, and Francis Seeburger, in *Addiction and Responsibility*, do not even raise the issue of shame. A notable exception to my generalization about nonaddicted writers is Robert H. Albers's *Shame: A Faith Perspective*.

26. See George Lindall, "A Shame-Based Model for Recovery from Addiction," in Shenk and Everingham, *Men Healing Shame*, 190–200.
27. Ibid., 192f.
28. Paul Tillich, *The Shaking of the Foundations* (New York: Scribner's, 1948), 162.
29. Kurtz, *Shame and Guilt*, 3.
30. See ibid., 27.
31. Bill W.'s statement can be found in a 1958 *Grapevine* article, quoted in Fitzgerald, 39.
32. Gomes, *Sermons*, 161.
33. Cole, *Gifts of Sobriety*, 18f.
34. See Glenn Hewitt, "Sanctification," in Musser and Price, *A New Handbook*, 430f.
35. William Griffith Wilson et al., *Alcoholics Anonymous Comes of Age* (New York: Harper & Row, 1957), 74f.
36. Marcus Borg, *Meeting Jesus Again for the First Time* (San Francisco: HarperSanFrancisco, 1994), 87; cf. Kurtz and Ketcham, *Spirituality of Imperfection*, 46; and Smith, *Nativities and Passions*, 116.
37. Gomes, *Sermons* 182f.
38. Quoted in Fitzgerald, *Soul of Sponsorship*, 70.
39. Kurtz, *Shame and Guilt*, 11.
40. Bill W. said this frequently in letters. See those to Howard C., Patricia N., and Bob C., cited in ibid., 17.
41. Quoted in Delbanco and Delbanco, "Annals of Addiction," 60.
42. Cole, *Gifts of Sobriety*, 50.
43. Moore, *Care of the Soul*, 37.
44. I am indebted to Martin L. Smith's interpretation here. See *Nativities and Passions*, 64ff.
45. Cf. John 10:17–18.
46. Though not speaking about recovery, Moore, *Care of the Soul*, describes this phenomenon well, p. 136.
47. See Tanner, *Jesus, Humanity and the Trinity*, 75.
48. For a helpful discussion of gratitude see Kurtz and Ketcham, *Spirituality of Imperfection*, 179ff.
49. As reported in *The New York Times*, 11 December 1986. Cf. Kurtz and Ketcham, *Spirituality of Imperfection*, 184.

Chapter 8: God and the Self

1. See Christopher D. Ringwald, *The Soul of Recovery: Uncovering the Spiritual Dimension in the Treatment of Addictions* (New York: Oxford University Press, 2002). This entire study is a useful survey of the pervasive presence of "spiritual transformation" in addiction recovery in the United States. On "approaches without God," see 147ff.
2. *Alcoholics Anonymous*, 62.
3. The struggle over inclusiveness of A.A. in regard to understandings of God had something of a parallel in the development of Tradition Three ("The only requirement for A.A. membership is a desire to stop drinking"). There were those in A.A.'s early years

who argued that only "pure alcoholics" should be admitted—people with "no other complications." *Twelve Steps and Twelve Traditions* caricatures this position: "So beggars, tramps, asylum inmates, prisoners, queers, plain crackpots, and fallen women were definitely out. Yes sir, we'd cater *only* to pure and respectable alcholics!" (p. 140). Apparently one of the effective challenges to the restrictive position came from a gay man, Barry L., long active as an A.A. speaker.

4. Delbanco and Delbanco, "Annals of Addiction," 59. For a detailed history of these developments, see Kurtz, *Not-God*, chap. 3.

5. James's pragmatic theory of religion was based on his answer to the question, "What kind of being would God be if he did exist?" James's answer was that God must be conceived as "a power not ourselves . . . which not only makes for righteousness, but means it, and which recognizes us." William James, *The Will to Believe* (London: Longmans, Green & Co., 1904), 20, 122. Cf. Kurtz and Ketcham, *Spirituality of Imperfection*, 208.

6. See H. Richard Niebuhr, *Radical Monotheism and Western Culture* (New York: Harper & Brothers, 1960), and James M. Gustafson, *Ethics from a Theocentric Perspective*, vol. 1 (Chicago: University of Chicago Press, 1981).

7. Quoted by Lane, *Solace of Fierce Landscapes*, 20.

8. Ibid., 12.

9. Quoted in ibid., 68. In various of his novels John Updike has pursued an argument with "soft immanence." One of his purple passages comes in *A Month of Sundays* in which the Rev. Thomas Marshfield, a lapsed vicar seeking divine transcendence, is exasperated with the squishy immanence of his young assistant, Ned Bork. Marshfield describes Bork's theology as "a perfectly custardly confection of Jungian-Reichian soma-mysticism swimming in a soupy caramel of Tillichic, Jasperian, Bultmannish blather, all served up in a dime-store dish of his gutless generation's give-away *Gemutlichkeit*." Not wanting any religion created by human needs, Marshfield declares, "Let us have it in its original stony jars or not at all!" John Updike, *A Month of Sundays* (New York: Alfred A. Knopf, 1975), 13, 25.

10. See Sam Keen, *To a Dancing God* (New York: Harper & Row, 1970), 44.

11. Niebuhr, *Radical Monotheism*, 25.

12. I have examined the practical dynamics of polytheism, henotheism, monotheism, and their resultant identities in my book *Moral Nexus: Ethics of Christian Identity and Community* (Louisville, Ky.: Westminster John Knox Press, 1996).

13. Quoted in Kurtz and Ketcham, *Spirituality of Imperfection*, 130.

14. Niebuhr, *Radical Monotheism*, 89.

15. H. Richard Niebuhr, *The Responsible Self* (New York: Harper & Row, 1963), 126. I have summarized this interpretive process in *The Responsible Christian* (Philadelphia: United Church Press, 1969), and in my Foreword to Randall, *Walking through the Valley*.

16. See Ringwald, *Soul of Recovery*, 125.

17. See Elizabeth Liebert, "Ignatian Spirituality," in Rodney J. Hunter, ed., *Dictionary of Pastoral Care and Counseling* (Nashville: Abingdon Press, 1990), 568f.

18. Suzanne Farnham et al., *Listening Hearts: Discerning Call in Community* (Harrisburg, Pa.: Morehouse Publishing, 1991), 23. Cf. Fitzgerald, *Soul of Sponsorship*, 75.

19. The reference is to Hebrews 13:2 and the phrase is as expressed in the King James Version. The message is about hospitality to strangers, though in one sense this applies to alcoholism—not that the addiction per se is welcome, but once it is at one's door it should be seen as a visitor to be understood through eyes of faith.

20. Moore, *Care of the Soul*, 168.
21. The words are from Phillips Brooks's "O Little Town of Bethlehem." I am indebted to the Rev. Lark Hapke for directing me to Marion Woodman, who uses the powerful image of the birth of the Holy Child within. See *Conscious Femininity: Interviews with Marion Woodman*, ed. Daryl Sharp (Toronto: Inner City Books, 1993), 46.
22. From Bill Wilson's correspondence of 1953 and 1959, as found in Kurtz, *Not-God*, 214, and Fitzgerald, *Soul of Sponsorship*, 71f.
23. Tillich dealt with these concepts in a number of his works. A convenient summary may be found in Alexander J. McKelway, *The Systematic Theology of Paul Tillich* (Richmond, Va.: John Knox Press, 1964), esp. 76ff. and 89ff.
24. These emphases are particularly Ignatian in their spirituality. See *The Spiritual Exercises of St. Ignatius of Loyola*, trans. Louis J. Puhl (New York: Knopf, 2000). See Mercadante, *Victims and Sinners*, 175f.
25. See esp. Tillich's *Morality and Beyond* (New York: Harper & Row, 1963).
26. See Niebuhr, *Radical Monotheism*, 123f.
27. Dietrich Bonhoeffer, *Letters and Papers from Prison*, rev. ed. (New York: Macmillan Co., 1967), 192f.
28. Sallie McFague, *Models of God* (Philadelphia: Fortress Press, 1987), 178.
29. In the last century, the most influential theological statement to this effect was Anders Nygren, *Agape and Eros*, trans. Philip S. Watson (London: SPCK, 1957), see esp. 75ff. Nygren postulated a fundamental opposition between divine love (*agape*, which is spontaneous, unmotivated by its unworthy object) and human love (*eros*, which is self-seeking and egocentric). One of the fundamental processes of redemption, hence, is the elimination of *eros* and the triumph of *agape* in the redeemed life. I have discussed this at greater length in *Embodiment*, 109–114.
30. *Alcoholics Anonymous*, 62.
31. Douglas Federhart, in personal correspondence with the author, by permission.
32. Quoted in Fitzgerald, *Soul of Sponsorship*, 44.
33. Quoted in Kurtz and Ketcham, *Spirituality of Imperfection*, 185. I am indebted to these authors for their treatment of humility in chap. 13.
34. Dag Hammarskjold, *Markings* (New York: Ballantine, 1964), 151.
35. Ernest Becker, *The Denial of Death* (New York: Macmillan-Free Press, 1973), 58.
36. Smith, *Nativities and Passions*, 140f.
37. See Lane, *Solace of Fierce Landscapes*, esp. 171–173.

Chapter 9: Journey and the Home

1. A helpful summary of the aesthetic perspectives of Aquinas, Edwards, and others may be found in Walters, *Godlust*, chap. 3.
2. Quoted in Kurtz and Ketcham, *Spirituality of Imperfection*, 233.
3. Grof, *Thirst for Wholeness*, 9.
4. Ibid., 10.
5. Ruth Duck, "Lead On, O Cloud of Yahweh," in Ruth Duck and Michael G. Bausch, eds., *Everflowing Streams: Songs for Worship* (New York: Pilgrim Press, 1981), 77, italics added.
6. Dietrich Bonhoeffer, *Ethics*, trans. Neville Horton Smith (New York: Macmillan Co., 1955), 30ff.

7. Parker Palmer, *Let Your Life Speak: Listening to the Voice of Vocation* (San Francisco: Jossey-Bass, 2000), 7f.

8. Quoted in Verne Becker, ed., *Recovery Devotional Bible* (Grand Rapids: Zondervan Publishing House, 1993), 1140.

9. See Walters, 55ff. for a more thorough discussion of the uses of *aletheia*.

10. Tillich, *Shaking of the Foundations*, 116.

11. Norman Pittenger, *Cosmic Love and Human Wrong* (New York: Paulist Press, 1978), 96.

12. See Moore, *Care of the Soul*, 10; cf. Cole, *Gifts of Sobriety*, 52.

13. Quoted in Kurtz and Ketcham, *Spirituality of Imperfection*, 1.

14. Cole, *Gifts of Sobriety*, 52.

15. See Kurtz and Ketcham, *Spirituality of Imperfection*, 152.

16. See Søren Kierkegaard, *Concluding Unscientific Postscript to the "Philosophical Fragments,"* trans. David F. Swenson, ed. Walter Lowrie (Princeton: Princeton University Press, 1941), 265.

17. See Cole, *Gifts of Sobriety*, 19ff. for a helpful description of this phenomenon. Cf. Twerski, *Spiritual Self*, 115; and Kurtz and Ketcham, *Spirituality of Imperfection*, 214.

18. I am indebted to Paul Tillich's interpretation of this passage in *The New Being* (New York: Charles Scribner's Sons, 1955), chap. 21.

19. Bishop John Shelby Spong expresses these things well and in detail in *Why Christianity Must Change or Die* (San Francisco: HarperSanFrancisco, 1999), see esp. 190.

20. See Paul Tillich, *Systematic Theology*, vol. 1 (Chicago: University of Chicago Press, 1951), 192ff.

21. Gomes, *Sermons*, 84. In this paragraph and the next I am indebted to Gomes for his interpretation of this particular passage in John and for his suggestive ways of interpreting the resurrection faith.

22. Quoted in Kurtz and Ketcham, *Spirituality of Imperfection*, 177.

23. *Alcoholics Anonymous*, 83.

24. Smith, *Nativities and Passions*, 141f.

25. Ibid., 34.

26. I have found Wilfred Sheed, *In Love with Daylight*, very suggestive in his descriptions of our prerecovery images, and I am indebted to him.

27. T. S. Eliot, "Choruses from 'The Rock,'" *Collected Poems, 1909–1962* (Harcourt, Brace & World, Inc., 1963), 101.

28. See Cole, *Gifts of Sobriety*, 62; cf. Kurtz and Ketcham, *Spirituality of Imperfection*, f.n. 6, 262.

29. Singer, *Message in a Bottle*, 284.

30. Fitzgerald, *Soul of Sponsorship*, 105.

31. Private correspondence of Wilson to Mildred O., 14 November 1946, quoted in Kurtz, *Not-God*, 121.

32. Tanner, *Jesus, Humanity and the Trinity*, 92.

33. *Twelve Steps and Twelve Traditions*, 10ff.

34. *Arizona Daily Star*, 30 January 2001, A2.

35. Statistics are taken from the on-line services of the National Council on Alcoholism and Drug Dependence (NCADD), *www.ncadd.org*, dated June 2002; and William C. Moyers, "The Personal Should Be Political," *Hazelden Voice* (Summer 2002): 8.

36. *Arizona Daily Star*, 15 March 2001, B1.

37. Lane, *Solace of Fierce Landscapes*, 172f.
38. Quoted in Lamott, *Bird by Bird*, 18.
39. I gratefully acknowledge my indebtedness to Peter Gomes in these reflections on Moses, King, and the vision. See his *Sermons*, 158.
40. I have adapted this sentence from words of Vaclev Havel, which I copied some time ago and for which I now cannot find the source.

Index